THE
Maid
AND THE
Socialite

THE BRAVE WOMEN BEHIND GREEN BAY'S
SCANDALOUS MINAHAN TRIALS

Lynda Drews

LITTLE CREEK PRESS
AND BOOK DESIGN

MINERAL POINT, WISCONSIN

Little Creek Press
5341 Sunny Ridge Road
Mineral Point, WI 53565

To contact Lynda directly:
lyndadrews@gmail.com or www.lyndadrews.com

ORDERING INFORMATION
Quantity sales. Special discounts are available on quantity purchases
by corporations, associations, and others. For details, contact
info@littlecreekpress.com

Orders by US trade bookstores and wholesalers.
Please contact Little Creek Press for details.

Printed in the United States of America

Cataloging-in-Publication Data
Names: Drews, Lynda, author
Title: The Maid and the Socialite
Description: Mineral Point, WI Little Creek Press, 2023
Identifiers: LCCN: 2023902028 | ISBN: 978-1-955656-47-4
Classification: HISTORY / United States / State & Local / Midwest

Book design by Mimi Bark and Little Creek Press

Dedicated to:
The strong women in my family—
Jess, Emily, Brinley, Josie, and my mother Dana
And to the compassionate men—
Jim, Collin, Chris, and Crosby

Prologue

Chicago & Northwestern Railroad Bridge crossing the Fox River in Green Bay, Wisconsin (Postcard)

AT THE END of the nineteenth century, amid the buzz of sawmills, the bellow of steamships, and the whistles of trains, cities around the world were rife with syphilis. Rumors spread that U.S. president Abraham Lincoln, French author Guy de Maupassant, and Dutch painter Vincent van Gogh had contracted the "unmentionable disease." But no test could prove it.

Two women in Green Bay, Wisconsin, found their lives destroyed by that simple fact.

Mary Cenefelt, an illiterate maid, and Mollie Bertles, a college-educated socialite, fell victim to the physical violence and mental abuse of celebrated surgeon Dr. John R. Minahan. He undercut their voices by claiming they had the shameful and dreaded disease, syphilis. He sought to manipulate and silence them by exploiting his power.

Dr. Minahan was the most influential member of a brilliant family, a family that dominated Green Bay's professional, business, political, and social arenas from 1892 to 1954. The surgeon lived and worked in the prestigious Astor Heights neighborhood, Green Bay's current Astor Historic District, still filled with magnificent homes built by craftsmen from days gone by. Before the elms died and the streetcars ceased, Dr. Minahan strolled comfortably on those mansion-lined streets. It was in Astor Heights where Mary and Mollie suffered, and it was in Astor Heights where they fought back publicly with great boldness despite high personal stakes.

While history lost, or perhaps erased, Mary's and Mollie's courageous stories in the century between their lives and now, Dr. Minahan's fortune built a stadium, science hall, and six-story office building—all named for him. Disturbingly, these women's intimate narratives embody the same battles dominating headlines today: men's entitlement versus women's liberty, wealth versus poverty, and false information versus scientific fact. This is a story of power, abuse, and seeking justice. It is the story of Dr. Minahan versus the maid and the socialite.

NOTE: All quotations are provided from archival records, letters, or other written documents. No changes have been made other than altering the word "plaintiff" and "defendant" to pronouns or names. Mary's and Mollie's thoughts and scenes are extrapolated from the same sources, as imagined by the author.

THE Maid

"The day must come when man,
who robs virtue from its innocents,
shall suffer not less than the
victim he damns."

—HENRY DUKE, Chicago evangelist, 1892

The Fateful Meeting

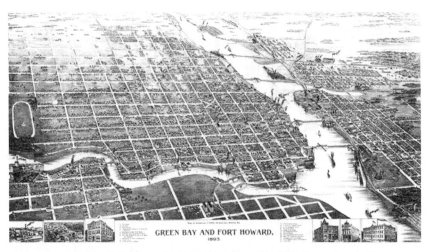

1893 Map: Green Bay (left of Fox River) and Fort Howard (right). East River is the tributary. (Courtesy of the Neville Public Museum of Brown County)

THE GREEN BAY Winona & St. Paul train screeched to a halt on January 9, 1893, its cowcatcher encased in ice, and Mary Cenefelt stepped off with a small suitcase in each hand. She had lived on her sister's Minnesota farm for three months, accepting her charity, and Mary had returned to the cities of Fort Howard and Green Bay seeking employment and hope.

She had no way of knowing the hell that awaited her.

Snow fashioned a white shawl over her black traveling cloak and small-brimmed hat, which was pinned to her dark, tightly coiled knot of hair. Train attendants unlocked the baggage car and its sliding doors rumbled open. Nearby, livery drivers cursed and soothed their horses. A porter trotted past with a luggage cart, his penny tips jingling inside his coat pockets.

Twenty-five-year-old Mary sucked in the air's frosty tang, the below-zero wind gusts nearly freezing her eyelids shut. She lifted her hand to flag down a coach and her body seized. For two years, she had suffered from stomach pain, a gnawing, burning, most excruciating agony that never relented. During the train's blizzard-condition crawl from her sister's home to northeastern Wisconsin, Mary's cramped and lumpy seat had strained her back, adding to her misery.

She realized she could not wait any longer. She had to see a doctor.

Until her stomach issues surfaced, Mary had been an industrious girl, strong, hardy, and cheerful. From the age of nine, she had performed a man's work beside her papa and brothers on her parents' Wisconsin farm. At age sixteen, Mary left home in the winter months to work in Escanaba, Michigan, first at a private home, then as a kitchen girl at a boarding house attached to a saloon. That pattern of procuring domestic winter employment and returning to her family's Cooperstown village for the planting and harvesting seasons had continued for nearly ten years. She had made good money and supported herself while aiding her immigrant parents. Like other farming families in the years following the Civil War, her parents' livelihood had suffered from long droughts, rising equipment costs, falling crop prices, and high-interest rates.

Mary's fragile health suddenly threatened the careful balance upon which her family's survival depended.

A coach outfitted with snow runners pulled up. Mary told the driver her destination and climbed in. She could speak and understand both her parents' native Czech and the English of her country of birth. But lacking any formal education, she could only read and write her name in either language.

Mary's hand slipped beneath her cloak to confirm the $35 sewn into her petticoat pocket was still safe ($1,200 in current valuation). As a young woman traveling alone, she knew she was a prime target for pickpockets and thieves, and she could not afford to lose a penny of what she had saved.

Mary's carriage glided east onto the Mason Street Bridge. Clouds parted and the quarter moon illuminated the frozen Fox River below. The bridge was one of three that connected the city of Fort Howard to Green Bay, its cross-river rival. Five miles to the north, the Fox River emptied into the waters of Green Bay that serviced the critical steamship route to the Great Lakes ports.

The lingering scent of cigar smoke from a former carriage passenger made Mary sneeze. She gritted her teeth as another surge of pain doubled her over, and the horse cantered off the bridge.

Mary's last job had been at the Green Bay Reis Hotel which had ended three months ago. Her duties—serving 150 Catholic conventioneers their meals and sewing twenty-five yards of heavy white cloth into a cover for the hotel's horse and hack—had been too much for Mary's worsening health. She had gone to her sister's Minnesota farm to recuperate. There she had tried home remedies such as cabbage juice, honey, and a concoction of baking soda and cider vinegar. Nothing had helped. A doctor, a luxury for a farm girl like her, was her last hope.

Mary's coach veered north onto Washington Street, Green Bay's downtown thoroughfare, recently paved with cedar blocks because they were safe, durable, quiet, and clean. In front of Joannes Bros. wholesale grocers, a lamplighter ignited the gas jets atop the cast-iron street poles that had been installed after the Civil War.

Civil War veterans had returned to the prosperous communities in 1865, the rail yards and wharves clogged with shingles and lumber. The hum of steam and water-powered saws had been the sweet sound of money. Both cities astride the Fox River had enjoyed a vibrant social life centered in their fourteen churches primarily established by Irish, Dutch, German, and Belgian immigrants. But gin mills and "houses of ill-repute" had also flourished, catering to the sawyers, lumberjacks, and lake sailors.

Three decades later, within Green Bay's prosperous commercial district, saloons and "disorderly houses" continued to thrive.

Mary's carriage crossed Walnut Street, where Mrs. R.W. Raymond, alias Nightingale, owned a "disorderly house," as did Mrs. Sadie Gans. The police frequently arrested both madams and ordered them to pay $20 court fines or spend fourteen days in the county jail.

Most citizens associated those houses with the much-feared syphilis and the other "unmentionable disease," gonorrhea. Rumors about catching a venereal disease in other ways fueled paranoia. People erroneously believed that syphilis chancres could pop up on the gum after a dentist pulled a tooth, sprout on the chin from a contaminated barber's razor, or appear on the genitals from a dirty lavatory or outhouse seat. It *was* a fact that the disease could be contracted by kissing a person with a syphilis chancre on the lip, mistaken for a cold sore. Dr. William Brady's local "Health Talk" newspaper column warned: "A girl of normal mentality should not do promiscuous kissing."

The two communities had reason to fear the disease. Syphilis's first stage was mild, but if left untreated, the disease could spread to the eyes, ears, brain, and nervous system. The symptoms could include blindness, hearing loss, severe headaches, muscle weakness, and dementia, which could place a victim in an insane asylum.

Mary's coach slowed, trailing a sleigh loaded with cords of pine stacked high.

Lumber companies had depleted most of the regional timber, and Green Bay's economy had stagnated. That reality had made local businessmen, primarily cautious conservatives, suspicious of new ventures. But by 1893, after the city realized its mistake by turning away industries like Carnation Milk, which had settled near Milwaukee, Green Bay leaders had changed their tune. Investors were erecting new business blocks. Manufacturing plants like the Allouez Bike Company were generating new jobs. Private citizens were building impressive homes inside the Astor Heights neighborhood, nicknamed "The Hill," and St. Vincent, the community's first hospital, had opened five years earlier. The Wisconsin Telephone Company had expanded its switchboard, construction crews had nearly completed the electric streetcar system, and the city's powerhouse had recently updated its equipment.

Brown County Courthouse (A Souvenir of Green Bay 1903)

Green Bay had emerged as the region's premier service and transportation hub with a population of nearly 8,000, the largest Wisconsin city north of Milwaukee. Fort Howard had developed into the Fox River Valley's manufacturing center with hopes of surpassing Green Bay in size.

At the new Citizens National Bank building, Mary's carriage turned east onto Cherry Street. The bronze-cupola-vaulted Brown County Courthouse, Mary's destination, came into view at last. Newly elected Sheriff John Bartelme and his family had moved into the ground floor residence of the three-story white brick courthouse, where Mary's driver reined in his horse. The county jail cells abutted the family's living space, and Mrs. Bartelme provided meals for the inmates. The Bartelmes had two daughters, Nettie and Josephine, both seamstresses in their twenties, and the family rented extra bedrooms to boarders, one of whom was Mary's educated younger sister, Carrie.

Mrs. Bartelme, who had relatives in the sisters' Cooperstown village, answered the door and warmly greeted Mary. Weary yet excited to see her younger sister, she hung her damp cloak and followed Mrs. Bartelme into the wallpapered dining room filled with female chatter and the scent of cabbage. Carrie pushed back her chair and stood. She crushed Mary into a hug, and Mary cringed. Both sisters had pleasing faces, though their body frames differed. Mary's large bones efficiently carried her 165 pounds within her home-spun dress while Carrie, still clad in her ready-to-wear black skirt and white shirtwaist Jorgenson-Blesh clerk attire, was so petite she could nearly encircle her waist with her hands.

1900 photo of Cenefelt family. Seated are parents: Catherine and John. Standing left to right are: Carrie (Mrs. Joseph J. Stangel), Catherine (Mrs. John S. Wanish), Joseph, Mathias, Mary, and Julia (Sister M. Clarissa). Note: This is the only known photo of Mary, poor as it is. (Courtesy of Rev. Harry E. Cenefeldt)

Mary joined the other boarders at the dining table.

Mrs. Bartelme kindly brought a pillow for Mary's back, asking after her ailments. The stout woman, known to be a gossip, said she had just served dinner to a new jail inmate temporarily housed there by Judge Brice. As she fed Mary, Mrs. Bartelme explained that the homeless man had worked odd jobs, but illness had overtaken him. "It was an act of kindness to send him where he could at least have food and shelter," she quoted from that evening's *State Gazette*. Mrs. Bartelme had called Dr. John R. Minahan to treat the man. She told Mary that if the physician had time, she would ask him to see Mary as well.

In that era, it was not uncommon for men claiming to be doctors to in fact be quacks or charlatans with no formal education. Not the twenty-nine-year-old Dr. J.R. Minahan, Mrs. Bartelme assured the sisters.

He had been born into his Irish immigrant family's nine-sibling clan, and his parents believed in education. Dr. Minahan had graduated from Chilton High School, attended Oshkosh State Normal School, and earned his medical degree at Chicago's prestigious

Dr. John R. Minahan (Roger Minahan Papers)

Rush Medical College. Even though he had not received academic honors, he had been elected president of his graduating class thanks to his charisma.

That evening, the six-foot-three physician with ginger curls and a bristling mustache did indeed have time to see Mary. After treating the jail inmate, Dr. Minahan strutted into the courthouse residence like a theater star. The prior year, he had left his successful Casco, Wisconsin medical practice and arrived in Green Bay. Minahan had secured St. Vincent Hospital's attending physician and surgeon position, much to the chagrin of certain local physicians competing for that spot. Since then, animosity had grown between Minahan and some of those doctors. They grumbled about the upstart. They agreed that Dr. John R. Minahan was aggressive, ambitious, and aloof—a reputation he seemed to enjoy.

What was more, Dr. Minahan had established a lucrative private practice. His reputation for handling complex cases was well-known around town, as was his willingness to do charity work. Both traits had provided him a heavy patient load. In addition to stockpiling $12,000 in savings, far more than a physician's yearly salary, Minahan had accumulated a land and rental property portfolio, quite an accomplishment at his young age.

As Mrs. Bartelme ushered Dr. Minahan into an unoccupied bedroom, Mary joined him. He closed the door, and his commanding pale-blue eyes met hers.

Mary later testified, "He looked at my tongue, and looked on my pulse, and gave me medicine." Minahan told her she had digestion problems, dyspepsia, a kind of gas on her stomach caused by ulcers, and the pills he provided would cure her condition.

Mary gazed up at that man of power and prestige and felt an overwhelming gratitude. He was the first person who had given her hope after two bleak years.

The Doctor's Power

GREEN BAY'S temperature danced below zero on the morning of January 16, 1893. Mary gingerly walked west on the Cherry Street plank sidewalk, a scarf tied over her mouth, her warm breath forming ice crystals on the itchy wool fabric. A Wisconsin Telephone Company shift change was in progress. Young ladies known as "The Centrals" stepped out of the WTC building and blinked at the glare of daylight on the snow. During Mary's sleeping hours, these women had been hard at work, repeatedly launching switchboard calls with the refrain, "Number, please."

Mary envied them. They had something she sorely needed: a job.

The Depression of 1893 had just begun and would continue for eighteen more months. Unemployment was 8 percent, and many women were vying for the same domestic jobs as Mary. If she did not regain her health, she knew it was doubtful that anyone would hire her, and she would need to live on her family's charity again.

The Beaumont House across from the Parmentier Block where Dr. J.R. Minahan's office is on the second floor. (A Souvenir of Green Bay 1903)

She could not, would not, think about that possibility.

In her first week in the city, Mary had shared her sister's bed for three nights and slept four at her Aunt and Uncle Loukotka's Green Bay home near the East River. "I took all the medicine [Minahan] prescribed for me the first time, and then he told me I should come again to the office." Mrs. Bartelme instructed Mary to walk to the Parmentier Block's Queen Anne building, identifiable by its turret and decorative ironwork. The three-story building was on the corner of Washington and Main, two blocks north of the Citizens National Bank, and across from the Beaumont House. Minahan's second-floor office sat above Raphael Soquet's Drugstore and across the hall from the Athletic Association and Gymnasium.

If that club's new director, C.P. Doherty, deemed a "gentleman of good appearance," had passed Mary as she climbed the stairs that day and headed down the hall, she would not have acknowledged him, nor any men coming in and out of the offices. "I never spoke ... to any man that I don't know his name." Mary knew her manners and station.

She entered Dr. Minahan's crowded waiting room, and Mrs. Emma Nolan greeted her. The doctor's office lady kept a tight ship, maintaining the proper patient rotation according to their arrival time. She had to be alert in her supervision; patients would try to squeeze into Minahan's consultation room when he opened the door. However, there were exceptions to the order kept by Mrs. Nolan. Minahan could provide certain individuals direct access through his private office hallway door to avoid scrutiny.

Minahan knew the secrets of many Green Bay residents. The two "unmentionable diseases," syphilis and gonorrhea, were just as prevalent among the wealthy as the poor, and their treatment was among Minahan's specialties. Two decades later, he would be interviewed by a Wisconsin Legislature committee for the *White Slave Traffic* report and would state: "I would not wonder if the percentage of males who at some time during their life have had venereal disease would run as high as 80%. But in the cases of females, probably from 40 to 50%."

German physician Albert Neisser discovered the bacteria that caused gonorrhea in 1879. The syphilis microorganism, however, remained a mystery. Syphilis treatments existed, primarily in the form of mercury tablets. But excessive use could cause loss of hair, teeth, and nails, kidney failure, brain damage, and even death. Gonorrhea treatments, like sandalwood oil, simply reduced genital inflammation and discharge. No gonorrhea or syphilis cures existed. Minahan had no patience for the aforementioned quacks who claimed to have found them, such as Dr. Bohannan's Vegetable Syphilis Cure and Acker's Blood Elixir, "A sure cure for Rheumatism, Syphilis, and all blood disorders."

Even trained physicians had a difficult time identifying syphilis from other conditions like smallpox, psoriasis, leprosy, epilepsy, and rheumatism. On the other hand, Dr. Minahan could mistakenly diagnose an individual with syphilis when they did not even have it. That could be a costly mistake, as the diagnosis carried a heavy weight and stigma.

Professor Alfred Fournier
(Welcome Collection,
Public Domain)

A male patient preparing for marriage might come to Minahan for counsel. According to France's nineteenth-century syphilis expert, Professor Alfred Fournier, the young man might say, "Doctor, I have not always been discreet in my bachelor life, and, what is worse, I have not always been fortunate. I contracted syphilis at such a time. I have been treated in such and such a manner. The matter is now a serious one for me. I have come to ask you if I am thoroughly cured and, if I can, without danger for my wife, without danger for my prospective children, contract the union which I propose."

In Dr. Minahan's professional opinion, if he believed the man's disease was active, he would condemn him to celibacy, depriving him of a wife and children. Even if his patient's syphilis had been latent for some years, the man risked giving his virtuous young bride syphilis as a wedding present, subsequently causing her to miscarry their children or have them be born with the disease.

The young man's serious question required a serious answer. Minahan held considerable power and responsibility. And he knew it.

With limited means and education and the swirl of medical misinformation in the world, Mary was vulnerable to the doctor's power. She trusted him, a highly educated man, one whom the two communities' only hospital endorsed.

While Mary waited to see Dr. Minahan, Mrs. Nolan and others in the reception area perhaps discussed the Chicago World Columbian

Exhibition. It was the talk of the town, due to open in four months. Many Green Bayites, including Mrs. Nolan, had plans to attend. Once it began, weekly steamboat excursions would leave the city's harbor to arrive at Chicago's Jackson Park, where the finest architects had constructed more than 200 classically designed buildings. A midway highlighting the much-anticipated "Ferris Wheel" was nearing completion, and each U.S. state had erected an imposing structure. Wisconsin's resembled one of Green Bay's Astor Heights mansions. A key feature on its first floor would be a twenty-two-thousand-pound block of cheese.

That fair would celebrate, among other things, Christopher Columbus's arrival in the New World. From Dr. Minahan's medical studies, he knew the Italian explorer's return to Europe after his expedition offered a prime candidate for the syphilis bacteria's introduction to the *old* world.

Wisconsin State Building at Columbian Exhibition (Courtesy, Field Museum. GN90799D_CON_167S)

A mild form of the "unmentionable disease" had been observed in Hispaniola (Haiti) before 1492, which had little effect on the natives due to adaptations in their immune systems. But when Columbus and his three ships arrived, his crew had no resistance. Upon Columbus's return to Barcelona, Spain, sailors displayed a strange illness. Ulcers and pustules had appeared on their genitalia. Scaling pimples surfaced on their bodies. Advanced stages destroyed nasal cartilage, tracheas and permanently bent and shortened hand and leg bones. Some crewmen lost their minds.

The initial outbreak spread throughout Europe, estimated to have killed over one million people. Although syphilis had become less virulent by the late nineteenth century, "the leprosy of lust" still carried a badge of shame.

When a patient stepped out of Minahan's private office, Mrs. Nolan waved Mary in. She could not read the diplomas on the wall, but Mary knew what they meant: Dr. Minahan was a very smart man. She felt fortunate to have stumbled into the physician's capable hands.

The Biggest Mistake

Corner of Crooks and Adams. The Presbyterian Church steeple is shown. To the church's right would be its parsonage and then the Minahan home. (Postcard)

FRIGID WIND SCENTED by industrial fumes nipped at Mary's cheeks. She had been in Green Bay for ten days, the last three spent at the Bartelme courthouse residence with her sister. Mary's savings were running out. But thanks to Dr. Minahan, the dyspepsia pills he had refilled at his office seemed to be working, giving Mary miraculous hope. If she was healthy, she could find work, and soon.

Lucky for Mary her friend, a Miss Nye, had a lead.

The two young women trod carefully down Adams Street, bordered by bony elms planted in soldierly ranks after the neighborhood's 1880 fire. They were on their way to the Minahan home. It was quite a coincidence when Miss Nye had told Mary the wife of the doctor treating Mary for dyspepsia needed a maid. Miss Nye had perhaps met Mrs. Minahan, the former Elizabeth Dollard, when the two had lived in Casco, Wisconsin, 25 miles east of Green Bay.

Miss Nye told Mary it was a temporary position, only until Mrs. Minahan's cousin took the job sometime in March. But the short-term placement was still imperative for Mrs. Minahan to fill. A housewife could not hope to maintain her proper community status without employing at least one domestic.

Mary was desperate for a job, but a private home placement might not have overjoyed her. She faced perils like so many other women in her position. In Mary's very first job in Escanaba, Michigan, she had stayed with that family for just a few weeks. Perhaps her mistress had been cruel to sixteen-year-old Mary. Maybe her master had not kept his hands to himself. In any case, Mary had left and found work at Mr. Fontaine's boarding house for the rest of that winter season.

Urban reformer Jane Addams wrote, "Never before in civilization have such numbers of young girls been suddenly released from the protection of the home and permitted ... to work under alien roofs."

Mary and Miss Nye stepped onto the porch of the Minahans' 425 S. Adams Street two-story clapboard home next to the Presbyterian Church parsonage. A woman about Mary's age answered the door. According to a letter Mary allegedly dictated to Josephine Bartelme some years later, Mary stated, "Dr. Minahan might have had more taste than to pick out such a wife—a little scrumpy being."

It is possible he hadn't had much choice in the matter.

Miss Nye told Mary that the doctor's wife had met her husband in Chicago when he had been in medical school and moonlighted as a railway horsecar driver. Dr. Minahan had boarded at a rooming house owned by his future mother-in-law. The community had judged Mrs. Dollard's reputation by her tenants' moral upkeep. Of utmost importance was her eighteen-year-old daughter's virtue, put in peril, if Minahan and the young Elizabeth struck up an affair. If rumors spread that she had lost her virginity to Minahan, Mrs. Dollard would surely have threatened the medical student to make Elizabeth his wife. The pair married on January 1, 1887. Whether by choice or threat is not known.

Miss Nye introduced Mary to Mrs. Minahan. She invited the two women into the loveliest home Mary had ever seen. Richly patterned carpet covered the sitting-room floor, walnut shelves of books lined one wall, and an elegant gas lamp hung from the ceiling. A candlestick telephone, a status symbol, stood on a table beside a brown leather chair. Above it hung a painting of a lion, its mane the same rusty color as Dr. Minahan's hair.

Mary inquired whether Mrs. Minahan still needed a temporary maid. If so, while her health was on the mend, Mary had a proposition. "The way I had it made with his wife, I was going to stay only a short time until I got a place, and I told her that I didn't ask for any pay," only room and board.

For Mrs. Minahan, whose husband scrutinized all expenditures—among other things—the handsome young woman's offer was a perfect arrangement.

Everyone, it seemed, was getting exactly what they wanted.

THE MINAHANS' Adams Street block contained nearly identical homes, all grand and modern, but all without indoor plumbing. Mary began her days by tending to the sitting room and kitchen stoves. After her employers awakened, she emptied the slop buckets and provided fresh pitchers of water and sponges for the bedroom washstands. She put up the breakfast, washed the dishes, and made the beds. Mary swept and dusted all the rooms and the halls before scrubbing the kitchen and privy floors on her hands and knees. After securing the groceries and running errands, Mary started supper, served it, and cleaned another set of dishes. The days were long and hard and sometimes Mary wished she had held out for a factory job, where she would have had more time at the end of the day to do as she pleased.

Although Mary was working for no pay, for the time being she had all she needed: a place to stay, food, and a growing sense of health. She felt honored to be employed by the city's talented surgeon. Indeed, Dr. Minahan's local reputation continued to rise. The Weekly Advocate's January 26, 1893, issue included two articles about Dr. Minahan that reported he had surgically treated a man for varicose leg veins and amputated another man's cancerous leg. He was clearly a hero.

To Mary's surprise, Mrs. Minahan did not feel the same about her husband and criticized him constantly. She called him a "brute." Night after night when he returned from house calls, Mrs. Minahan said he seemed to have purposely forgotten his house key, so he could rouse her from her sleep to let him in. Even though she complained, when the doctor arrived home for the dinner hour, Mrs. Minahan scurried to pull up his footstool, helped him remove his boots, and asked him about his day. But Minahan barely acknowledged her, and when he did, it was only to berate her for minor things such as neglecting to polish his shoes, forgetting to buy his new underclothes, or not drawing the drapes correctly. And he certainly did not seek out his wife's opinion on his financial endeavors as he did with his male friends, most recently at a poker party. While Mary waited on the men, she noticed how Minahan sought out the card players' approval for his purchase of an expensive racehorse. And even after Minahan received the men's glowing praise for his smart acquisition, the doctor only seemed to crave more admiration and praise from his peers.

IN MARY'S SECOND WEEK of employment, she helped Mrs. Minahan pack for a trip to Madison and Milwaukee. All the while, her mistress seemed to have something on the tip of her tongue to tell Mary—something serious and urgent. But when Dr. Minahan informed his wife their coachman was waiting to take her to the train station, those words remained unsaid.

Mary completed her duties in Mrs. Minahan's absence. Other than when she served the doctor meals, Mary rarely saw him. On those occasions, his coachman, a lame fellow named Henry Drissen, hovered at Minahan's side, always at his beck and call.

Mrs. Minahan returned to Green Bay with a few thoughtful trinkets for Mary, and she told her mistress everything had gone smoothly.

The lines on Mrs. Minahan's forehead relaxed, and she told Mary not to worry, she was not traveling again until March—and only for a few days. "Mrs. Minahan said she was going to Casco," where Dr. Minahan and two of his brothers owned a camp, "when they was making maple syrup, when they was tapping the maple trees."

Mary chewed on Mrs. Minahan's words. Why should she worry? Why should it matter that Mrs. Minahan be close by and not gone for very long? Mary felt safe and secure in the Minahans' home. Also, by March, her stomach issues should be a thing of the past, and she could find a paying job.

IN MID-FEBRUARY, Mary walked down Washington Street on her way to the grocers. The sidewalk planks often came loose in the winter months. If she did not take care, she could suddenly sink, and the board's opposite end would rise and hit her, a painful error should she misstep. She shopped at George D. Nau & Company and F. De Cremer's, where she scheduled deliveries of her selected cuts of meat and other groceries for later in the day. On the way home, Mary was pleased when she bumped into an acquaintance who asked about Mary's current domestic position. She could not hide the pride in her voice when she said she worked for Dr. Minahan. But her friend reacted in a most unexpected way. Rather than impressed, she looked horrified and, through a sharp gasp, told Mary to watch out. She heard he "liked the women," and the doctor had gotten into trouble with a servant girl in the past.

And yet, despite her friend's urgent warning, Mary would not listen to any gossip about her doctor. He had been a perfect gentleman when his wife had been away for an entire week. Mary had no reason to doubt Dr. Minahan's reputation or intentions.

ON TUESDAY, March 7, 1893, the maple tree sap started to run. Mary was on the move as well. She fussed with her hair, put on a bit of rouge, and slipped into the new dress Nettie Bartelme had sewn. With vigor in her step, Mary returned to Dr. Minahan's office, her good health resurrected. His wife was adamant: Treating anyone at the house, including those they employed, was off-limits. But Mary was not there for medical treatment. She wanted to settle up what she owed Dr. Minahan for her prior visits and to tell him she had found a paying job at the home of Mr. and Mrs. John D. Lawe.

According to Mrs. Bartelme, who had recommended Mary to the family, Mr. Lawe's grandfather, Judge John Lawe, was famous. Born to an English navy commander from Yorkshire and a Jewish mother, he had been a pioneer fur trader for John Jacob Astor's American Fur Company, a land speculator, a sawmill owner, and a Green Bay territory judge. When Mr. Astor platted what would become Astor Heights in 1838, he even named one of the streets for Judge Lawe.

Mary was relieved to have secured her new job. She knew it was only a matter of time before Mrs. Minahan's cousin arrived to fill Mary's position.

While she waited her turn in Minahan's reception area, Mary chatted with his office lady. Although they had talked only once before, Mary considered Mrs. Nolan a friend. If Mary showed kindness to others, she assumed they would return that favor. In Green Bay's class system, this was not always the case, but Mrs. Nolan seemed ready enough to offer kindness to Dr. Minahan's maid.

Mary's turn arrived, and she stepped into the physician's private consultation room. He gave her an appraising look and inquired whether her dyspepsia had returned.

"I told Minahan I felt strong," Mary later testified. "I didn't need any more medicine." She handed him two dollars for her earlier medical treatments. "I told him … I [had] hired out at this place, Lawes'."

Minahan was taken aback. He asked Mary when she planned to leave. "I told him I was taking the place on Monday." But her last workday would be on Thursday, only two days away. She wanted to visit her family in Cooperstown before starting her new position.

Dr. Minahan seemed visibly rattled, a crimson flush creeping up his neck and saturating his cheeks. He told Mary she must reconsider her decision. He and Mrs. Minahan had just discussed keeping Mary on and paying wages. His wife's cousin had decided not to take the job.

Mary wrung her hands. She said she was sorry, but the doctor's offer had come too late. She had already committed to Mrs. Lawe.

"[Minahan] says his wife spoke about going to Casco." He asked whether Mary would stay at least until she came back. Mrs. Minahan planned to depart on Thursday and return on Saturday. If Mary left, Minahan said he would have no one to make his meals or answer the telephone.

He needed Mary.

She could not leave him in such a bind.

The doctor's words tore into Mary. He had done so much for her. She could not disappoint him.

Mary gave in to his plea.

Lost Innocence

MARY FED white cotton fabric under the needle of Mrs. Minahan's treadle sewing machine. Its velvety click created a calming sense of satisfaction. The doctor's wife, freshly glowing and scented from her weekly bath, was seated in a chair beside Mary. Mrs. Minahan held up the first nightgown the two of them had made for her husband. She told Mary she appreciated her willingness to stay until Saturday.

Her mistress's brow looked troubled, although Mary could not understand why.

Mrs. Minahan said since Mary had managed the first time she was away, she hoped her three-day absence would also go smoothly.

Mary's feet paused on the treadle, and her hand halted the small silver wheel. She gave Mrs. Minahan a reassuring smile and told her not to worry. Her home and the doctor would be in good hands.

Mary made bread after Mrs. Minahan's Thursday morning departure. The doctor insisted that his dinner table be "kept in good shape, and it couldn't be without homemade bread." While the loaves baked, Mary put together an Irish stew of mutton, bacon, cabbage, and potatoes. The previous day, a new coachman, Patrick Mahoney, a gray-headed Irishman, had unexpectedly replaced the old coachman. Mahoney ate dinner in the kitchen while Mary served the doctor in the dining room. She refilled his water glass and ladled a second serving of stew into his bowl. Minahan used a chunk of bread to soak up the last bit, then pushed back his chair and stood. He stepped into the kitchen and instructed Mahoney to hitch up his team. Minahan said he had house calls to make.

Mahoney went out to the carriage house, leaving the home quiet and still.

Minahan asked Mary to join him in the sitting room. He paced, his palms smacking his thighs, the harsh sound echoing through the heated space. "He asked me if I done up his nightgowns. I says, yes ... Then he asked me if I knew anything about his collar. That his wife was going to have it changed a little. I says I had brought it back from the store, and he says, where is it?"

She crossed the sitting room and entered the Minahans' bedroom.

Rapid footsteps followed Mary, the sound like pelting hail on a carriage roof.

Her head turned as Minahan's arms crushed her to his chest. He kicked the door shut and hauled Mary toward the bed, heaving her onto his lap. "I didn't know what was the matter with him—that he acted so queer, and I asked him if he was crazy."

Minahan grunted yes, he thought he was crazy, that something was the matter with him.

Mary twisted forcefully to get out of his arms, telling him to leave her alone. She wanted to get out of the room. She wouldn't stay with a crazy man. Her panicky eyes found the door. If she could only escape and use the telephone. Or what about the new coachman? Any moment, he might come searching for Minahan.

Those wishful thoughts evaporated when the doctor threw Mary onto the bed. Her bones chilled as she realized what Minahan planned to do.

His hands shoved up her skirts as she wrestled to keep them down. Mary's hands targeted Minahan's head, pinching and beating at his face, telling him to stop, to keep away from her, to mind his own business: anything to get him off of her.

But Minahan was stronger and larger. He yanked down her drawers and gripped her arms, pinning her to the bed.

Tears pooled in Mary's eyes as his body humped hers. "[But] he couldn't do anything with me ... He took me in his arms ... and threw me on the floor."

Mary sobbed, but her cries seemed to enliven him. He mounted her again, and she screamed from the ripping, tearing pain as he thrust inside her.

Minahan jerked away and told Mary to shush. He lumbered to his feet and reached down to help her up.

Mary slapped away his hand. "I told him he was no man at all ... I never had anything to do with anybody." She said she was a good girl.

Mary kept telling him she was a good girl as she pulled up her drawers, arranged her skirts, and crawled to her feet. Through tears, she said she wouldn't stay on at the house with a man that acted the way he did.

Minahan hung his head. He said he was ashamed. He didn't know what had come over him. He'd never acted like that with any girl before. He told Mary he would go away if she stayed.

"I told him he ought to be ashamed of himself, and I was going to tell his wife."

Minahan lifted his chin, and his eyes narrowed. "He says he didn't care if I would tell his wife, that if she wasn't satisfied to live with anything he could give her, she could go where she wanted." And without another word, Minahan swung open the door and left.

As soon as Mary heard the back door slam, she stumbled toward the sitting room staircase and used its handrail to drag her battered body up to her second-floor bedroom. Even having heard her friend's warning, she never would have believed Dr. Minahan capable of such a violent transgression. That the respected and powerful doctor she knew could rape her.

Confused and terrified, Mary held back sobs as she wedged a chair below her door handle in a pitiful attempt to make herself safe. She could still smell Minahan's oniony breath, his bleached shirt scent, and her own sweat. She fought back the urge to vomit.

Mary did not know what to do. She had always felt capable, able to handle any problem.

Now she was lost.

Through the window, Mary watched Minahan's carriage head down the street. Should she go to Mrs. Bartelme's to stay with her sister? Or should she hike the long way to her aunt's house? Conflicting emotions filled Mary's head, but shame overpowered the others. She could not reveal Dr. Minahan's unspeakable acts to those closest to her. If she stayed until his wife returned and told her what her husband had done, Carrie and her aunt would never have to know.

That was what Mary decided to do.

She removed her torn housedress by rote, her corset and tattered petticoats, her stockings and drawers. She cleaned her private area, the pain intense. When the sponge color turned red, she bent over and moaned.

For twenty-five years, she had been a good girl.

Now, she feared, she no longer was.

Foolish and Fearful

RAIN PINGED against the windowpanes, and dawn's first light crept into Mary's room. She had barely slept, terrified that Minahan would return and attack her again. Mary removed the chair still wedged under the door handle and took a deep breath. Dressed for the day, she hobbled down the stairs. At the bottom, her worst fears materialized. Dr. Minahan sat on his leather chair, reading the newspaper. He calmly looked up and asked Mary for his breakfast.

She made it to the kitchen on shaking knees. Mary broke two eggs into a bowl and dropped the third onto the floor. She bent down to wipe up the gooey mess. Her eyes darted toward the kitchen door. Mary held her breath and listened. She burned the toast and started over. Bacon grease spattered and scorched her hand.

Mary announced that breakfast was on the dining room table and dashed back into the kitchen to hide, refusing to wait on Dr. Minahan. She counted the seconds until she heard him push back his chair. He entered the kitchen, and she shrank against the counter. "[Minahan] told me I shouldn't be foolish enough to go and tell this to anyone. That he was going away. That I should stay till his wife come back."

Mary's body trembled, and Minahan departed.

Her resolve to tell Mrs. Minahan wavered.

MARY WAS NOT the only woman raped that week. Newspapers documented the crimes with relative frequency, though police did little, and it's safe to assume that innumerable assaults like Mary's went unreported. In England, *The Yorkshire Herald's* March 10, 1893 edition stated that a traveling optician had conducted a felonious assault upon a farmer's domestic servant. On that same day, in New York City, *The Evening World* reported that a man had threatened to stab a fifteen-year-old girl if she did not submit while he forced himself on her. Closer to home, as Mary fed the coachman his supper, Mahoney told her about a *Gazette* article concerning a burglar in Pullman, Illinois, who had climbed into a kitchen window where a female domestic worker was sleeping on the couch. He had chloroformed her and sexually assaulted her before choking her to death. Since Mahoney had the night off and would not return until breakfast, he warned Mary to lock all the windows and doors.

Before Mrs. Minahan's departure, before her husband raped Mary, the doctor had granted Mary's request to go out that Friday night, and she and her sister had made plans. If Mary did not show up, Carrie would worry.

Under a waning crescent moon, men and women gathered outside the Adams Street Roller Rink for the three-mile Brown County Championship Race. Mary threaded through the crowd to meet her sister at Mrs. Bartelme's. Although Mary craved to reveal to Carrie what had happened, how could she? It was a given: unmarried women had no choice but to stay chaste until marriage. The community would not pardon her from that strict expectation, no matter the circumstance. Mary would be ruined. She had to lock her shameful experience away. Perhaps she could attempt to tell Mrs. Minahan when she returned, but with Carrie, Mary chose silence.

It took all of Mary's willpower to keep up a good front as the two sisters traveled to their aunt and uncle's home. They passed Mrs. Frankie Peepcorn's Cedar Street "disorderly house." In Mary's state of mind, she might have felt she was no different than one of the home's residents. Everyone knew the police had recently jailed Mrs. Peepcorn for two weeks. But before her release, Mrs. Bartelme had told Carrie that a physician had examined the woman and deemed her insane due to her syphilitic condition. It was no surprise when a Brown County judge committed Mrs. Peepcorn to the Oshkosh Northern Hospital for the Insane.

When the sisters reached their Aunt and Uncle Loukotka's home, a cozy fire warmed the front room. The companionable conversation of Mary's family enveloped her, yet she shivered. Mary was a changed woman, distanced from her sister.

On Mary and Carrie's return trip, they passed The Green Bay House, a two-story hostelry frequented by traveling salesmen. Raucous laughter drifted out from its open tavern door, but Mary was quiet. All evening, Carrie had asked whether something was bothering Mary. As they neared the Bartelme courthouse residence, Carrie asked again.

This was Mary's chance.

Her decision to keep her secret faltered.

Maybe, just maybe, Carrie could help.

Mary began to speak, but she could not find the words, and the moment passed.

She arrived back at the Minahan house at about 9 p.m. carrying homemade sausage sent by her parents. Her aunt had returned with the gift after a recent Cooperstown visit. Mary used her key to unlock the kitchen door. She paused and listened. The wall clock's sleepy tick was the only sound she could hear. She relocked the door and headed for the sitting room where she had left one gas lamp lit. Mary checked the front door and the first-floor window latches. To keep the stove burning all night, she riddled the coals with a poker, then dumped the panful of ashes over the hot embers. Only twelve hours remained until Mrs. Minahan's return.

Mary was afraid to go to bed. She would be the only person in the house. She knew she could never sleep in her upstairs bedroom while listening to the home's creaks and the windows' rattles, imagining the worst. Instead, she settled by the sitting room stove for the night. Lulled by the gas lamp's hiss, Mary dozed fitfully.

A knock at the side door startled her wide awake. The knocking continued. Mary entered the kitchen, slippery with nervousness, and checked the clock in the dim light. It was almost 11 p.m.

Mary placed her ear to the door. "I asked who it was, and [Minahan] said it was him."

Moonlight scattered in through the window, and his shadow appeared, vast and dark.

Dr. Minahan told Mary he did not have his key, and he commanded her to let him in.

What could Mary do? The house was his. What choice did she have? What choice did she ever have?

Mary unlocked the door, and the dank scent of wet wool seeped into the kitchen.

Minahan brushed roughly past her and headed for the sitting room.

Mary's guarded steps followed but stopped short in the dining room.

The doctor stood by the stove. "And he says that I should step in, that he wants to talk to me. And I told him ... he could talk to me from his room to my room, that the door was open. And he says ... I shouldn't make such a fool of myself to stay in a cold place, where I could go where the stove was."

Mary took one timorous step, then three more, her hands clenched at her sides, her breath raw in her throat. She stopped on the opposite side of the stove and angled her body toward the staircase, prepared for flight.

Minahan inquired about the telephone calls.

Mary managed to tell him what had come in as he took off his hat, coat, and vest.

He asked whether she had gone out during the day.

Mary lied and said, "No," fearful he would think she had told someone about his assault.

A slow smile crossed Minahan's lips. His hand darted out and grabbed Mary's wrist. She struggled to break free, but he wrenched her around, snaring her body in his arms.

"Leave me alone!" she cried as Minahan dragged her toward his bedroom, pushing the door open with his back. He landed heavily on the bed, Mary on his lap.

Her fists pounded his thighs. Her heels kicked his shins. "I told him to leave me alone ... that I have heard he had trouble with someone else."

Minahan's grip tightened. "He said it was nobody's business what he done. He was ... going to have satisfaction anyhow."

He tossed Mary onto the bed, and his hands grabbed her skirts. He had her sprawled on her back, her feet dangling off the side. She scratched and beat at his face, her cries coming out in pitiful gasps. Pins came loose from her hair. Snot ran from her nose. The button to her drawers came off.

Mary screamed, begging him to stop.

Minahan's words, smooth like ice, coaxed her to keep quiet and still. "He said I was a girl, quite an age, and that I never had anything to do with a man. And some girls, when they get that age, if they ain't married, they get consumption and different sickness. And some of them, if they have something to do with a man, they get all well and all such nonsense talk. It was a shame to listen to."

Minahan's lies were cruel, but Mary had no energy to respond, no strength to resist.

Tears ran down her cheeks and into her hair as he penetrated her.

She cried for her mama.

She prayed to God...

MINAHAN'S THRUSTS and grunts finally stopped. "He told me that I had to stay with him all night." But once his breathing settled into quiet snores, Mary escaped up the stairs and wedged the chair below her door handle.

She heaped her tainted clothes into a pile inside the frigid room. Her shaky hand poured water from the pitcher into the washstand bowl. Mary used a sponge and soap to scrub her body until her skin was raw. She pulled on a thread-worn nightgown and curled up under the bedcovers. Terrifying thoughts reeled inside her head: Minahan's hands, his scent, his collar still around his neck as he raped her a second time.

ON SATURDAY MORNING, Mary pulled stockings over her tender inner thighs and slid a housedress over her bruised upper arms. She packed up her belongings and labored down the stairs, avoiding the squeaky boards. Mary peeked around the landing's corner, and her heartbeat slowed. Minahan's coachman was the only person in the sitting room. Mahoney said the doctor had spent the night in De Pere (a city on the Fox River about five miles south of Green Bay).

Mary did not contradict him. Minahan's wife was her only interest. Mary had decided to tell Mrs. Minahan what her husband had done—twice.

Mary made breakfast. When the coachman finished his, he stepped outside. The kitchen door opened, and Mary looked up from the dishes. Dr. Minahan entered and Mary cowered.

"He asked me when I was unwell the last time," inquiring about her monthlies. If Mary had been flowing, she believed that might have stopped him from raping her. But her "time" had finished about three days before his wife had left for Casco. Mary kept her eyes focused on the floor as she shared that fact.

"He told me, well, you come to my office and let me know how you get along."

Then Minahan's voice turned threatening. "He told me I shouldn't dare to tell anything. If I would ... he didn't know what he would do with me."

Taken from Her

MARY FLED NORTH on Adams Street, outpacing a farmer's team pulling a hay wagon. She went as fast as she could, faster, her suitcases banging against her knees. Mrs. Minahan had just returned from Casco, bringing butter and maple syrup, and Mary had not told her what her husband had done. Dr. Minahan's threat scared Mary. She knew what he was capable of, and it would have been her word against his. Nobody would believe an illiterate maid over the famous Dr. Minahan.

Mary could only run.

She crossed Main Street, where laborers in overalls, suspenders, and flat caps worked to install the steel tracks for the new streetcar system. She sped past the two-story Reis Hotel, her last place of employment. Mary stifled a sob. If she had remained in that position, rather than going to her sister's Minnesota home to attempt to recuperate, the nightmare of the past two days would never have happened.

Mary arrived at her aunt and uncle's small wooden house. To ward off images of Minahan, his pounding body on top of hers, Mary immersed herself in chores. She beat the rugs hung over the backyard clothesline, washed the soot-covered windows, and killed and plucked a chicken for the Sunday meal.

Mary wiped down the gas lamp chimneys and trimmed the wicks, giving them new life. And though she was devastated, she felt a power surge up inside her. She needed to reclaim her life. She was a strong girl, smart at simple things. The doctor's pills had cured her dyspepsia. On the farm, she was every bit as capable as her brothers and papa. The past few days could not control her life. Minahan had had his way with her, but nobody would ever know if she kept her secrets to herself.

When Mary stepped into Mr. and Mrs. John D. Lawes' Cherry Street home on Monday morning, she buried Dr. Minahan's sexual assaults away and embraced her new position. She would not grant him power of her.

Mrs. Lawe kindly greeted Mary and helped carry her suitcases up to the third-floor bedroom. Mary's new mistress had hired her knowing she would only work for about two months, until Mary's return to Cooperstown to help her family with the planting season. The Lawes' son, Leo, a twenty-two-year-old Citizens National Bank teller, also lived in the home.

On Mary's second day of employment, winter sent one last rip through Green Bay. The week's high reached twenty-six degrees on Friday, March 17, St. Patrick's Day. Mary knew the Irish celebrated that holiday, but she did not know the specific date it fell on, a critical detail that would later hurt her.

Mary's positive attitude continued, especially after a weekend visit to family in Cooperstown, where she and her youngest brother John had likely danced to polkas at Zeddie's Hall.

But then Mary missed her period, and her anxiety returned in force. She could think of little else as she tried to go about her work. "I was afraid because they came so regular." She knew she might be in the "family way" and what that would mean for her future. "I was old enough to know that much ... I had not had morning sickness, but I was so sleepy—kind of faint ... More like weak."

Mary knew she had to see Dr. Minahan. If she was pregnant, he was the man responsible.

She would make him responsible.

The Tuesday before Easter, Mary walked up Washington Street crowded with horses, drays, and carriages. Manure and garbage odors oozed from puddles. The Salvation Army women and men in their gray bonnets and pillbox caps were out, waging war against hunger and sin. Mary kept her head up. Their attentions should be turned to Dr. Minahan, not her.

Mary reached the Parmentier Block and climbed the stairs to the doctor's office. She took a seat and tapped her boot until Mrs. Nolan admitted Mary into Minahan's consultation room. "I [told] him that I was in trouble with him ... That it was about a week over my time to have my sickness, [and] I never went over my time by more than two days."

Minahan pursed his lips, his pale-blue eyes meeting Mary's. "He says I had better wait a couple of days yet, before he gave me any medicine. And he told me I should go home and take a foot bath and some hot tea, ginger tea, and so I did."

Two fretful days passed. Nothing changed. "I went back in his office and told him that I have not been around yet. Well, he says, there is something the matter ... I believe you are caught. And he wrote a prescription and [says] I should go downstairs and have those pills put up."

Mary trudged out of Dr. Minahan's office. "I knew [those pills] was something to bring on monthlies." Mary perhaps knew another Catholic girl who had taken herbal or medicinal pills, called emmenagogues, to relieve an unwanted pregnancy. But other violent purgatives were also used like turpentine, veterinary medicine, or gin. If all else failed, the pregnant woman could participate in a controlled fall down a flight of stairs.

In Mary's era, Wisconsin Statues prohibited all abortions except those done to save a pregnant woman's life. If the expectant mother, whose life was not in danger, had perceived fetal movement, called "quickening," and an abortion was performed, the doctor and mother could both be charged with first- or second-degree manslaughter. Each could serve one or more years in prison and be given heavy fines. In Mary's case, her pregnancy had not "quickened." Even so, if she took Dr. Minahan's prescribed emmenagogue pills, which induced her fetus to successfully abort, that act would be deemed a felony. She would be fined $100 or serve one to six months in the county jail, while Dr. Minahan would serve six months and pay at least $250.

Because Mary was Catholic, she would also have considered the Papal Rulings. Before 1884, the Church only excommunicated the doctor who performed an abortion, not the mother. But since that year, the Holy Office's position had hardened, condemning the mother as well.

Perhaps both of those fears were why Mary, knowing the full weight of her choice, returned to the Lawes' home without filling the prescription and hid it inside a cigar box where she kept her family photos.

That night, Mary did not know how she would cope with her situation. Once her pregnancy showed, the Lawes would certainly dismiss her for being a sinful woman. She could go home, but what would her parents say? And what about her younger sibling, Clarissa, who had taken her vows at Silver Lake Holy Family Convent? Now she was a teacher at St.

Joseph's School in Kellnersville, a few miles south of Cooperstown. Her parents were proud of Clarissa. Mary knew her pregnancy would bring her family nothing but shame.

Would her parents attempt to arrange a quick marriage to a neighboring farmer's son, offering him a dowry to keep quiet? Mary could never allow her parents to squander their hard-earned money and humiliate her.

Mary had heard whispers about a Wisconsin maternity home, where she could live until her baby arrived. Of course, she would have to give it up for adoption. Bearing a child out of wedlock would condemn her to an impossible life. Everyone would know she had lost her virtue if she kept her child.

On March 31, Good Friday, the day after Minahan had given Mary the prescription, she plowed through the rain to reach his office. In water-logged shoes, she waited her turn, wet strands of hair glued to her neck. "I told him that I wouldn't take these pills."

Minahan scowled and even more so after Mary mentioned the maternity home and his financial responsibility.

Dr. Minahan had definite opinions about Mary's decision, as he would later state in a 1914 Wisconsin report. "There are two types of women who, as a result of immoral acts, give birth to illegitimate children. First, those who are too ignorant of the practices of abortion ... and second, those who prefer to give birth to an illegitimate child rather than to destroy the embryo." The report assumed the women, primarily "domestics," were "immoral," rather than attributing any of their pregnancies to sexual assaults like Mary's.

That day in the doctor's office, Minahan told Mary, since she was moving forward with her pregnancy, she needed to return to his office on Monday after four o'clock, so he could perform an examination.

Mary and her sister attended St. Francis Xavier Cathedral for the Easter Sunday service, where the "floral decorations were beautiful." Right Reverend Bishop Messmer celebrated the Pontifical High Mass while Mary's pregnancy consumed her thoughts.

She arrived at Dr. Minahan's office on Easter Monday at the assigned hour. Mary was about two weeks over her time. She stepped into his private office, and he locked the door.

The room's focal point was an oak-framed leather examination chair. Beside it, a table held a speculum, a probe, and a little curved knife to open boils. Minahan rarely required other instruments when treating patients at his medical office. He conducted all surgeries at St. Vincent Hospital to provide a sterilized environment, anesthesia, and nursing care.

"The doctor told me that I would have to get in the chair. That he had to examine me through a treatment."

Mary did as he instructed. The idea that she could question or contradict Dr. Minahan did not cross her mind. But as she used her weight to push the chair back, her head tilted down, the realization that Minahan would probe the area he had violated made her skin crawl.

"He put my feet in some kind of hooks," Mary later testified, and when Minahan placed a cloth over her face, she balked. It had no hint of chloroform, the potent anesthetic commonly used in surgeries since the Civil War, so she was conscious when Dr. Minahan began. "I couldn't see anything, only I felt."

A cold instrument spread Mary's private area apart. Another one slid within her. When it twisted inside, like a barbwire-wrapped wooden spoon, Mary screamed. "I told him that he should leave me alone ... that I couldn't stand them pains. I told him that was more than the examination going on."

Mary yanked off the face cloth. She lifted her head and hands. With her feet strapped in, she could not move her lower body. "He told me ... that I was with child, and he was going to remove it."

Minahan jabbed Mary again, and she begged him to stop. She thought he was digging out her organs. "I thought he was cutting my heart out." Mary continued to struggle, and Minahan grabbed her leg. "He told me I should be still, quieted me as much as he could ... otherwise the pain would be worse."

Mary did not know how it could be any worse. She had already lived through such horror, but this ... It was just too much. "I told him that he should leave me alone, that I wanted to get out of the chair." But Minahan said it was too late. "He says he had it so far [and] he couldn't leave me alone."

Mary writhed about, whimpering like a beaten-down dog until Minahan finished and removed her feet from the stirrups. She was flowing blood, and he gave her a towel to stuff inside her drawers. "He told me I should hurry home, that I would get awful sick yet."

In shock and alone, Mary stumbled out of his office with nowhere to turn.

She headed back toward the Lawes' home, a half-mile away. An abdominal contraction caused her to bend over, and she bit her lip to hold back tears—not only for her physical pain but for her heartbreaking loss. Even though she had planned to put her child up for adoption, she had imagined it would have had a life.

Mary gazed up at the heavens and sobbed.

All because of Dr. Minahan, her child's life had been snuffed out before it could draw a single breath.

A Bloody Mess

MARY SNUCK IN through the Lawes' side door, desperate to avoid seeing anyone. She crawled up the back stairway, then up the second flight of stairs. Inside her tiny attic bedroom, its ceiling angled and scent musty, Mary hid the bloody towel and her drawers in a bucket under her iron-framed bed. She cleaned her private area, and the washstand's ceramic basin of water turned apple red. She poured it into the bucket and attached two homemade menstrual flannel cloths to a belt at her waist.

Mary finally struggled into clean undergarments and pushed through her pain to return to the kitchen before she was missed at work. While the stew she had made that morning simmered, Mary bent over on a chair and stared at the pine floor, panting, feverish and in agony. She made sure the family did not catch a glimpse of her until she had placed dinner on the table.

Mary told Mrs. Lawe she was not feeling well and asked if she could wait until morning to do the dishes. Although she did not want to let her mistress down, Mary feared she might faint if she worked another moment. Mrs. Lawe agreed with concern. Slowly, painfully, Mary made her way up to her bedroom. She dropped the saturated cloths into the bucket and secured two new ones into place. A metallic scent filled the room. Mary climbed into bed and moaned, unable to find a comfortable position. "Mrs. Lawe came there that night to give me some whiskey at about 9 or 10 o'clock before she went to bed."

Mary could not get up at dawn to prepare the family's breakfast.

They let her rest.

At about 10:00 a.m., Mary stripped off the blood-stained sheets and hid them in the same bucket, planning to wash all the gory evidence when Mrs. Lawe was away.

Using the handrail and wall for support, Mary staggered downstairs, two new menstrual cloths in place.

She simply had to get better.

She had to move on.

She had to forget what Minahan had done, forget what she had lost.

That was the only way.

But how could Mary forget as blood dripped down her inner thighs while she attempted to do the chores. In the afternoon, she went to bed. To get up to make supper, she lifted each leg onto the floor, one at a time, then changed the sodden flannel cloths again. After serving dinner, Mary was too weak and in pain to stand. "I had to sit down to wash my dishes," she later testified.

Over the next three weeks, Mary's condition showed no improvement. She bled constantly and could not do all her work—no matter how hard she tried. By applying different dressings at night, she managed to keep the blood off her bedclothes. But as her health continued to worsen, Mary was too weak to go on. She had no choice but to see Dr. Minahan. Any other physician would want to know what had occurred, and Mary was too ashamed to tell her terrible secrets to anyone else.

Sheets of rain fell on Cherry Street, turning the thoroughfare into a muddy stream. Horses staggered, and wagons stalled. Mary had borrowed Mrs. Lawe's umbrella. On the walk to Minahan's office, Mary paused to rest multiple times. After the slow trek, she arrived, exhausted, only to discover the doctor was not there. Mrs. Nolan informed Mary that Minahan was away in Appleton, attending the Fox River Medical Association meeting, and he would return the next day. With pride in her voice, Mrs. Nolan added that the doctor had been one of seven physicians elected to attend Milwaukee's upcoming American Medical Association meeting.

Mary shuffled back to the Lawes' home, defeated and in worse shape than before. Bitterly, she reflected on how Minahan's career proceeded in high fashion while her life leeched away, all because of him. No matter how famous and successful he was, he could not get away with what he had done to her. Even in Mary's weakened state, she had to fight back.

She had to live.

The next day, Mary entered Minahan's consultation room and stood squarely before him, mustering what little strength she had left. She told him her pain and blood flow were constant. She could hardly work to support herself. If he did not do something to help her, she would tell others what he had done.

Perhaps a momentary tick of fear crossed Minahan's face before he assured Mary her condition was temporary. He removed a corked bottle of pills from a cabinet and handed the glass container to her. Minahan instructed Mary to take one pill three times a day to control her pain and stop the bleeding.

She followed his instructions in the coming days, to no effect. Mary sent her sister to Minahan's office, and Carrie brought back another bottle. "I took all those pills and waited almost a week again, but my pain and blood flow didn't stop."

Mary had to confront Minahan again. Unable to walk farther than out to the street in front of the Lawes' house, she climbed aboard a hired coach and asked the driver to drop her off at the doctor's office. Mary rested on each step ascending the stairs, still prepared to act on her threat. But inside his consultation room, she could only think about her pain. Mary clung to the back of his examination chair and said he had to do something to help her.

Minahan brushed off her desperation. "He told me I have to keep off my feet. I have to go to bed. And I told him, I couldn't do that at the [Lawes'] house when I was working [for them], I couldn't do it. So, he says that I should try it anyway for a day or so."

Leo Lawe (Courtesy of the Neville Public Museum of Brown County)

Mary remained in bed for two days, but her pain continued to rage, and her blood flow never slowed. She feared she would lose her job before her planned departure in mid-May. But Mrs. Lawe continued to show concern for Mary, believing she was dealing with "female issues."

At around that time, Catharine E. Beecher and Harriet Beecher Stowe published a manual to guide women in the management of their households. The manual included instructions on the proper way for housewives to handle domestic servants. "It is not by merely giving them comfortable rooms and good food ... and privileges, that the attachment of domestics is secured; it is by the manifestation of a friendly and benevolent interest in their comfort; ... in guarding their health; ... and [supplying] the place of a parent."

Mrs. Lawe subscribed to their instructions. She had taken on the role of Mary's mother and the Lawes' son, Leo, that of a younger brother. Their kindness was a gift Mary badly needed.

Leo was worried about Mary and contacted her sister. When Carrie arrived at the home, Mary could scarcely prop herself up. "I only told [Carrie] that I had terrible cramps. And she asked me if I wanted to see [Dr. Minahan]."

Mary said, "Yes." She knew no one else to turn to other than the man who had raped her and savagely aborted her child.

"Minahan came there that evening at 9 o'clock, and he told me that I have to be ready in the morning to go to the hospital."

Original St. Vincent Hospital at 626 S. Quincy Street (Courtesy of St. Vincent Hospital)

THE FOLLOWING DAY, on May 4, 1893, Minahan's driver, Patrick Mahoney, transported Mary to St. Vincent Hospital at 626 S. Quincy Street within the Astor Heights neighborhood. Formerly, the twenty-three-room mansion had been the residence of Dr. A.H. Van Norstrand of the Civil War's Fourth Wisconsin Regiment. Five years earlier, the Green Bay Businessmen's Association had recognized the community needed a hospital, and Bishop Frederick Xavier Katzer of the Green Bay Diocese contacted the Sisters of the Third Order of St. Francis in Springfield, Illinois. After Brown County residents raised enough money to purchase the Van Norstrand home, five Sisters of St. Francis arrived to turn the mansion into the city's first hospital.

St. Vincent now contained fifteen beds and the Sisters provided attentive nursing care. They frequently gave up their own beds to incoming patients when the hospital was full, "retreat[ing] to the leaky attic" to sleep on the floor. The Sisters followed the hospital's charter: to care for patients of any creed or nationality. And yet, they would not admit patients with contagious infections or venereal diseases. Instead, the Sisters provided private home care to those suffering from such diseases in order to allay inpatients' fears of contracting a contagion.

Dr. Minahan allocated his hours between his Washington Street medical office and St. Vincent Hospital depending on his surgery schedule and the hospital's patient load. As St. Vincent's attending physician and surgeon, he had the final responsibility for all inpatient care—even that given by a subordinate.

Minahan's driver helped Mary climb the hospital's front steps and supported her across the porch. Inside the foyer, a Sister took over and admitted Mary. When Dr. Minahan entered her room, he checked her blood flow. Mary could not look at the man. Instead, she stared into the Sister's compassionate eyes. Mary desperately wanted to reveal what Dr. Minahan had done, but how could she when she depended entirely on him for her care?

The next morning, only the Sister entered Mary's room to check her blood flow. Mary's gaze focused on the doorway. She saw Minahan pass, his white coat flapping, his eyes purposely looking away. Day after day, that pattern continued. Anger bubbled up inside Mary. Dr. Minahan should not be allowed to ignore her. He must be held accountable for her condition. She was determined to report him to the authorities and have him arrested. He should have to pay for his dreadful acts. She told the Sister she needed to talk to Dr. Minahan privately. During Mary's twelve-day hospital stay, which included no treatments or surgeries, nothing but bed rest, he ignored her request.

When the hospital discharged Mary, her bleeding had stopped, but after her harrowing month, she still lacked energy. Mary's $25 hospital bill also loomed, more than she could earn in three months. She had figured Minahan would pay her hospital charges, but the Sister said she knew nothing about that.

Before Mary returned to Cooperstown, she stopped at Dr. Minahan's office. Her resolve had only grown. "I told him I would have him arrested."

With a smug smile, Minahan shook his head. "He says I couldn't do it. That I had no money. That he had money and could fight it any day."

His words drained all the spunk out of Mary, and her will to fight dissipated.

Minahan was right: He had money and power.

Mary had neither.

The Statement

Mary's Village of Cooperstown, Wis. Wanish General and Wanish Tavern on left and St. James Church on right. (Courtesy of Lee Verkuilen, USMC)

MARY'S COACH neared Cooperstown, twenty-five miles south of Green Bay. Her bleeding had not returned, but she was weak and discouraged through and through. Mary did not know what options she could pursue to make Minahan accountable, and she was unwilling to ask her family for advice, unwilling to risk their shame, and unsure if they could help her anyway.

Still, as she neared home, the scents of prairie grass, moist soil, and manure perked Mary up, welcoming her back to her rural community. The horses whinnied as her coach rolled to a stop by St. James Church in the village center. A tornado had recently torn off the roof, leaving the white steeple intact but damaging the interior. Even though the church was under repair, its tower bell still rang at noon and six.

The Wanish General Store and the Wanish Tavern to Mary's left were both owned by her brother-in-law John Wanish and her eldest sister Catharine. Mary entered the spice-scented store, where a delight awaited around every corner. The couple stocked provisions like flour, hardtack, and coffee on shelves and displayed candy inside the glass counter at a youngster's eye level. There were cigars for men and fabrics for women. There were lamps and utensils and even stoves for furnishing a kitchen. Near the front door, three farmers chewed tobacco by a spittoon. The store served as the local information center. After Sunday church service, Wanish General was where families gathered to stock up for the week.

Mary's brother-in-law, also the Cooperstown postmaster, greeted her warmly. He removed his apron and offered to drive Mary to the family farm while her sister minded the store. The Wanish home and barn were just beyond the tavern. John went around back and hitched a horse to his rig and Mary climbed up beside him. With a flick of his reins, they were off.

Mary's grandparents, Joseph and Margaret Cenefelt, had arrived in New York with their six children in 1856 from Zahorany d Pilsen, located in the Stanetice Roman Catholic Parish of the Prague Archdiocese. They immediately set out for Wisconsin, where friends had written the land was cheap, the taxes low, and the soil adaptable for growing maize, rye, wheat, oats, and vegetables, all familiar to the Czech husbandman. Mary's grandparents bought 150 acres of land about one mile south of Cooperstown for about $1.25 an acre, and there they built a farmhouse, barn, and a split rail fence.

Cenefelt farm between Cooperstown and Kellnersville
(Courtesy of Lee Verkuilen, USMC)

Soon after, her grandfather gave the farm to his eldest son John, Mary's father, when he married her mother, Catherine Vogeltanz, from Kdyne Nova, Bohemia, the current Czech Republic. The couple produced ten children, Mary being the seventh. Two siblings had passed away in infancy. The rest lived in Minnesota, Green Bay, and in and around Cooperstown, four of them married with families of their own.

Over the summer months of 1893, Mary's energy steadily increased as she helped cultivate her parents' hilly land and milk their dairy cows. But as is true for many rape survivors, the unseen effects of her trauma lingered. She made excuses when her youngest brother John asked her to go to Zeddie's Hall for a social. The idea of any man touching Mary while dancing an innocent polka made her want to throw up. She wondered whether that physical reaction to the mere suggestion of intimacy would ever change and whether she wanted it to. She saw couples at the newly reopened church with their sweet little offspring. After the brutal abortion Minahan had performed on her, Mary questioned whether she could have children, a necessity in any farming family.

St. James Church in Cooperstown prior to 1914 (Courtesy of Lee Verkuilen, USMC)

Mary's parents provided her with free room and board, but that would not pay her delinquent hospital bill. Mary knew Minahan should be responsible for it. But now that she felt healthy and independent again, ready for the future, she wanted to erase that horrific chapter from her life and move on. Instead of confronting Minahan, Mary decided to find work in Green Bay and slowly pay off the bill herself.

In late August of 1893, Mr. and Mrs. Dorr Clark hired Mary. They lived in Astor Heights in a rambling Queen Anne at 936 S. Monroe Avenue. He was a cattle dealer and stockbroker married to Allie Robinson, the *Green Bay Advocate* newspaper founder's daughter. They were a good family. In addition to securing free room and board, Mary would make about $8 a month.

But her optimism soon faded. Sharp pains cropped up on her left side, and abnormal bleeding returned. If she wanted to receive medical care, she would have to see Minahan again. She knew no other doctor who would treat her once they discovered the source of her distress.

When Mary entered Minahan's consultation room he eyed her and his face pinched tight. Three months had passed. He likely thought he had seen the last of Mary Cenefelt. She told him about her abdominal pain, and he curtly told her to remove her drawers and sit. Minahan then instructed Mary to recline in the same chair where he had destroyed her baby. He used a speculum to hold Mary's vaginal walls apart and inserted a cystoscope containing a light and lens system to examine her uterus. Minahan told Mary she had "inflammation of the womb." To treat her condition, he said she would need to inject medicine into her abdomen twice a day.

That devastating news reignited Mary's conviction to expose Minahan's crimes. "I told him I was going to have him arrested."

Minahan calmly wiped his hands on a towel. He informed Mary he would provide the drugs she needed and could not afford, but not if she told anyone. Minahan opened a cabinet and removed a box of syringes and a bottle of liquid medicine. He paused, then asked Mary for her decision.

OVER THE NEXT four months, Mary continued to see Dr. Minahan "a good many times." She had no other choice financially, yet her abdominal pain never diminished. "He used to say that I wasn't sick, that I was lazy. I was like an old woman ... and I got discouraged." Before traveling back to Cooperstown at Christmastime, she told Minahan she planned to see another doctor when she returned to Green Bay. He warned Mary not to do so. No other doctor could help her but him.

While Mary lived in the country, she took the pills Dr. Minahan had given her and the monthly refills he sent by stagecoach mail, yet the pain on her left side steadily increased. Only able to nibble at her mother's cooking, Mary cinched her skirts tighter and tighter at the waist to keep them from falling as she grew thinner and thinner.

All the while, Dr. Minahan's surgical success continued to elevate his community status. The *State Gazette* provided details about two operations Minahan had performed "which promise to be of great interest to the medical profession." The first was on Mr. Ed Willits to cut out a cancerous tumor from his leg. The second was on Martin Thor. Minahan removed an abnormal growth from the farmer's nose and skillfully patched it with skin harvested from the man's upper arm. Dr. Minahan's surgical ability had begun to spread beyond Brown County. The Wisconsin State Medical Society invited Minahan to present a paper on his "Surgical Treatment of the Varix," or the excision of varicose leg veins.

Mary returned to Green Bay on Sunday, September 2, 1894. She moved into her sister's room at the Bartelme courthouse residence while Carrie spent a week in Cooperstown. Mary had lost thirty pounds, and her "womb trouble" had sapped her vitality. Dr. Minahan had told Mary he was the only doctor who could help her. She finally realized: He *needed* her to believe that. Mary also worried whether the medicine she was taking was making her "crazy." She felt "queer" and off. She needed another physician's opinion to see whether she should continue to take Dr. Minahan's pills.

Dr. William E. Fairfield
(Men Who are Making
Green Bay 1897)

The next day, September 3, 1894, Labor Day, Mary entered Dr. William E. Fairfield's waiting room on the second floor of the Citizens National Bank building. The thirty-three-year-old physician was a Canadian native who had taken a prominent place among local doctors. He had graduated from Quebec's Bishop's College first in his class. That honor had led to his position as house surgeon for the Montreal Women's Hospital where he had treated females suffering from mishandled abortions.

Mary knew nothing of that. She had ended up in Fairfield's office at the recommendation of her thirty-year-old brother. Although he had recently passed away, likely from tuberculosis, the nation's leading cause of death at the time, Mary knew her brother had trusted Fairfield's medical care.

Dr. Fairfield's office girl admitted Mary into the physician's private consultation room. The kind-eyed man with a slim build and neatly trimmed beard and mustache asked Mary to sit. In his soft, French-accented voice, he then inquired how he could help her.

Mary handed him the pharmacy bottle containing the pills provided by Dr. Minahan. She asked Dr. Fairfield whether he could identify the drugs. He checked both sides of the glass container and extracted one pill. Fairfield said he was sorry. Without a prescription label, there was no way to tell.

For seventeen months, Mary had suffered. Nobody other than Minahan was privy to what he had done to her, though Mary's family and employers had certainly guessed that something was seriously wrong.

Enough was enough.

Mary took the risk in Dr. Fairfield's office to reveal the truth. Finally, painfully, desperately, she told him about Minahan's assaults, the forced abortion, and her resulting medical problems.

Dr. Fairfield stood there, processing Mary's story. Unbeknownst to her, he was one of the city physicians who did not care for Dr. Minahan. At the Fox River Medical Association meetings, Dr. Fairfield and his two colleagues, Dr. Abbott Slaughter and Dr. Fred Brett, would privately criticize Minahan for being too boastful.

Fairfield asked Mary whether she wanted him to examine her, and she said she did.

Using a system similar to Minahan's, Fairfield gently examined her uterus then stepped back, his face grim. "He says that I was in a bad condition."

His words confirmed what Mary had already known.

Even though Fairfield was not confident he could improve her health, he asked Mary whether she wanted him to treat her, and she said, "Yes."

To do so, Fairfield said Mary would need to make a written statement concerning Dr. Minahan's abuses. The document was for Dr. Fairfield's protection as Mary's new physician and hers.

Minahan's threat that Mary should not "dare to tell anything" made her hesitate before she agreed.

Dr. Fairfield stepped out of the office while Mary waited inside. She worried whether she had made the right decision. When the doctor returned with a Brown County justice of the peace, Mary felt she had no choice but to forge ahead.

The justice of the peace swore Mary in and told her to think carefully and tell the truth.

Mary followed his instructions, summoning all her courage. When she was unsure how to phrase something, the two men aided. The justice of the peace read Mary's completed statement back, and she signed her name underneath it.

After Fairfield handed Mary a prescription for injectable medicine, she asked what he planned to do with her statement.

The doctor said he would take it to his Jackson Street home for safekeeping.

Mary clutched the prescription, hoping for relief.

Perhaps her statement would be safe, but *she* did not feel safe.

If Dr. Minahan discovered what she had done, what would he do to her?

Making Lies

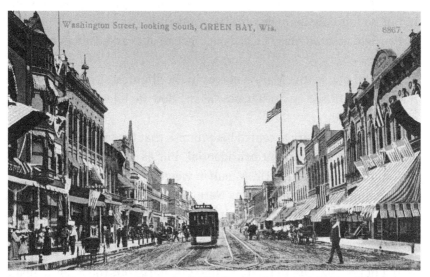

Washington Street looking South—Dr. Fairfield's office is on the left side within the Citizens Bank Building. (Postcard)

SMALLPOX FEARS gripped the community in 1894 as the fall semester of school approached. The disease had spread to Milwaukee after an infected steamboat passenger had arrived from Chicago. Fort Howard and Green Bay could be next. The Brown County health officer mandated that "every student be vaccinated" for that viral disease which killed thousands each year, could cause blindness, and created pustules that left permanent scars on survivors.

Even with a plague looming, a different fear gripped Mary. Yet the reality of the smallpox threat was unavoidable when she stepped into Dr. Fairfield's waiting room on September 4. It sounded like a Saturday afternoon matinee, where mothers in hats trimmed with satin flowers, lace, and ribbons attempted to control their noisy offspring, awaiting a jab in the arm. Mary did not need much of Dr. Fairfield's time. In fact, she wasn't there for medical attention. Mary was there for reassurance.

She trusted the physician would keep her statement confidential. But she wanted to confirm the justice of the peace would do the same.

As Mary waited, she looked out the window onto Washington Street. In front of Knox & Wilner's shoe store, she saw Dr. Minahan and Dr. Fairfield talking.

Mary's mouth went dry.

A short time later, Fairfield entered his waiting room, and Mary bolted to her feet. He ushered her into his consultation room. "I asked him if he told Minahan about my statement."

Fairfield assured Mary he had not. He had only asked about her prior treatments.

That did not soothe Mary's nerves in the slightest. Dr. Minahan had told her not to see any other physician. Now he knew she had talked to Dr. Fairfield.

Nevertheless, Mary accepted his promise that the justice of the peace would keep her statement confidential. But as she left Dr. Fairfield's office, her worries about Dr. Minahan weighed on her still.

Standing outside the Citizens National Bank building, Mary paused to think. The bank and other businesses would close the next afternoon to provide their employees time off to enjoy the Brown County Fair. The Bartelme sisters had asked Mary to attend with them. She knew the fair held a horse race where the top three finishers split the "gentlemen's driving purse." When Mary had worked for Dr. Minahan, he had talked about his horses participating in that kind of race. Mary's fear of running into him had kept her from accepting the Bartelme sisters' invitations. But Mary's circumstances had changed. She suddenly realized there was no reason for her to worry about Dr. Minahan. She had secured a new physician. Mary was no longer under Minahan's thumb. If she wanted to attend the fair, she should. Rather than dodging him, Mary decided to face Dr. Minahan head-on. She wanted him to know about her statement. She wanted him to worry.

Mary crossed the dusty thoroughfare where a city street cleaner swept horse droppings into a handcart. She headed up Washington Street and climbed the stairs to Minahan's second-floor office. While Mary waited for Mrs. Nolan to call her name, she kept reframing her thoughts and words.

"I told [Minahan] that I wasn't going to doctor with him no more. That I didn't know if he was giving me the medicine to keep me well.

He says, yes, I heard that you went to Dr. Fairfield … What did you tell him? And I says I told him all that was done to me. [Minahan] was kind of excited about it." He asked Mary whether she had told Fairfield he had had "anything to do with her."

"I says, yes, I told [Fairfield] all about it, and he has got it down on paper … that I signed my name to it."

Mary could tell Minahan was "fretting about it," and she was pleased.

"He says I made a damn fool of myself to go and tell such things. [And] I says, I didn't care if I was a fool or not, I said it."

Minahan stood there, his eyes hooded in thought. He asked Mary what else she planned to do.

"Well, I says, I was going to have him arrested … Because he ruined me."

Minahan shook his head, his lips tight. He said she couldn't do that. It was a damage case, not criminal, and Mary had no money to put up.

Mary did not understand the difference between a criminal case and a damage suit, also called a civil suit. Only in a criminal case would Mary, as the plaintiff, receive free representation from the state, or in Mary's case, Brown County's District Attorney. Since Mary had never reported Minahan's crimes to the authorities, it was unlikely she could succeed at a criminal trial. Minahan knew that. The state would have to prove her case "beyond a reasonable doubt" without any physical evidence: no photos of Mary's rape injuries taken with that era's Kodak camera, no samples of her tattered clothing, nothing. Mary's only option would be a damage suit, where she would need to hire an attorney. That lawyer would have to convince a jury there was a greater than 50 percent chance that Mary's assault claims and her non-consensual abortion were true. If a jury found Minahan liable for those acts of wrongdoing, she could receive financial compensation from him. But he would never serve a day of prison time.

Minahan reached into his pocket and handed Mary a silver dollar to pay for Dr. Fairfield's office visit.

Mary told Minahan she did not want his money.

He reminded her that Dr. Fairfield's injection prescription, which she was now responsible for purchasing, was most likely the same medicine Minahan had given her for free. Mary should also consider her ongoing cost of Fairfield's office visits.

But, if she had Fairfield burn her statement, Minahan said he would give Mary $20 *and* continue to provide her free office visits and medicine.

In any case, Minahan said she could keep the silver dollar while she considered his proposition.

Mary left his office. She did not know what to do.

The sun was high, and Washington Street steamed. The previous day, several hundred working men led by a police squad and a trombone band had paraded down the roadway to celebrate Labor Day. The men belonged to unions—the Brewers, the Longshoremen, the Masons, the Machinists, the Carpenters, the Coopers, and the Cigar Makers—that provided their workers guidance and protection from injustice.

Mary had no one to call upon for similar support. No community and no resources. As a domestic, she belonged to the country's largest women's workforce, yet grievances about poor wages, long working hours, and physical and sexual abuses similar to Mary's fell upon deaf ears. Progressive women's organizations tirelessly advocated for protective labor legislation for female factory workers, but even those initiatives excluded domestics. Any laws which could invade their middle- and upper-class homes' privacy could gain no traction.

Mary felt trapped.

Dr. Fairfield had said he was not sure he could improve her health. Mary was not certain that Minahan could either. But his office visits and medicine cost nothing. Mary realized she could not afford her daily necessities if she had to pay for Dr. Fairfield's office visits and prescriptions.

Despairingly, Mary felt she had no option. She had to accept Minahan's terms.

Mary returned to Dr. Fairfield's office the next day and handed him the silver dollar for her prior office visit. Scuffing her toe on the plank floor, she looked down. Mary told Fairfield she wanted her statement burned.

He gave Mary a somber smile and reminded her he had taken it to his Jackson Street home. He would bring her statement back to his office the next day. At that point, Mary could decide whether she wanted him to destroy her statement.

Over the past twenty-four hours, Mary had shuffled back and forth between the two doctors' Washington Street offices, suffering from pain, her weary arms and legs pulling her up steep flights of stairs. After all the agony and helplessness, she took a moment to consider her plight. "I asked [Dr. Fairfield] if I could have [Dr. Minahan] arrested.

And he said he couldn't tell [me] anything about it. That I would have to go and see a lawyer."

Mary left Dr. Fairfield's office feeling alone and unsure, yet seeing a lawyer seemed like a good idea to her.

LEO LAWE was still a teller inside the ground floor lobby of the Citizens National Bank building. He had been kind to Mary while she worked for his parents. Perhaps he was the person who had given Mary Attorney Patrick H. Martin's name. Or perhaps Mrs. Bartelme had mentioned Mr. Martin since he prosecuted many of the jail inmates she fed. No matter how Mary had found him, she would soon find herself in Martin's office, trying yet again to stand up to Dr. Minahan. Unfortunately for Mary, Green Bay was a smaller town than she realized.

Mr. P.H. Martin was the Brown County District Attorney, and he had a private practice in a second-floor office across from the Parmentier Block. Born in Brown County to Irish farming immigrants, he had graduated from De Pere High School, taught in the village of Allouez, and married Mary Wigman, a Green Bay attorney's daughter. Martin's next job was in the railway mail service, where he was off every other week. Martin used that time to clerk for his wife's father and study law. When the Wisconsin Bar admitted Martin, he returned to his father-in-law's firm, and its name changed to Wigman & Martin.

Patrick Martin never drank or smoked. Neither did his close friend and fellow Irishman, Dr. John R. Minahan. Both were fond of outdoor sports like hunting and fishing, and both were charter members of Elk Lodge No. 259. Martin was one of the few who had cracked Minahan's cool reserve to become a true friend, and they were abidingly loyal to each other.

Attorney Patrick H. Martin (Men Who are Making Green Bay 1897)

Martin also handled Dr. Minahan's legal work.

The district attorney's assistant admitted Mary into Martin's private office, and a breeze drifted in through the open window. Martin sat behind his desk, his curly hair parted on the side in the current fashion, his handlebar mustache waxed. He asked Mary how he could be of assistance.

Her story spilled out: how a man had ruined her by physically assaulting her, then aborting her baby against her will; how she was permanently injured and could barely work. "I didn't mention Minahan's name, nor my name ... [Mr. Martin] asked me if that was a curly-headed doctor."

Mary thought the question was strange but said, "Yes." He was a curly-headed man. "[Martin] asked me if he had any property, and I says, no, all I know is that he had his own horses ... Then [Martin] said it was a damage case."

Mary nodded and asked whether he could help her.

Without uttering a word, the district attorney turned in his swivel chair, and dust motes spun in the air. Martin looked out the window, his back to her. He did not speak another word.

Mary had her answer. If the district attorney would not help her, Mary believed no attorney could. Her only option was to yield to Minahan's demand and have Dr. Fairfield burn her signed statement.

The following morning, she asked him to do so. As her accusations turned into ashes, a sense of loss enveloped Mary.

Defeated anew, she slogged toward the Parmentier Block behind two women, their laughter riding on the wind. Mary was only twenty-six, yet she could foresee little happiness in her future.

Back inside Minahan's private office, Mary said she had done what he had asked.

Minahan shook his head. He said that was not enough. If Dr. Fairfield ever decided to use her accusations against him, Minahan said Mary had to sign another statement. He wrote it down and told her it included his promise to provide Mary free medicine and treatment for as long as she was unwell.

Minahan knew Mary could not read.

After she signed the statement, Minahan read it back to her. "But there was a difference," Mary later testified.

In substance, it said: When Mary first saw Dr. Minahan at the Bartelme courthouse residence in January of 1893, he treated her for "womb trouble," caused by an "unmentionable disease," and whatever she told Dr. Fairfield was false. There was no mention of Minahan's free medicine and treatment promise.

Panic gripped Mary.

How could she have trusted him?

"I told Dr. Minahan, that is a lie! And he says, we have to make lies sometimes."

Under His Thumb

GREEN BAY'S *State Gazette* ran monthly advertisements for Dr. Turpin, "The celebrated surgeon and specialist of Diseases of Women and Men," formerly from the Imperial Hospital in Vienna, Austria. One day each month, Dr. Turpin took up office at the Beaumont House on the corner of Washington and Main. He provided free, "strictly confidential" consultations for diseases like blood poisoning, gonorrhea, syphilis, rheumatism, fits, and dyspepsia. Each patient was to bring four ounces of urine passed first thing that morning for "chemical and microscopic examination." The inspection could diagnose some of those diseases—though not syphilis.

Mary perhaps noticed those patients standing in line when she stepped out from the back entrance of Dr. Minahan's office building onto Main Street. At an upstairs window, the physician might have watched the Beaumont House with interest as well. Minahan knew a urine test could prove Mary did not have gonorrhea. Not until the mid-twentieth century would scientists identify other sexually transmitted diseases like chlamydia and herpes. For Minahan's statement lie to hold up to scrutiny, it meant Mary's "unmentionable disease" could only be syphilis, which no existing urine or blood test could prove. For centuries, the only way for a doctor to diagnose syphilis was to examine the patient for known symptoms and to ask pertinent questions.

Minahan followed the work of the syphilis experts. English venereologist Jonathan Hutchinson called the disease "the great imitator" because of its varied presentation. Canadian physician William Osler said syphilis was a "versatile thespian," capable of acting out roles in any part of the human body.

Fannie C. Hart Steamship
(A Souvenir of Green Bay 1903)

Minahan knew if a woman had a diseased uterus and a doctor ruled out gonorrhea as its cause, syphilis would be the likely diagnosis. If she was unmarried, she was automatically heralded as a woman of loose morals.

Mary watched passengers disembark from the Fannie C. Hart steamer while she scolded herself for signing Minahan's statement, filled with lies. Even after Fairfield had burned her initial statement, Minahan had not given Mary the promised $20. Worst of all, she feared he would no longer treat her now that he could falsely claim she had an "unmentionable disease." The Brown County District Attorney would not help her. Even if she found the courage to tell her family, what help could they offer against Minahan's influential position in the community?

Mary decided to turn to a place of last resort: a Catholic priest. Carrie was acquainted with Father Michael J. O'Brien, who officiated at St. Patrick's Church in Fort Howard. Mary knew the priest was Irish like Minahan, although she had heard the doctor deride the Catholic religion to his wife. Minahan might not listen to a priest, yet Mary had to take that chance. It was the only idea she had left.

Breathing in black dust from the Hurlbut coal yard, Mary limped across the Main Street Bridge, heading toward St. Patrick's Church.

Back in 1862, the arrival of the Chicago and Northwestern Railroad had brought an influx of workers into Fort Howard to support the roundhouse and shops. Most of them were Irish, and among those immigrants were five families who gained Milwaukee's Rt. Rev. Archbishop Henni's support to build a church inside the "Irish Patch." Fort Howard's first Catholic parish, Saint Patrick's, opened in 1865 at 211 N. Maple Avenue. When its pastor Father William Verboort was transferred to St. Willebrord Parish in 1893, the thirty-four-year-old Father

St. Patrick's Church (A Souvenir of Green Bay 1903)

Michael J. O'Brien arrived to fill his shoes. With "characteristic Irish energy," he convinced his congregation they needed a new house of worship and he promptly secured the necessary funding.

Mary stepped off the Main Street Bridge and St. Patrick's beautiful steeple, topped by a gold-leaf cross, guided her toward the Gothic Revival church. Scaffolding surrounded the cream-colored brick building with red accents, still under construction.

Mary entered through the arched doorway and stepped inside a nave furnished with oak pews. Incense permeated the air. There were seven stained glass windows depicting biblical scenes on either side, and colorful beams of light filled the nave. In a radiant pool of light stood two men. One was a priest in a black cassock and white collar. The other was a workman, his clothes coated with plaster dust and a flat cap held respectfully in his hand. Mary dipped her fingers in the holy water and made the sign of the cross.

The confessional booth was off to the side, but that would not serve Mary's purpose. She was there to make an accusation, not a confession. As the workman departed, nodding her way, she approached the priest with a strong face and black hair parted on the side. Mary introduced herself and asked whether Father O'Brien could spare some time to discuss a confidential matter. He agreed, and they sat on one of the pews. Mary's emotional floodgate opened, and a

Rev. Father Michael J. O'Brien (Men Who are Making Green Bay 1897)

flurry of words poured out about her rapes, including Dr. Minahan's name.

Father O'Brien's eyes darkened. He told Mary he could not understand why she hadn't left after her first assault. Mary said she knew it was foolish, but Minahan had told her he was leaving town. When she told the priest about her non-consensual Easter Monday abortion in Minahan's office, "[Father O'Brien said] he didn't know how I stood it."

Mary had no answer.

He agreed to talk to Dr. Minahan.

That night, alone with Nettie Bartelme, Mary finally revealed her secrets to her friend. Stunned by the revelations, Nettie pulled Mary into a hug and promised not to tell. Even if Carrie had not been in Cooperstown, Mary would have confided in Nettie. For Mary, telling a friend instead of a family member felt less shameful, far safer, as if falling into a bed of hay rather than onto a dirt floor.

THE NEXT AFTERNOON, Mary made her way to the Parmentier Block. She opened the street door beside Raphael Soquet's drugstore. Its front window featured a perfume display of Rogers & Gallet, "known the world over as the best." She climbed the stairs to Minahan's office, hoping for the best. When Mary entered his consultation room, he gave her a resigned sigh.

Father O'Brien had kept his word and talked to Minahan. The doctor said he had told the priest that in addition to providing Mary the promised $20, he would give her $15 more, enough for Mary to finally pay off her delinquent hospital bill and live on for one month. Minahan would also provide Mary free ongoing treatment and medicine. Finally, he handed her a gold ring.

Mary examined it and the engraved initials inside. When she had worked at the Minahans, her mistress had worn that exact ring and she told Dr. Minahan that. He nodded and said it had originally belonged to a lady who had used it as payment for her medical treatment conducted by him. He told Mary to keep the ring. But said if anyone asked her where she had gotten it, she was to say she had "found it."

Mary stepped out onto Washington Street, the money in her pocket and the ring on her finger. She raised her face toward the sky, tears stinging her eyes.

Minahan had done more than she had expected. He had given her the gold ring. He had paid money she sorely needed, and he would continue to treat her condition free of charge. But Mary did not feel the relief she had expected, no gratification at what she had accomplished, no closure. She realized, with a flash of anger, that nothing had changed.

Threats and Accolades

AFTER YEARS OF deep-seated rivalry, the cities of Green Bay and Fort Howard voted to consolidate on April 2, 1895. At the foot of Pine Street, a cannon boomed farewell to the old and rang loud greetings to the new as thousands of citizens lined both sides of the Fox River. Their cheers, whistles, and kazoos echoed across the water. Bands played, processions marched, and the celebration continued until dawn. With the stroke of a pen, Green Bay's population had jumped to approximately 18,000 citizens.

Mary heard the revelers from the Clarks' home, but she had nothing to celebrate. Seven months had passed since Dr. Minahan had paid her $35, given her the ring, and agreed to treat her for free. He had kept the agreement, but her health had not improved. Each day, as she scrubbed the Clarks' floors, fed their coal stoves, and gathered the ashes and cinders, Mary felt razor-sharp abdominal pain on her left side.

Her life seemed hopeless.

She could see no way to free herself from the past so she could seek a better future—or any future at all.

In Minahan's consultation room in late April of 1895, he had the nerve to claim that Mary's womb trouble was all in her head. He said there was nothing more he could do for her. Mary stood there in disbelief. Her every waking hour was defined by her pain. Sometimes it seemed more real to Mary than anything else. "I scolded him. Because as long as he got me in this trouble, as long as he was the doctor that he could injure me so for my life, how could he have left me alone afterwards?"

Minahan was unmoved. He pointed toward the door and told Mary to get out.

She left, yet she could not give up. Nettie Bartelme recommended that Mary get another opinion from Dr. Austin F. Olmsted. She had heard good things about him. After graduating from the Cleveland Homeopathic Hospital College, he had earned quite a reputation in Green Bay as a trusted homeopath, specializing in pregnancy, childbirth, and women's reproductive health.

Unfortunately for Mary, his excellent work in the city's medical community had also earned him a spot within Dr. Minahan's tight circle of selected physician friends.

The post office building's second floor housed Dr. Olmsted's office. Mary entered the street vestibule and climbed the stairs. "I went to [Olmsted] to know from one doctor that didn't know anything about it, what he would say ... I just told him I wanted to know if I had any female trouble."

Inside Olmsted's private consultation room, he examined Mary. "And he says, yes ... There was some inflammation, but he couldn't just tell me just what it was ... only there was some trouble way back."

Olmsted asked Mary whether she had been seeing another physician. "I told him I had doctored two years with Minahan."

Olmsted peered at her through his spectacles. He said he could prescribe hot water and medicine injections, although he did not believe any treatment could reach the injured spot. He told Mary she would be "wasting money" to ask him to treat her if not even Dr. Minahan could help her.

Dr. Olmsted's words did not discourage Mary. His examination had proved her troubles were not imagined, bolstering her confidence. She marched back to Minahan's office and said, "You better do something to help me, or I'll tell Dr. Olmsted everything you done to me."

Mary's threat worked. Minahan promptly admitted her into St. Vincent Hospital for the second time. Each day, during her four-week stay, she soaked in hot baths and took cod liver oil.

By the end, Mary could climb in and out of the tub with no discomfort. She had to borrow money from Carrie to pay her bill, but Mary told her sister, Minahan's treatment for her "female trouble" was worth every penny. Mary could still not tell Carrie the cause of her problems—but if Mary could continue to heal, she thought she might never have to.

The Clarks welcomed Mary back after her hospital stay since they had not filled her domestic position. Mary's sallow cheeks turned pink, and her hair's rich chestnut sheen returned. She cautiously imagined the life she deserved had finally arrived. Mary had never wanted much. Just the opportunity to support herself and aid her parents through steady work for a kind employer like the Clarks.

When they gave Mary a night off, she and the Bartelme sisters often met to tell fortunes. Mysticism and fortune-telling were popular amusements at the time, especially with young ladies. Josephine would play the seeress role, shuffling standard playing cards and looking wise and mysterious as she dealt a three-row, five-column card arrangement, each card faceup. On one occasion, when Josephine revealed the Queen of Clubs, representing Mary, the nearby King of Hearts, her future blond admirer, and the Ace of Spades, designating the two would have children, Mary felt a surge of optimism. Now that she was feeling back to her old self, that promising future seemed possible for the first time in years.

IN THE SUMMER of 1895, Green Bay's middle- and upper-class women pedaled bicycles around the city in bulky skirts and white pique hats with black ribbon bands. The new "safety" bicycle, with two wheels of the same size and a chain-and-sprocket drive, had ignited the craze. Theirs was a newfound freedom. At long last, women could control their vehicles and travel without a man's supervision. They had to combat naysayers who believed a bicycle seat could be sexually stimulating for women and lead to a "loose lifestyle," but it was not enough to stop them.

Men were also biking and not only for pleasure. The city's Water Works superintendent stated, "I have lots of work all over the city, and I have always used a horse and carriage. But I am convinced a bicycle beats a horse for speed, convenience, and cost. My son can go to De Pere and back on his wheel while I only make it one way. They may say what they will, but the wheel has come to stay."

The increase in bicycle usage and other new modes of transportation translated into additional business for Dr. Minahan. He was in a prime position to capitalize on the accidents caused by the industrial age's new inventions. Minahan treated a Green Bay Athletic Association member injured in a Washington Park race track bicycle crash. The physician tended to a young man who, when leaning out on a crowded streetcar, had smashed his shoulder as a car on the opposite track hit him. The surgeon also operated on a brakeman's hand, crushed while he had been coupling an engine to a rail car. Dr. Minahan attended to nearly all Green Bay rail workers. The Chicago and Northwestern Railroad and the Chicago, Milwaukee, and St. Paul Railroad had named him chief surgeon.

All that recognition heightened Dr. Minahan's community stature. And the best was yet to come. To aid the Sisters of St. Francis in constructing a larger St. Vincent Hospital, Minahan donated money to purchase land for the new building on the northwest corner of Webster and Porlier. He also agreed to buy the old hospital to refurbish into his residence, launching him into the elite ranks on "The Hill."

In September of 1895, the Sisters invited local physicians to a reception to inspect the new seventy-bed hospital. Reverend J.J. Fox, the Green Bay Diocese Vicar General, and Dr. Minahan conducted a tour before the latter showcased his new surgical procedures in the large, airy operating room. Minahan leveraged his good favor with the Sisters to control and hand-select the physicians who operated at the city's only hospital. Dr. Fairfield, who had prompted Mary's statement of Minahan's wrongdoings, was not among them.

St. Vincent's Hospital, Green Bay, Wis.

Established December 13, 1889.
Opened the present building September 24, 1895.
This institution is open to all physicians in Green Bay
and the surrounding country.

DR. J. R. MINAHAN is the attending Physician and Surgeon.

Advertisement in the 1895-1897 Green Bay Gazette

As Minahan achieved greater and greater success, Mary's abdomen pain returned. For nearly four months, she had savored the sweet taste of good health, but suddenly it had curdled like sour milk. She could not keep up her work at the Clarks', and she moved into the O'Neil Hotel at 348 S. Washington Street (the current Fox Harbor Pub & Grill). Mary had Nettie Bartelme write letters to Dr. Minahan. "Just a few lines—that I wasn't through with him yet." Mary pestered Minahan so much that in late October of 1895, he admitted her into the new St. Vincent Hospital for an operation. Dr. J.F. Doyle and Dr. Olmsted assisted him. The former had studied at Chicago Polyclinic Medical School, and Dr. Minahan had recently hired him as his assistant.

"Dr. Doyle examined me—just my outside, on the left side," Mary later testified. "Then I took chloroform, so I don't know what Minahan and Olmsted did to me, but it was something for my womb trouble.

I was there three weeks and two or three days." At Mary's discharge, Minahan promised to pay her current hospital bill. "Doctor Minahan [also] gave me $35 to pay back my sister for my second hospital stay."

BROWN COUNTY had been loyally Democratic since its territorial days. But in the 1896 presidential election, the county switched parties. The community's now-conservative political leaders feared the bimetalism theories of the Democratic Party's candidate, William Jennings Bryan, and instead supported William McKinley, the Republican Party's candidate, who championed the gold standard.

Dr. Minahan did not align himself with either party. He expressed an "American Individualistic Philosophy" and rejected the autocracy of church and state. He believed he possessed the freedom to define himself based on his talents, abilities, and ambition, and he rolled over anyone who got in his way, including Mary Cenefelt.

A year had passed since her surgery at the new St. Vincent Hospital. Mary's periods were regular again, although their flow and color were light. She felt hopeful, especially after Nettie told her about a recent *Gazette* article highlighting the city's notable physicians and surgeons. Dr. Minahan received the most accolades, including his success in performing "some of the most difficult and dangerous operations known to medical science."

Mary had returned to Green Bay after the 1896 fall harvesting season and found work at the home of Mr. and Mrs. Oliver Tennis, a Belgian couple who ran a grocery store. But Mary's abdominal pain resurfaced in late-November.

She faced the terrible truth: the surgery had failed.

On December 8, Mary received a collection letter for her third hospital stay. She threw the letter on the floor.

It had been nearly four years since she had first met Dr. Minahan. Four years since he had raped her and butchered her womb. Four years of pain and suffering. Four years of secrets and shame. Four years.

Mary could not wait any longer.

It was time for her to expose Minahan's crimes.

It was time for Mary to seek justice.

Brave Decisions

MARY TREKKED past the Chicago Bargain Store on Washington Street, sleet stinging her cheeks and pain searing her abdomen. She was on a mission. She had to find an attorney to represent her against Dr. Minahan. To complete her housework at the Tennis home was a struggle, and once her savings ran out, she would not be able to afford further medical treatment. She refused to be a lifelong burden to her family. Minahan had to pay for his criminal acts—for destroying her life. There was no other option.

Mary asked a long-bearded man sprinkling salt on the plank sidewalk whether the Greene, Vroman & Fairchild law firm was on the building's second floor. He said it was, and she opened the adjacent door and slowly climbed the stairs.

Perhaps Leo Lawe, the son of her former employers, had given her Attorney Charles E. Vroman's name. He was a director at the Citizens National Bank where Leo worked. Or perhaps Mary's friend Nettie had told her about the attorney. His firm's name and Washington Street office location were advertised in the Gazette's business section.

In any case, Attorney Vroman might not have been Mary's best choice for a lawyer since he and Dr. John R. Minahan lived directly across the street from each other in Astor Heights.

Mary entered Mr. Vroman's cigar-scented second-floor Washington Street office heated by a coal stove and lined with stackable cabinets. The attorney politely stood and offered her a chair. A green-shaded gas lamp lit the desk where Vroman took a seat. He was an active Presbyterian and a fine pianist. At social gatherings, he performed solos such as "Bonnie Dundee."

The attorney asked Mary how he could help her. She took a deep breath and relayed her entire emotional story. Dr. Minahan's rapes, her nonconsensual abortion, her infected womb, the statement she had given in Dr. Fairfield's office, and how she could barely work.

As Mary spoke, Attorney Vroman tapped a pen on his desk blotter, raising his eyebrows on more than one occasion. When Mary finished, she bravely asked him whether he would take her case.

Mr. Vroman hesitated. He told Mary her claims were disconcerting. Before making any decision, he said he would need to talk to Dr. Fairfield about her allegations.

That worried Mary. More than two years had passed since Dr. Fairfield had burned her statement. He had only treated her once. She questioned whether Fairfield would care about her problems, especially since there was no evidence her statement had even existed.

TEAMS OF MEN shoveled snow off Washington Street as Mary traipsed back to Attorney Vroman's office two days later. Anxious thoughts filled her head. Would he take her case? Or, would he send her away asserting her accusations held no merit?

When Attorney Vroman asked Mary to take a seat, she felt a spark of hope.

The attorney said he had not known what to think about her story, but things had changed. Vroman picked up a document from his desk and handed it to Mary.

She peered down at the paper, but the only words she could read were her signature on the bottom.

He told Mary it was her original statement, dated September 3, 1894, given under oath inside Dr. Fairfield's office. The document Mary had watched him burn had been a copy. Fairfield had saved the original and even shared its contents with two of his medical colleagues.

Vroman's revelations astounded Mary. The document in her hand now proved her current story matched her initial sworn facts.

Dr. Fairfield had not let her down.

When Attorney Vroman said he would take her case, Mary was incredulous. She had done the impossible. She *believed* she had found an attorney—one that would help her seek justice against Dr. John R. Minahan.

THREE DAYS PASSED. Mary sat across from Attorney Vroman once again as a muffled train whistle filtered in through the closed window. "He told me that he'd called Minahan into the office and that [the doctor] denied everything." But Vroman said that Minahan would rather lose some money than have the case come to court. He would settle privately with Mary for $1,000.

She gave a startled gasp. That was more than Mary could make in five years, though unbeknownst to her, Minahan's medical practice could recoup that sum in less than one month. Dr. Minahan had likely agreed with his neighbor, Mr. Vroman, that $1,000 would be a small sacrifice to shut Mary up.

Attorney Vroman told Mary he believed Minahan's offer was a fair figure.

She considered his words. Mr. Vroman was an educated man. He had to know what was best for her. Mary agreed to accept Minahan's offer.

THE NEXT DAY, at Minahan's request, passed along by Attorney Vroman, Mary entered the physician's private consultation room all alone. If Mary had been a lady of different social status, or if her offender had not been her attorney's peer and neighbor, Mr. Vroman would undoubtedly have insisted that he accompany Mary on this visit to look after her interests.

Nevertheless, as Mary looked Minahan in the eye, she felt confident she would soon leave with her settlement, confident she would never have to see the man who had raped her and aborted her child, again. "I know you don't like to have this come to a court," she told Minahan. "[Let's] settle it privately for one thousand dollars."

Minahan nodded, yet Mary noticed a crafty glint in his eyes. He told her that settlement would be hers, but only after she fulfilled certain conditions: She had to meet with Dr. Fairfield *and* Father O'Brien and tell each of them that her stories about Dr. Minahan were all lies. Then Mary could return to his office to receive her settlement.

Mary was no longer the meek girl Minahan had dealt with in the past. She could see through his strings-attached promise. She would not be fooled again. "I says, if I would go now and deny it, then you would have me in a trap ... then I don't believe I can do it." Mary swung open Minahan's door and left. She descended the stairs and stepped out onto the plank sidewalk. How could her attorney have sent her into Dr. Minahan's office all alone to fend for herself? How could she trust Mr. Vroman after he had done such a thing? Especially, after she had recently discovered from his servant girl who shopped at the Tennis grocery store that Mr. Vroman and Dr. Minahan were neighborly friends.

Father O'Brien had helped Mary before. Maybe he would do so again. She crossed the Main Street Bridge to reach St. Patrick's Church and located the priest inside the rectory. "I told him that Dr. Minahan sent me there to get back what I said about him ... And I says, Father O'Brien, I can't deny it ... Whatever I said here, it is true ... But if I only knew, that is, if I could make sure [Dr. Minahan] would help me, I would tell Minahan I have denied it."

Father O'Brien released a heavy sigh. He said he would talk to Dr. Minahan. Mary was to come back the next afternoon, and the priest would counsel her on what to do.

MOONLIGHT SNUCK under Mary's bedroom curtains inside the Tennis home. She had not told her employers she had hired Attorney Vroman. If she could not settle privately, Mary feared the couple would dismiss her if her claims came out in the press. They had their reputation to uphold, as well as their grocery business livelihood. They could not employ a young woman who claimed to have been raped, one who had lost her virtue.

Mary walked the mile and a half back toward St. Patrick's Church the next day. The railroad gate was down as a train passed, giving Mary time to rest. Some boxcars likely contained tramps coming to the city's workhouse for a warm bed and food, more than Mary might have if she could not settle privately with Dr. Minahan.

She located Father O'Brien attending to his vestments. He said he had talked to Dr. Minahan. If Mary denied her accusations to the priest *and* Dr. Fairfield, she could report that to Minahan. He had promised Father O'Brien that he would then give Mary the $1,000 settlement.

Mary stood there, conflicted. Minahan's money could soon be hers. Yet she suddenly realized she could not accept his financial offer. She had to tell the truth. "I told [Father O'Brien] if I would take it back ... [Dr. Minahan] could have me arrested for running his name down ...

So, I could never take it back."

Mary returned to Minahan's office and told him she had not denied her accusations to Father O'Brien nor Dr. Fairfield since they were true.

Minahan called her a fool and told her to get out.

Mary descended the stairs, her head held high. She crossed the street and climbed the stairs to Attorney Vroman's office. "I told him that Dr. Minahan wanted me to deny it, and I couldn't do it ... What I swore to it once, it is there, and I could never take it back."

Attorney Vroman frowned. He told Mary unless she was willing to serve Dr. Minahan an official complaint and potentially go to trial, there was nothing more his firm could do for her.

Mary studied Attorney Vroman's eyes, which would not meet hers. She did not know whether she could trust him to move forward with her case. She worried whether he had ever had her best interests in mind. Mary told him she needed to get another opinion before making a decision.

She stepped outside his office. Other than confiding in Nettie Bartelme, Mary had been going it alone. Men in power had offered her little help. She needed to talk to an educated female, one who had been right under Mary's nose. One she should have told immediately after her first sexual assault. Her sister, Carrie.

On Christmas Eve, beneath a star-filled sky, sleighs passed with tinkling bells and singing carolers draped with robes. Trees with electrified lights or candles glowed through the windows of nearly every home. Aromas of hot mulled cider and cocoa wafted into the street. Carrie and Mary walked toward the Cathedral for midnight mass. Mary cringed not only from her physical pain but from her stored-up shame as she told Carrie everything. She was the sister who had shared Mary's bed when they were children, the sister Mary had whispered secrets to in the dark. But nothing could compare to the secrets Mary revealed that night.

Mary's shocking words ignited Carrie. She said Dr. Minahan could not get away with what he had done to her sister. The famous surgeon had to pay, and Carrie was convinced an attorney she knew could make that happen.

J. CALVIN STEWART practiced general law in Sturgeon Bay, Wisconsin, but he was young and green, never having conducted a trial in circuit court. Carrie had perhaps waited on Mr. Stewart at the

Jorgenson-Blesch dry goods store where she clerked. Many Sturgeon Bay citizens shopped in the "big city" of Green Bay where there was a better selection.

The two sisters traveled by train to Sturgeon Bay, about forty-five miles north of Green Bay, to meet with Attorney Stewart. A ship canal completed in 1882 split the community of about 3,000 citizens in half. That waterway provided a safe passage from Lake Michigan to the waters of Green Bay to avoid the dangerous Porte des Morts strait at the peninsula's tip.

Before agreeing to take Mary's case, Stewart told her that three respected Green Bay physicians would first need to confirm that Mary's womb was diseased.

After Dr. Benjamin Brett, his son Dr. Fred Brett, and Dr. Abbott Slaughter each examined Mary, the two sisters met with Attorney Stewart again. He said that all three doctors had confirmed Mary was indeed suffering from womb trouble. Based on their examinations, Stewart said he would take Mary's case.

She gripped Carrie's hand. All because of her sister, Mary had finally found a lawyer to represent her, one with no hidden loyalties to Dr. John R. Minahan.

But the reality of what lay ahead set in for Mary.

Stewart warned her about the community repercussions she should expect once her official complaint accusing the city's renowned surgeon came out in the press. Most people would believe a truly virtuous woman would have avoided rape at all costs, and, knowing the sexually explicit courtroom testimony she would have to provide, Mary would never have willingly proceeded to trial. Also, not only her reputation but that of her family would be judged.

Mary shared a pleading glance with Carrie. Mary said she knew what she and her family were up against, but she could not back down. Dr. Minahan had to be held accountable for her humiliation, pain, and suffering.

Much to Mary's relief, her sister agreed.

ON APRIL 19, 1897, Mary's attorney officially served Dr. Minahan her damage suit complaint that stated the following: In March of 1893 while Mary was a single, twenty-five-year-old woman, she had worked at the Minahans' home. In that month, Dr. John R. Minahan, with "force and arms," made an indecent assault upon her and "defamed, debauched and carnally knew her," whereby she became pregnant with child. That on or about Easter Monday of 1893, at Dr. Minahan's office, without her knowledge or consent, and "with force and instruments," Dr. Minahan removed Mary's child, or "so-called fetus or embryo, and committed feticide and abortion upon her ... to conceal the fact he had carnally known her."

Consequently, Mary "has suffered and will always suffer great pain; her health has been ruined and will always so remain; her ability to work at her accustomed business and earn money has been, and always will be, greatly impaired; she has suffered and will always suffer from the shame and disgrace caused by the acts aforesaid." Further, Dr. Minahan had treated Mary for the injuries he caused, "for which he charged her nearly nothing."

Mary's attorney demanded damages of $15,000 for his client to be paid by Dr. Minahan, enough to support Mary for most of her life.

To douse Mary's slanderous allegations, Dr. Minahan engaged Attorney Patrick H. Martin, Brown County's former district attorney, the same man Mary had sought legal counsel from three years earlier without success. On May 6, 1897, *The Green Bay Gazette* provided the first whiff of what could transpire. It summarized Mary's complaint and included Attorney Martin's response. "Within the next day or two," Martin stated, "the defendant's answer, in the case of Mary Cenefelt vs. Dr. J.R. Minahan, will be filed. It will be brief and to the point, denying each and all of the allegations ... and asking for judgment dismissing the action with costs. It is my belief that the woman is insane and not responsible for her actions. She has told and denied this and similar stories several times within the past few years ... It is my belief she is mentally incompetent and influenced by others to commence this action."

Mary and her attorney now knew what challenges lay ahead—unless the court ruled there was insufficient evidence to proceed to trial.

In mid-May, Attorney Stewart met with Mary, his youthful face full of cheer. He said the judge had not dismissed her case.

Mary clasped her hands together.

She would finally have her day in court.

Seeking Justice

INSIDE COURT Commissioner Cady's Washington Street office on May 14, 1897, a month after Mary's complaint had come out in the press, Mary and her attorney stood by a window facing the Fox River. While awaiting the arrival of Dr. Minahan's attorney for her pretrial deposition, Mary watched the commotion on the water occurring to the north. The lifting power for the Main Street bridge appeared to have given out as a steamer approached. The bridge tender was rapidly hoisting the bridge by hand while dock workers tossed a line to the steamer to secure her to the shoreline piles, and the vessel's engines reversed.

Mary realized the bridge tender's quick action had saved the ship from disaster. She glanced over at her attorney, J. Calvin Stewart. Mary counted on him to do the same for her during her deposition that day and at her upcoming trial.

The former Brown County district attorney Patrick H. Martin strode into the room and Mary clenched her hands to suppress her anger. If he had helped her years before rather than turning his back on her, Mary's life could have been far different.

Court Commissioner Cady swore Mary in, and she and her attorney took seats across from Attorney Martin. Under section 4096 of Wisconsin's Revised Statutes, Cady said that Mary would give her sworn deposition verbally as he recorded Mr. Martin's questions and Mary's answers into shorthand. After the court commissioner transcribed the proceedings into a typed document, the same participants would meet again. Since Mary could not read, the commissioner said he would read her testimony back to her to confirm its accuracy. At that point, Mary would sign her name on the document.

Attorney Martin gazed across the table at Mary. He told her he would be asking her questions similar to those he would use at trial. But he did not share that her answers would formulate his overall strategy and courtroom plan of attack, where he would hope to catch her in a lie or an omission. Depositions were extremely useful to opposing counsel. Although Mr. Martin had talked to Mary in 1894 when he had been the Brown County District Attorney, he would now delve deeper into those details and educate himself on any events which had transpired since.

One crucial question Martin asked Mary during her two days of deposition was: "Do you remember the date when [Dr. Minahan] had this to do with you?"

"I remember it was on them days when his wife was away. I don't know what those days were, but they were in March. It must have been around the tenth or twelfth sometime."

A WEEK LATER, under Sheriff John Bartelme's surveillance, a court official randomly drew thirty-six male jurors' names for the September 1897 Brown County circuit court calendar from a male citizen pool. In Wisconsin, women would not sit on a jury until 1921, based on the belief that females lacked intelligence, were too sensitive, or needed to tend to their homes. But an all-male jury was far less apt to understand Mary's humiliation, fear, and suffering—adding to the already high odds stacked not only against her but all women of that era seeking similar justice.

The U.S. Constitution guarantees the right to a trial by jury for all criminal cases and any civil suits exceeding twenty dollars. Mark Twain observed with cynic wit: "We have a jury system ... superior to any in the world, and its efficiency is only marred by the difficulty of finding twelve men ... who don't know anything and can't read." Brown County attorneys openly ridiculed the current jury selection process, and the Wisconsin state legislature had recently passed a bill to overhaul the procedure. Judge Samuel D. Hastings, who would preside at Mary's trial, had appointed three Brown County jury commissioners to choose 150 men for jury duty for the November 1897 court term. The commissioners would select those men based on their fitness to consider and weigh the evidence and to derive a just verdict for the litigation parties. The hope was that process would make trials fairer and just. But the change was too late for Mary. The Cenefelt vs. Minahan case would be one of the last trials to use the old jury selection process.

FOUR AND A HALF years had passed since Mary's sexual assaults and abortion. On September 21, 1897, the Cenefelt vs. Minahan civil trial commenced inside Brown County Circuit Court. Mary sat beside her attorney J. Calvin Steward at the plaintiff's table. Dr. John R. Minahan and his attorney Patrick H. Martin were seated at the defendant's table. On the bench was Judge Samuel D. Hastings.

As a lawyer, Hastings had represented large Wisconsin lumber, timber, and shingle companies. He was the board president for the Green Bay schools and the Rufus B. Kellogg Library. Brown County citizens had first elected Hastings to the Eleventh Circuit's bench in 1883 and had never failed to reelect him. His peers said he never deviated from the case's facts or the law owing to "influence, politics, or expediency."

Judge Samuel D. Hastings (Men Who are Making Green Bay 1897)

Mary would soon discover for herself whether those qualities attributed to Hastings were true.

Mary's sister Carrie and their twenty-year-old brother John, a Valparaiso University dental student, were present in the third-floor Brown County courtroom to give Mary support.

Nothing had been in the press since Mary's initial complaint and Minahan's attorney's response. There were plenty of open seats in the gallery. The first *Green Bay Gazette* article about the trial appeared on September 24. Mary's testimony received little coverage, but the press noted one thing: Mary testified she had already been working at the Lawe home on St. Patrick's Day.

The Daily Advocate included a brief portion of Dr. John R. Minahan's testimony. Under oath, he said, in January of 1893, he had first met Mary at the Bartelme residence. "You have a slight cough," he had told her. "And I asked her to come to my office for an examination. She visited me in two or three days, and I found her in a bad condition, suffering from a disease of the womb. It was difficult for me to tell the cause of the disease, for there must have been a history of the case extending back sometime."

Minahan then testified that in September of 1894, Mary returned from Cooperstown and sought Dr. Fairfield for his opinion on the drugs Minahan had provided to her. "She visited my office, and told me, she had found out I was treating her wrongfully. She told me of making a statement to [Dr. Fairfield] ... At one time, I performed an operation at St. Vincent on the plaintiff and was assisted by Dr. Olmsted. She had complained of great pain in the lower extremities, and it was thought advisable to operate on her womb. It was cut open, and nothing but a little inflammation was found in its upper part. We told her that her illness was mostly imaginary, and she partly concurred with us. She then returned to her home in Cooperstown, and that was the last time she was treated by me."

Mary took the stand multiple times, suffering constant abdominal pain and holding her face turned down to hide her humiliation. Many in the courtroom would have deemed her modesty a performance staged to secure an innocent man's conviction.

Their sentiments played into Attorney Martin's strategy—to sully Mary's character by inferring she was a prostitute. His goal was to prove Mary never had dyspepsia, only the "unmentionable disease," syphilis. Because Minahan had not cured her, Martin argued, she had fabricated her sexual assaults and abortion to blackmail him.

Minahan's attorney handled the judge far better throughout the trial than Mary's, who primarily played to the twelve jurors' emotions. The panel included three men from Green Bay: Joseph Beth, a German grocer; John Kittner, a fireman; and James Oliver, a co-owner of J. Saunders wholesale fish company. The nine other jurors were farmers from De Pere, Wrightstown, Holland, Denmark, Howard, Glenmore, Preble, and the Town of Green Bay. They or their parents were immigrants from Luxemburg, Canada, and Germany. Those country jurors could have received only rudimentary education and, due to language barriers, may not have fully understood the proceedings. That was one of the argued defects within the jury selection process.

The case went to the jury on Saturday, September 25, 1897 after four days of arguments and testimony. The jury rendered a verdict Sunday, and it was opened in court on Monday. Friends of Minahan reeled with astonishment, their lips curled in disgust when Judge Hastings announced the verdict that favored Mary. He ordered Dr. Minahan to pay her $5,000 in damages (about $180,000 in current valuation) and Mary's trial costs.

Mary swayed in her chair, intoxicated by the judge's words, unable to absorb the marvelous verdict. Even though her settlement was far less than $15,000, it exceeded her expectations. Just as importantly, Minahan's crimes had been exposed to the public. The jurors' decision proved they believed Mary's testimony rather than Minahan's lies. She would have money to support herself and pay for ongoing medical treatment. She could hold her head up high. Her life had not been destroyed as she had feared.

But Mary's joy was short-lived.

Attorney P.H. Martin stood, his face flaming. He made a motion to set aside the verdict as "perverse and contrary to the testimony's weight." While he argued those points for nearly an hour, Mary attempted to follow the legalese batted around—yet his intentions were clear to her.

Judge Hastings finally announced he had made up his mind. No verdict for the plaintiff should be allowed to stand. It was indeed a perversion to the submitted testimony. Hastings pounded his gavel and granted Attorney Martin's motion to set aside the verdict.

Mary's lawyer, bristling with anger, sprang to his feet and informed the Court, "A new trial will be held!"

Mary was stricken with the realization she was back to where she had started. Her siblings gathered around. Both placed a hand on her slumped shoulders. Mary gazed at Dr. Minahan as his friends gave him congratulatory backslaps. That sight and her trial's injustice drove Mary to her feet.

A similar sentiment was brewing inside Madison, Wisconsin, Attorney John M. Olin, who perhaps sat in the spectator seats or had followed the courtroom proceedings published in the press. That highly respected prosecutor was known statewide for his proclivity to defend downtrodden clients with just cases.

Even if Olin had not been present, he and Mary's attorney talked within the next few weeks. Both agreed the Brown County Circuit Court had carried out a grave injustice. Attorney Stewart realized the odds of losing Mary's subsequent trial were high unless he paired up with another lawyer with as much courtroom experience as Mr. Patrick H. Martin.

Mr. John M. Olin agreed to be that attorney.

Bold and Badgered

ON TUESDAY, December 14, 1897, a boisterous crowd pushed through the Brown County Circuit Court door, all scrambling for a prime seat, or any seat at all, to attend the second Cenefelt vs. Minahan civil case. In the two months since the former trial, much had been in the press about its shocking details and Judge Hastings' controversial ruling. Not only curious spectators filled the wood-paneled courtroom, but professional men and respected farmers were present. Everyone wanted to watch what the *Green Bay Advocate* promised to be "one of the most interesting and sensational trials ever known to the history of Brown County... where two intellectual giants," Patrick H. Martin and John M. Olin, would meet "in mortal combat."

Mary sat at the plaintiff's table closest to the jury box, her hair in a neat bun and a satin ribbon tied around the neck of her high-collared dress. Beside Mary were her two attorneys, J. Calvin Stewart and John M. Olin. The latter was born in Lexington, Ohio, graduated from Williams College in 1873, and earned his law degree at the University of Wisconsin, where he continued to lecture. Olin was a "profound prohibitionist" with a fondness for Bach chorales. He indulged in no "flights of fancy or figures of speech," noted

Attorney John M. Olin
(Courtesy University of
Wisconsin Library)

Wisconsin Supreme Court Justice Burr W. Jones, "but spoke with such eloquence and earnestness that no one could doubt his absolute sincerity."

Mary's attorneys would be up against a formidable force. Attorney P.H. Martin had partnered with Dr. Robert Emmet Minahan, the defendant's thirty-nine-year-old brother, who would assist with the medical testimony. At six feet tall, with silvering hair parted in the middle, and the pale-blue Minahan eyes, Dr. Robert E. Minahan, better known as R.E. or Dr. Robert, was a physician and lawyer practicing in Kewaunee, Wisconsin. He earned his degrees at Chicago's Rush Medical College and the University of Michigan, where he had been president of his law class. "All of the Minahans were intelligent, highly gifted, and strong-willed individuals ... arousing strong emotions," stated Green Bay historian Jack Rudolph.

Dr. Robert E. Minahan
(Roger Minahan Papers)

Since the two Minahan brothers had joined forces under Martin's leadership, Mary's attorneys knew they were in for a bloody battle.

At exactly 9:00 a.m., the court sheriff's voice boomed, "Hear ye! Hear ye! Hear ye! This Court is now in session. Silence is demanded." Judge Hastings mounted the short steps leading to the bench, his black robe swishing, and he took his seat. After Mary's first trial, she had discovered that Judge Hastings lived up on "The Hill," at 827 S. Monroe Avenue, just blocks from Dr. Minahan and Mr. Martin. All three men attended the same social functions and were temperance movement supporters. Mary felt those factors could have influenced Judge Hastings' decision in her first trial. Now he would preside over her second trial.

The attorneys had selected twelve jurors from the 150 male Brown County residents the commission had vetted. Mary gazed at the new panel, about ten feet to her right. Those twelve educated jurors held Mary's life in their hands unless Judge Hastings intervened. To attend her first trial, Mary had depleted her savings and resigned from her domestic position at the Tennis home. Between that trial and her second, she had not looked for work. Mary knew it would have been difficult to find a new position when many in the community believed her reputation was in doubt. Instead, Mary's parents had sent her money to pay the Bartelme family for her room and board.

From the bench, Judge Hastings gazed out at the spectators and announced, "All minors must clear the courtroom." Amid grumbles, teenage boys, eager to witness the scandalous trial testimony, dragged their feet as they departed through the courtroom door.

Minahan's attorney stood before the jury to make his opening argument. Mr. Patrick H. Martin vehemently denied all the case's charges and said he would prove there was nothing wrong in the interactions between Dr. Minahan and Mary Cenefelt. Martin spoke eloquently for thirty minutes, highlighting the doctor's achievements and community status before sitting down beside his client.

Attorney Olin ambled over to the jury box to make his opening statement. His face was smooth-shaven, and his warm eyes crinkled at the corners. His unpretentious voice delivered Mary's history, how she had worked as a maid and on her parents' farm, how she had first met Dr. Minahan at the Bartelme residence and secured employment within his home. On the day before Mary had left his service, Olin said, her second assault had taken place. That rape had resulted in a pregnancy, and the defendant had criminally aborted Mary's child to hide that fact. Olin said he would prove that Mary had physically and mentally suffered from those brutal acts ever since, and she would continue to suffer for the rest of her life.

Olin paused while every eye in the courtroom focused on Mary. She rubbed her damp palms back and forth on her skirt until Olin finally broke the silence by calling Dr. Minahan as his first witness. Unlike a criminal trial, in a civil action, if the plaintiff's attorney calls the defendant as a witness, they are required to testify.

Whispers erupted as Minahan approached the witness stand. He placed his hand on the Bible and swore to tell the truth. But as a man who was known to "ridicule religion ... and all that is held sacred by Christians," one might wonder whether he would have any qualms about lying.

A whiskerless Dr. Minahan settled onto the oak chair behind the witness rail. He nodded his curly head toward the jurymen, men he had undoubtedly talked to at one time or another.

Attorney Olin handed Dr. Minahan a slip of paper marked as exhibit "A" and asked him to identify it. Minahan said it was Mary's emmenagogue pill prescription. On it, his written instructions stated she was to take "one pill after each meal."

At Mary's May 1897 deposition, her undated prescription, "to bring on monthlies," had been submitted into evidence. Mary had dug through her cigar box of treasures to find the unfilled script Minahan had given her in late March of 1893 after he had confirmed she was pregnant.

Olin asked Minahan for the approximate date he had written the prescription.

Minahan testified he had given Mary the script on her first visit to his office in January of 1893 "to enrich the blood" for her diseased womb.

Mary's gaze fixed on Minahan. She found it hard to believe that his eyes had not even wavered as he lied. But on second thought, that actually made sense to her. When she had worked for him, she had heard his poker friends claim they could never tell whether Minahan was bluffing.

Mary's attorney retrieved the prescription and then offered a plain gold ring into evidence before handing it to Minahan.

Soon after Attorney Olin had agreed to represent Mary, he had asked her whether Dr. Minahan had given her anything, besides money, to entice her not to reveal his crimes. Mary had held out her hand and showed Olin the ring.

On the stand that day, Minahan examined the gold ring with engraved initials inside and said it was his.

The doctor's response seemed to startle Attorney Olin. He had likely expected Minahan to deny ever seeing the ring. Instead, Minahan claimed that Mary had stolen it from him when she had worked at his house. He said the ring had been given to him by a lady patient as payment for her treatment.

"You didn't testify to anything about this ring in the former trial, did you?"

"No, sir."

"Why didn't you?"

"I wasn't asked to."

Attorney Olin raised his brows and looked at the jurors. Minahan's response made no sense. If Mary had indeed stolen the ring from Dr. Minahan's home, as he claimed, why wouldn't his attorney have introduced that evidence at the first trial to further tarnish Mary's character?

Olin smiled as he dismissed Dr. Minahan from the stand. Olin would later tell her, he had accomplished what he had set out to do. He had caught Minahan in his first lies.

THE CLERK OF COURTS swore Mary in. She sat up straight in the witness chair, ignoring the pain in her abdomen. Her eyes located her two siblings, Carrie and John, seated directly behind the rail on the plaintiff's side. Their presence provided Mary courage as in her first trial.

But her second trial was different. She had two attorneys, one with ample courtroom experience who had provided Mary tips. Mr. Olin had warned her that the jury would scrutinize her every move to determine whether her testimony was truthful. They would watch her facial expressions, gestures, and body movements. In particular, the jurors would read lack of eye contact as deception.

Attorney Olin placed two photos of Mary into evidence. She said the first had been taken just before her abortion, when she weighed around 165 pounds. The second had been taken two years later, when she weighed about 135 pounds.

Mary's attorney also produced a small white barber towel banded in red and marked as exhibit "Y." Mary testified she had saved that towel, which Dr. Minahan had given her on the day of her abortion, to absorb the blood flowing from her private area. When employed by the Minahans, Mary said she had washed and ironed the household hand towels. The one marked exhibit "Y" was similar to those.

Olin next handed Mary the gold ring and asked her to identify it. She said when she had worked at the Minahan home the doctor's wife had worn it. At some point, after Minahan had aborted Mary's child, she said the doctor had given her the ring and told Mary, if anyone asked her about it, she was to say she had found it.

The jurors seemed confused by the ring testimony. Either Dr. Minahan or Mary had lied. Yet, the jurors had to wonder why Mary's attorney would have risked introducing the ring in the first place if Mary had actually stolen it from the Minahan home.

After Olin returned the gold ring to the evidence table, he asked Mary whether she could recall when her sexual assaults took place.

"I remember it was on them days when Mrs. Minahan was in Casco, around March tenth. The way I figure because Mrs. Minahan said she was going there when they was making maple syrup, when they were tapping the maple trees."

There was no record of whether Olin had called any witnesses who could have provided proof about the Casco maple trees. A cool night, just below freezing, and a daytime temperature in the upper 40s is the best condition for sugaring. That temperature swing causes shifts in pressure outside the tree that sends sap flowing out through a tapped hole. In March of 1893, according to the *State Gazette*, the Casco maple tree camp owners could only have tapped their trees from March 7 to March 10 when the daily temperature ranged from 18 to 41 degrees.

Another way to pinpoint Mary's assault dates would have been to back into them using Mary's Easter Monday, April 3, abortion date. During Mary's pretrial deposition, Minahan's attorney had asked her the following questions:

"Now, with reference to the time of your periods when you had sexual relations with the doctor, how long after you had your monthly courses?"

"It was only about two or three days after I had my monthlies."

"Might it have been a week?"

"No, it wasn't a week. I remember because [Minahan] come out in the kitchen Saturday, and he asked me when I was unwell last time, and I told him."

"What Saturday?"

"The Saturday that I was going away when his wife was coming home."

"How long would [your monthly course] last?"

"Three or four days." That would have placed Mary's period start date on about Thursday, March 2, assuming Friday, March 10 was her second assault date.

"You were very regular, were you?"

"Yes, I used to come around every three weeks." That would have placed Mary's new period start date on about March 22. Mary testified she had waited approximately a week to see whether her period would start before visiting Minahan's office four times, spanning seven days. Given all that, Mary's abortion would have landed on Easter Monday, just as she had testified.

But at trial that day, Olin did not cement the Friday, March 10, 1893, second assault date into the jurors' minds.

That was a grave mistake.

Mr. Olin questioned Mary for more than eight hours, walking through her four years of misery. He primarily stood, only sitting for a short time to rest his legs and back. In Olin's closing argument, he would say, "As Miss Cenefelt told her simple touching story, with tears in her eyes, the courtroom got stiller and stiller. And I believe, gentlemen, that I saw some of you cover your faces. And speaking for myself, I could not bear to sit in my chair and listen to the story, so I got up and went to the further side of the room and looked out the window. You all remember this occurrence. Can you doubt the simple story told by this girl?"

ON THURSDAY, December 16, 1897, Mary faced Attorney Patrick H. Martin. He looked as if he had just come from the Beaumont House Barber Shop with his groomed handlebar mustache and neatly trimmed side-parted hair. Mary sat on the witness chair in the stagnant air, reeking from tobacco smoke and courtroom attendees' body odor.

The shrewd look in Attorney Martin's small eyes did not daunt Mary. She had gained experience from her first trial. Mary squared her shoulders, smoothed her housedress, and clasped her calloused hands in her lap. She was ready for his onslaught of questions.

Using a brusque style, Martin first asked Mary about her job in Escanaba, where she had worked at Mr. Fontaine's boarding house— attached to a saloon. He next delved into her employment at the Reis Hotel, noting its barroom. His goal was to attack Mary's "sexual respectability" since most people of that era believed the saloon was the prime institution for fostering prostitution.

Martin next dug into Mary's first meeting with Dr. Minahan at the Bartelme residence.

"Did you tell him what was wrong ... That you had trouble with your back?"

"I complained most about my stomach."

"Did you have cramps in the stomach?"

"No, but I had such a distressing, terrible distressing ... all the time."

"When you sat up in a chair there at Mrs. Bartelme's, you had to have a pillow to your back, did you not?"

"Yes, but my back was so tired from riding so far."

"Did he examine your private parts?"

"No, he only looked at my tongue, and looked on my pulse, and gave me medicine."

"Are you sure of that?"

"I am sure."

"What about at his office, shortly after. Didn't he examine your private parts there?"

"No."

"Wasn't he treating you for womb trouble?"

"No, stomach problems."

Martin was getting nowhere, and he switched paths. "On what day did Mrs. Minahan go away?"

"The first time?"

"Yes."

Mary said the doctor's wife had gone to Madison and Milwaukee for a whole week. "But she was away another time ... sometime in March. [Mrs. Minahan] went to Casco. That is what she told me. She left Thursday and came back on Saturday."

"Tell me about the circumstances when you first had sexual intercourse with Dr. Minahan."

Mary could not help but flush as she had the previous day. To reveal those humiliating details, not only to the jury but to the courtroom gawkers, still mortified her. Yet, she bravely lifted her chin. She had to push through. "It was that Thursday, same day when his wife went away to Casco."

"That was the first time?"

"Yes."

"Now, you are certain of that, are you?"

"Yes. I never was with [Minahan] before."

Martin crossed his arms, his lips pursed as if he did not believe her. "Where did you have this intercourse?"

"It was in his room."

"Did you sleep with him that night?"

"No. I didn't stay with [Minahan] at all."

"Didn't you?"

"No, the first night—he went out and made calls after that."

"Did you invite the doctor into the room?"

"No." Mary told Martin about Minahan's collar and how the doctor had followed her into his room—and all the heart-wrenching, stomach-churning details.

"Did you call for help?"

"I didn't call, but I told him if he didn't leave me alone, I would call—scream."

"But you didn't?"

"I cried when he threw me from the bed and onto the floor."

"But you didn't cry so that anybody would hear you, did you?"

"Of course, if anybody was near, they could hear me—I am not telling you a lie."

"You aren't?"

"No. I know what happened." Mary blinked back tears, attempting to stay strong, while the eyes of the jurymen focused on her.

Among them was thirty-seven-year-old George D. Nau, owner of Green Bay's largest tugboat line. Before that, he had run the wholesale and retail grocery business in the Nau Building, where Mary had shopped. Everyone in Green Bay liked the friendly and congenial George, who never said an unkind word about anyone—at least not in public. A person's social class obscured the vision of many in the community, but not George D. Nau's. According to the press, he seemed sympathetic to Mary. Another juror who appeared to be concerned about her welfare was Joseph DeGreef, a Preble truck gardener, known for his large strawberries—only eleven needed to fill a quart.

George D. Nau (Men Who are Making Green Bay 1897)

The other jurors' expressions remained unchanged, like those of the De Pere Riverside Brick Company owner, F.L. Smith, and Wrightstown farmer and town treasurer, James Joyce.

"If you looked out the bedroom window," Attorney Martin's gaze met Mary's, "what house would you see?"

"You see right to the minister's house."

"Why didn't you call the minister?"

"I didn't have time to call."

"Then he took you on the floor, did he?"

"Yes. But I commenced to cry, and he went."

"Then he didn't do anything to you that time?"

"He tried to."

"But he didn't?"

"Of course, I never had anything to do with anybody." Her head and shoulders drifted down as if that admission was too heavy to bear.

"You know he didn't do anything to you that time."

"He did. He hurt me, so I bled."

"Well, hadn't you done anything of that kind before ... with this man Doherty, who was at the gymnasium ... across from Dr. Minahan's office?"

Mary's brow furrowed. "I didn't know anybody there."

"You used to go with him, didn't you?"

"With whom?"

"With that man in charge of the Athletic Club?"

Mary shook her head. "I never went with a man in Green Bay."

"But when you worked at the Escanaba boarding house, you had sexual intercourse with men there, didn't you?"

"No, sir. Never."

As in the first trial, Martin intended to tell a tale of Mary's promiscuity. When Mary's testimony did not match Martin's intent, he huffed and squinted at his notes.

"Are there times when you don't know what you are doing?" His gaze met Mary's. "When you have your monthlies?"

"I always know what I am doing."

"There are times when you are troubled mentally, aren't there?"

"When I had high fever sometimes ... When I was very sick."

"And at such times, you scarcely know what you are doing, isn't that true?"

"Yes, but I ain't that way now."

Martin frowned, tapping his fingers on the witness rail. "Well, let's go back to the alleged assault. That's the only time that anything occurred between you and Minahan, isn't it?"

"No, there was another time."

"What? Did you stay there and let him try it again?"

"He said he was going away."

Mary described how on the second night Minahan had forgotten his key, so she had to let him in and everything that followed.

"You helped him take off your clothes, didn't you?"

"No. [Minahan] pulled them off till the button came off. I tried to keep them on and tried to keep my skirts down, and he was pulling them up."

"Didn't he ask you to take your clothes off ... to go to bed with him before he pulled them off?"

"No ... he just threw me on the bed."

The spectators strained forward, trying to hear every syllable of Mary's titillating testimony, far better than a dime novel's racy storyline as Martin continued. "You didn't screech, did you? Cry out?"

"I don't know what I done. I was so ashamed."

"Was that one of the times when you didn't know what you were doing?"

"I knew what he was going to do, but I got so scared."

"But you didn't know what you were going to do?"

"I didn't know what I could do ... if I could have got out of the room, I would have."

"But you didn't try to get out of the room?"

"I did. I tried to get out of [Minahan's] hands."

"Why in the world didn't you call for help? Shout out?"

"I don't know. I got so ashamed and scared that I—"

"Then did he have something to do with you on the bed?"

"Yes."

"You were perfectly willing, weren't you?"

"No, I wasn't willing, but I was all tired out."

"Then you did acquiesce ... You did submit ... Did consent that [Minahan] have something to do with you?"

"No, but he did, and then he wanted me to stay with him till morning since his wife was not home."

"Did he have intercourse with you the second time?"

Mary's cheeks burned as she said, "Yes."

"Do you remember the date when he had this to do with you?"

"It was on them days when his wife was away in March, around the tenth."

"Well, didn't you speak to anybody about it when it happened?"

"No, he told me I shouldn't dare to tell anything. If I would say anything, that he didn't know what he would do with me."

"You didn't tell any of your lady friends? Your mother, your sisters?"

"No, not anybody."

Martin rocked back on his heels and smiled, evidently pleased by Mary's response.

"How long did you work at the Minahans' all told?"

"It must have been about five weeks, but I can't tell for sure."

"Well, weren't you there as late as St. Patrick's Day?"

"No, I wasn't there on St. Patrick's Day."

"Didn't you pin a green ribbon on Dr. Minahan's coachman, Patrick Mahoney, that day?"

"No, sir. We don't celebrate that day."

"What is it that makes you think you were at Minahan's on Friday, March tenth?"

"I don't know."

"Well, couldn't it have been on Friday, March seventeenth instead?"

"I don't know." Mary did not realize St. Patrick's Day fell on that date, which Martin suspected and used to his advantage. He badgered her until she finally agreed that Friday, March 17, could have been her second assault date. Martin had accomplished what Olin had failed to do: Friday, March 17, 1893, was established as Mary's second sexual assault date for the rest of the trial.

Martin asked, "How did you come to go to Minahan's office from the Lawes'?"

"I went there to tell him I was in trouble with him, that he got me in the family way."

"You knew you were in the family way, did you?"

"I wasn't certain, but I thought I was." Mary explained how Minahan had told her to wait a few more days. But when nothing changed, she returned, and he wrote her the emmenagogue prescription. Since Mary could not read, she testified that Dr. Minahan had told her what the instructions said: to take "three pills at first, once, and then one after each meal."

"When you went to Minahan's [office] on Easter Monday, you got into the operating chair?"

"Well, he told me I had to go through an examination, through a treatment."

"Did you know what he intended to do?"

"No ... I didn't know there was any doctor could do such a thing."

"Was Dr. Minahan doing the work with an instrument?"

"Yes. I saw it afterward, when he laid it on a little stand. It was shorter than a fire poker, kind of sharp on one end ... a piece of steel, silver-colored."

"And did you feel as though he was cutting within you?"

"Oh, yes, terrible pain ... like digging inside me." Mary cradled her face in her hands.

"Did you screech so that people might hear you?"

"They—they could have heard me, yes. [Minahan] told me I should be still, quieted me as much as he could."

"But a woman never does what she is told, does she?"

Attorney Olin objected. He said Mr. Martin's question was argumentative. He was purposely badgering Mary, openly mocking her.

Judge Hastings agreed, sustaining the objection.

Martin shrugged and continued. "You cried out, didn't you?" He stepped closer to Mary.

"Yes."

"They could hear you on the street?"

"Not on the street, but in the next room."

"Did he remove something from you?"

"That is what he told me. And I could see the bloody towel he took away from me."

"You didn't see any substance on the towel?"

"He had it rolled up on a stand, and I didn't look in."

"Did he tell you how far gone you had been in the family way?"

"No, he didn't."

"Did you know?"

"I knew it was about two weeks over my time."

"Well, didn't you tell someone you were gone about two months?"

"No."

"Will you swear you didn't say to Mrs. Bartelme that Minahan first had something to do with you ... when his wife was in Madison?"

"I can swear that wasn't when it happened."

Martin's lips tightened. "What physician first advised you to go and see an attorney and bring this action?"

"There was no doctor told me to go to an attorney. I asked Dr. Fairfield if I had to live this way, and he says he couldn't say anything—that I'd have to see a lawyer."

"You hadn't consulted a lawyer at that time, had you?"

"Well, I spoke to you. I told you what Minahan done to me, didn't I?"

An uneasy rustling filled the courtroom.

"I ain't answering questions," Martin snapped back. "Did you threaten to sue Fairfield to get your statement back?"

"I knew he burnt it. I didn't know he had another copy."

"Didn't Dr. Minahan tell you that he would make both you and Dr. Fairfield jump for this?"

"No. All [Minahan] told me was that he has to make a paper so Dr. Fairfield could never have him arrested." Mary also said Minahan had told her the paper included his promise to provide her free treatment and medicine for as long as she was unwell. "After I had my name signed to it—[Minahan] made me sign my name to it ... he read it ... But there was a difference ... It said when I first came ... he had treated me for womb trouble, and whatever I told Dr. Fairfield, it was a lie."

"It was ... wasn't it?"

"No, it was not."

"Where is this paper?"

"[Minahan] told me I was going to get that paper ... and then after I signed my name to it, and he had altogether different writing on it, he folded it up and put it in his pocket."

"Did you ask him for it?"

"No, I never asked him for it."

Martin crossed his arms, shaking his head. "But the fact is, the doctor never had anything to do with you, did he? You made this up to get money out of him, didn't you?"

"God knows, Mr. Martin, I wouldn't have started this for no money if it was not true. There's not enough money in the state."

Outside the courthouse on December 17, holiday lights glittered on Washington Street. Inside the courtroom, darkness draped Mary like a mourning shawl. She cared little about the money, other than securing enough to pay for her ongoing medical bills and lost wages. Her prime goal was to prove she had been a wholesome woman until she had been defiled and tortured by Green Bay's celebrated surgeon, Dr. John R. Minahan.

Physician Factions

ON SATURDAY, December 18, 1897, Nettie Bartelme took her seat in the courthouse witness box, ready to testify for Mary. Two years earlier, Nettie had settled onto that same chair at the Thomas and Ruth Mooney trial, where she had identified the married couple the jury eventually convicted. Prominent businessmen had accused the pair of sending letters through the mail, claiming those businessmen belonged to the American Protective Association, an anti-Catholic secret society established by Protestants. That false allegation had impacted the Green Bay businessmen's livelihoods in a predominantly Catholic community.

Dr. Minahan's claims against Mary were exponentially worse. Not only could they affect her domestic employment opportunities, but they could brand her as an immoral woman for life.

With a pad of paper in hand, Attorney Olin approached Nettie. She testified, "I live in this city and have all my life."

Olin asked whether she could recall the night that Mary had arrived at the Bartelme courthouse residence in January of 1893. Nettie said she could and described Mary as being "quite sick, the trouble seeming to be in her stomach. Dr. Minahan was called in to see her ... I made a gown for her on her return, and the measurement would now, judging from her general appearance, be from three to five inches too big."

Olin asked Nettie whether she could recall another time, back in September of 1894, when Mary had returned to Green Bay.

"I heard about [her] making a visit to Dr. Fairfield's office and making a statement. Miss Cenefelt showed me some money. She had just returned from somewhere, where I don't know. The money was a five-dollar gold piece, a twenty-dollar gold piece, and a ten-dollar bill."

Olin would later weave that evidence into his closing statement to prove that Dr. Minahan had indeed given Mary $35 after Dr. Fairfield burned her statement and Father O'Brien interceded on Mary's behalf.

Attorney Olin asked Nettie to describe Mary's personality.

"She was of even temper, though I have seen her anger. I remember her visit to the hospital when her womb operation was performed. After the operation, she was very much depressed."

Minahan's attorney stood to cross-examine Nettie. He retrieved the gold ring from the exhibit table and asked her if she recognized it. Nettie said she did, that Mary had worn it. "Miss Cenefelt told both myself and my sister that she had found the ring."

Carrie took the stand, dressed in a Scotch plaid bodice, green skirt, and a black hat with plumes. Carrie testified to her sister's "honest and wholesome character" as did Mary's twenty-year-old brother John who was sworn in next. He also said that Mary was a "hard-working girl." Whenever she was home at the farm, he added, she always helped out in the fields.

After John gave his testimony, he sat down behind Mary and reached over the rail to place a hand on his big sister's shoulder.

WHILE THE Denessen and Hart pleasure boats were motored out to the Fox River's center channel for the winter months, the Cenefelt vs. Minahan damage suit continued. It was Monday, December 20. Spectators had filled the seats and about 100 people stood in the aisles and lined the walls. Among the crowd were most of the city's professional men: doctors to hear the outside physicians' expert testimony and lawyers to witness the battle between Attorneys Patrick H. Martin and John M. Olin.

Mary's September 3, 1894, statement, the one given in Dr. Fairfield's office, was read into the record:

Mary Cenefelt, being duly sworn, deposes and says: ... I am a female, unmarried of the age of twenty-six years. I came to reside in Green Bay in the month of January 1893 ... I had dyspepsia at that time and was not very strong, so I went to Doctor J.R. Minahan's home, spoke to his wife, told her how I felt and wanted employment. So, she told me I could come there and do her work until I got well. I had at that time been under the treatment of Dr. J.R. Minahan for dyspepsia.

I was there ... when his wife went away, leaving me the only lady in the house. The first night after his wife was gone, [Minahan and I] were in the house alone, the hostler being away. Minahan sent me to his room after collars. I went in his room, and he followed me ... and then assaulted me, he forced me, he took hold of me, and threw me down on the bed by force, and against my consent he then ... raped me, and committed rape upon me. The next night, [Minahan] called me in the sitting room, saying that he wanted to speak to me. I went, and he took hold of me and carried me in his bedroom, and then and there ... raped me.

The next day, I left the place. I there went to work at Mrs. Lawe's on Cherry Street. I then stopped going to see him for dyspepsia and did not go until the next time, when I should have had my monthly curses, or about eleven days after I left, at which time I discovered that I was pregnant and from him. And I never had intercourse with any other man. When I went to see Dr. J.R. Minahan and stated to him my circumstances, he did not deny it and said he would have to examine me. He then examined me and said I was pregnant with child. He then told me that I would have to undergo a treatment. I did not know what kind of treatment it was to be. He then and there took an instrument and made me submit to the instrument. He told me to keep very quiet. Otherwise, it would hurt me very much. As soon as he had used the instrument, I began to flow blood freely. It hurt me very much.

About three weeks afterward, I went again to see him. He then gave me medicine to stop the flow of blood. The medicine did not stop the flow of blood. Seven weeks after the operation was made, he came to see me over at the house. Then I was so weak that I had to be taken to the hospital in his buggy. The doctor's driver took me there with the Doctor's rig. I stayed there eleven days or thirteen days. I was there treated by him, Dr. Minahan ... The Sister was also there ... in the room with him and me. While I was in bed at the hospital, the flowing stopped, but after I got out, the flowing commenced again.

I have been unwell ever since and have been under treatment ever since. I am always very much inflamed all the time and have to take injections twice a day. The Doctor never asked me for any pay for his services.

MARY HAD DEFENDED her chastity and integrity on the stand.

Nine physicians would now spar over their differing "expert opinions" concerning Mary's purity and the cause for her womb trouble. Dr. Fred Brett took a seat in the witness box for the plaintiff's side and gazed out at the audience through frameless spectacles. He testified that he believed Mary was suffering from the physical effects of a criminal operation. Unlike Dr. Minahan, Dr. Brett said he would not prescribe emmenagogue pills to "enrich the blood."

Dr. Fred Brett (Men Who are Making Green Bay 1897)

Instead, he often used them to treat hormonal disorders in women and to help bring on their menses. But "midwives and quacks," he said, administered those pills to abort a woman's unwanted pregnancy.

A flurry of whispers erupted in the courtroom.

At the defendant's table, Dr. Robert E. Minahan leaned over and spoke to Attorney Martin. Martin stood to repair the damage. He asked Dr. Brett whether Mary's womb trouble could be from a "private disease" rather than a criminal abortion.

In public settings, instead of saying "unmentionable disease," the less offensive "private disease" was often used to describe venereal infections. That term could only mean syphilis in Mary's case since Dr. Brett would have tested her urine to prove she did not have gonorrhea.

Brett hesitated, then admitted that Mary's womb trouble could be from a "private disease."

Attorney Martin smiled, as did the two Minahan brothers sitting at the defendant's table.

Martin next wanted Dr. Brett to review a section of Mary's 1894 statement she had given in Dr. Fairfield's office. In it, she had said "about eleven days" after leaving the Minahan home, she had "discovered" she was pregnant. Attorney Martin asked Dr. Brett, as he would later ask all the other physician witnesses whether he could have determined whether Mary was pregnant on the eleventh day following her alleged assaults.

Dr. Brett admitted, as would all the other physicians, that he could not have confirmed Mary's pregnancy until she had reached about the two-week mark.

Mary realized her mistake. She should have told Dr. Fairfield and the justice of the peace that she believed she was pregnant. Then she should have explained her first trip to Minahan's office a week later and her additional two visits, leading up to her Easter Monday abortion. Mary could only hope the jury would remember and consider her earlier trial testimony, where she had provided that precise timeline.

Dr. Abbott Slaughter testified for the plaintiff, and his words mirrored Dr. Fred Brett's. Judge Hastings then addressed the jury. He said the defendant's medical experts, Dr. Hamilton, Dr. Buchanan, Dr. Beck, Dr. Olmsted, and Dr. Oviatt, would adjourn to Dr. Beck's 209 N. Washington Street medical office. Per Wisconsin Civil Deposition and Discovery procedures, the judge had granted Attorney Martin's motion to allow the defendant's doctors to physically and mentally examine Mary.

She struggled to her feet and Attorney Stewart accompanied her down the courthouse stairs. A sleigh awaited the pair and they traveled three blocks to Dr. Beck's medical building. Mary's attorney offered her words of encouragement as he helped her from the sleigh and up the stairs to Dr. Beck's office. Her attorney and the other physicians remained in the waiting room as Dr. Beck escorted Mary into his small consultation room. He told her

Dr. H. Max Beck (Men Who Are Making Green Bay 1897)

to slip off her drawers and lean back in his examination chair. Dr. Beck placed her feet into stirrups to spread Mary's legs apart and he shoved up her skirts.

He used a speculum to hold Mary's vaginal walls apart and slid a cystoscope containing a light and lens system into Mary's uterus.

She shuddered and tears pooled in her eyes.

Next came Dr. Hamilton...

Then Dr. Buchanan...

Then Dr. Olmsted...

Then Dr. Oviatt...

At last, Dr. Beck returned and instructed Mary to redress.

Her hands were shaking so much she barely could.

WHILE MARY'S mental examinations were in process, back in the courtroom, Attorney Olin recalled Dr. Fred Brett to the stand. He wished to correct the evidence he had given. He said he had erroneously testified that he had used a 32-degree lens instead of a 16-degree lens to examine Mary. That correction ran into a personal spat between Dr. Brett and Attorney Martin, who said, "Didn't Dr. Earls of Milwaukee, upon you going downstairs, tell you that there was no such lens made?"

"No, sir. I knew at the time that there was no such lens, but it was only thoughtlessness that caused me to make the misstatement."

"Didn't you say to Dr. Beck that we, the physicians, 'ought to clique and help the girl plaintiff, as she was poor and needed it?'"

"No, sir. No such statement was made by me."

Attorney Martin huffed. His goal was to portray the physicians testifying for Mary as inept. To place a conspiracy theory in the jurors' minds that the plaintiff doctors had banded together to destroy Dr. John R. Minahan, their major surgical competitor.

ALL THE DEFENDANT'S physicians had returned to the courtroom by 11:30 a.m. except Dr. Hamilton, who was still conducting a mental examination on Mary in Dr. Beck's office.

Dr. John B. Hamilton
(Wikimedia)

Attorney Olin called Dr. Fairfield to the stand. He was in a precarious position. From Attorney Martin's comments to the press and at trial, Fairfield knew the defendant's team believed he had encouraged Mary to initiate her damage suit against Dr. Minahan. Fairfield's reputation was on the line, as much as Mary's. As Fairfield provided his education credentials and Montreal Women's Hospital experience, the courtroom door opened and the ample-bodied Dr. John B. Hamilton, with his white walrus mustache and goatee, entered. He was superintendent at the Illinois Northern Hospital for the Insane and the surgery professor at Rush Medical College, the Minahan brothers' alma mater. Strutting down the center aisle, Hamilton peeled off his white gloves and took a seat behind Martin. In Attorney Olin's closing statement, he would say, "While Dr. Fairfield testified, Dr.

Hamilton was sneering, as if Green Bay doctoring was subpar to that of a Chicago physician like him."

Olin asked Dr. Fairfield a hypothetical question: Assuming Mary was pregnant, and took the initial dose of three emmenagogue pills, as she had testified, what would have resulted from her taking those pills?

"I believe the effects would result in an abortion."

Dr. Hamilton leaned over and muttered into Attorney Martin's ear. He nodded then asked Judge Hastings for a sidebar.

Attorneys Martin and Olin approached the bench. Martin said Dr. Hamilton's Chicago Rush Medical College duties were pressing. Martin requested that Olin temporarily rest the plaintiff's case so Dr. Hamilton could testify.

Much to Olin's apparent vexation, Judge Hastings granted Martin's request.

While Dr. Fairfield returned to his spectator seat, Mary and Attorney Stewart entered the courtroom and sat down at the plaintiff's table.

After Dr. Hamilton was sworn in, he provided his extensive credentials. Attorney Martin then asked the Chicago physician whether he had completed a physical examination on Mary that morning.

Hamilton said he had and he had found her womb to be inflamed. He could not tell whether Mary was a woman of unchaste character, but he thought she was.

All the jurors' eyes focused on Mary.

She steadied her breathing. The jurors' scrutiny was nothing compared to what she had just endured inside Dr. Beck's medical office.

Hamilton said he believed a "private disease" was the likely origin of Mary's womb trouble rather than a criminal operation.

The other doctors for the defendant would later state the same. But unlike Dr. J.R. Minahan, all of the physicians testifying for the defendant, including Dr. Hamilton, would state they would not prescribe emmenagogue pills to "enrich the blood."

Before the trial, Minahan's attorney had stated to the press, "It is my belief that the woman is insane and not responsible for her actions." The reasons cited for insanity could be fatigue, hysteria, premenstrual syndrome, unnatural sexual impulses like masturbation, or the third stage of syphilis that affected the nervous system and brain.

On the stand, Dr. Hamilton testified he believed Mary was of an "unsound mind," although he admitted he had never examined her until that morning. "I've had four years of experience handling insane and demented people," said Hamilton. "There are eleven hundred such patients presently under my care. Many of them have trouble sleeping at night, as the plaintiff does."

Minahan's attorney sat down while murmurs rippled through the courtroom.

Attorney Olin's jaw was tight, his eyes filled with disdain as he approached Dr. Hamilton. "Didn't you tell Dr. Brett, 'There is an epidemic of malpractice suits, and as soon as it becomes known that a doctor has any money, he is pitched upon by someone, trying to get a part of it? And that down in Chicago, one doctor would not testify against another. They help each other out?'"

"I—I did say that in part," Dr. Hamilton stammered, seemingly caught off-guard. "But I don't know whether or not I said all of it. But if I did, it was not my intention that my testimony would be anything but fair and truthful."

In Olin's closing statement, he would call Hamilton "this little bull toad" who came up to Green Bay to shatter the plaintiff's case. "You saw how he bristled up and asked the Court when the cross-examination got a little too much for him, 'Your honor, does a great and distinguished physician from Chicago have to be treated this way?' And how Judge Hastings very properly said, 'You answer the questions which are asked you.' He told us he was professor of surgery at the great Rush Medical College. Well, the truth of the matter is that Dr. Nicholas Senn is the professor of surgery. Dr. Hamilton holds his job by political pull. This great and learned physician ... He holds a clinic once a week of the little rag tail cases of the institution."

Dr. Fairfield returned to the stand and testified that Mary's condition showed some symptoms of being the subject of a criminal operation. Fairfield believed she was a woman of "chaste character," and her present condition would be permanent unless she underwent an operation. But in Mary's current state, he said an operation would be "hazardous to her life."

When Fairfield testified he would never prescribe emmenagogue pills to "enrich the blood," his sharp gaze sliced into Dr. Minahan, who was seated at the defendant's table.

During Attorney Martin's cross-examination, Dr. Fairfield admitted he "could not definitely say whether a criminal operation had been performed" or whether Mary's present condition had occurred from some "private disease." He also agreed, although reluctantly, that after undergoing a criminal operation, it was quite improbable that any woman could immediately return to work and keep on her feet as Mary testified she had.

Attorney Martin sat down looking smug, as did the defendant and his brother.

At the plaintiff's table, Mary longed to defend herself. Those men could not understand the dedication she committed to her domestic positions. That she had never wanted to be negligent in her duties, even after the man seated across the courtroom aisle from Mary had brutally aborted her child.

THREE DAYS BEFORE Christmas, men in felt hats and warm woolen coats, and women in bonnets, capes, and muffs, purchased last-minute gifts on Washington Street. Dolls at Theo, Muller & Company, books at Hoffman's Bazaar, slippers at Hoeffel Brothers Shoe Company, and fancy nuts, oranges, and apples at Corbett's. But inside the Brown County Courthouse, holiday activities were on hold as the crowd fought to access the best courtroom seats for the Cenefelt vs. Minahan trial.

Dr. Benjamin Brett with salt-and-pepper hair, beard, and mustache was sworn in. He told Olin he had practiced medicine in Green Bay for twenty-five years, and his son, Dr. Fred Brett, was part of his practice. The senior Dr. Brett confirmed he had ample experience

Dr. Benjamin Brett (Men Who Are Making Green Bay 1897)

with women's diseases and knew the ingredients in emmenagogue pills. He said ergot was weaker than ergotine, and the latter was used in combination with other chemicals within the drug, like oil of savon, to perform criminal operations. Another emmenagogue ingredient, black hellebore, produced vomiting. The final element, dried aloes of iron, should never be given to a pregnant woman.

"Doctor, what do you think would be the result of administering three emmenagogue pills containing those ingredients?"

"They would go through a patient like a sawmill."

The physician also said he would never prescribe emmenagogue pills "to enrich the blood," as Dr. J.R. Minahan had testified.

"Would you give these pills to a person whom you thought was pregnant?"

"No. Not unless I wished to commit a criminal operation."

The courtroom spectators murmured as Mary's attorney sat down and Minahan's stood. Mr. Martin's goal was to prove that when Dr. Minahan prescribed the emmenagogue pills for Mary, his purpose had nothing to do with inducing an abortion.

As Attorney Martin stepped through each of the pills' ingredients, he had Dr. Brett concur that each on its own could have been used to treat one of Mary's specific ailments. In particular, Martin focused on ergot.

Eventually, Dr. Brett agreed that ingredient could help induce sleep.

"Doctor, do you know of any reputable physician who would administer three of these pills, and one after each meal, for the purpose of performing a criminal operation?"

"No, sir. I know of no reputable physician who would do so."

Martin nodded. "Now, Doctor, doesn't hysteria and uterus trouble go hand in hand?"

"Well, they might, providing—"

"No provisions. Let us understand each other, at least before Christmas."

"Alright, Mr. Martin."

The witness and attorney, friends in everyday life, shook hands while an undulation of amusement ran through the courtroom.

Brett finally confirmed that uterus trouble and hysteria often occurred together.

Dr. C.W. Oviatt, who had performed a psychological examination on Mary, would later testify that he believed she had neurosis rather than hysteria or insanity. Neurosis was a mental illness with symptoms that included mild depression, anxiety, and hypochondria, but not a radical loss from reality. Two St. Vincent Sisters would also testify and state that Mary had displayed hysterical symptoms, becoming overwrought and emotional after her womb surgery.

Dating back as far as 1900 BC, doctors had considered hysteria an emotionally charged disease caused by the womb, leading to insanity. But Sigmund Freud had recently published a differing opinion: The brain, not the reproductive organs, caused hysteria, and both sexes could suffer from the disease. Another physician, Professor Alfred Fournier, thought syphilis was the driving force behind neurosis and hysteria. "As long as the true nature of syphilis, its cause, and possible cure remained shrouded in speculation," Fournier stated, "it could play the role of universal disease."

It could also be used as Dr. Minahan's defense against Mary.

Olin approached Dr. Brett again. "Do you wish to say that every woman who has uterus trouble is hysterical?"

"No, not hysterical but nervous to an extent." Dr. Brett also testified that Mary had not displayed any hysterical symptoms throughout the trial.

"Doctor, is hysteria naturally confined to a woman?"

"No, sir."

Minahan's attorney interjected, "We don't claim that such is the case. There are hysterical lawyers."

Olin turned toward Martin, seated at the defendant's table. "Yes, there are women lawyers."

"But there are none in Green Bay," Attorney Martin shot back.

Olin gave him a sardonic smile. "It is a good thing, perhaps. It might be difficult for them to practice here."

Olin settled back in his chair, shaking his head. He later told Mary, he believed the opposing team's strategy, to insinuate that she suffered from hysteria or insanity caused by an "unmentionable disease," was a trick to discredit her testimony—and Olin had "a holy hatred of all those tricks" which brought dishonor to the legal profession.

Friend or Foe

TRAFFIC BACKED UP on Washington Street on Thursday, December 23, after a rig transporting sewing machines tipped over and the sleigh broke. But the accident did not stop the crowd from entering the Brown County Courthouse. Dr. Minahan's team would place their non-medical witnesses on the stand that day, hoping to tear apart Mary Cenefelt's testimony once and for all.

Attorney Martin had previously led Mary into agreeing her alleged assault dates could have occurred on March 16 and 17 of 1893. Martin was now determined to provide proof that her sexual assault claims on those specific days were a fabrication.

At Mary's pretrial deposition, Martin had asked her about the two coachmen who had worked for Dr. Minahan. She had testified that he had changed men while she was there. "The first man, I don't know his last name. His first was Henry; he was a lame fellow. The other man was quite an old man. His first name was Pat; I don't know his last name. He is gray-headed. He must have been 55, 60 years old."

In the courtroom, "the lame fellow," Henry Drissen, Dr. Minahan's former coachman, was called to the stand and testified he had left the Minahans' employment on Tuesday, March 14, 1893. Attorney Martin showed Drissen an exhibit: the coachman's recommendation letter he had written, which Dr. Minahan had signed. It was dated Saturday, March 11, 1893.

According to Mary's initial testimony, March 11 was the Saturday Mrs. Minahan had returned from Casco following Mary's second assault.

Next, "the old man," Patrick Mahoney, Dr. Minahan's current driver, testified that he had started to work for Dr. Minahan on Tuesday, March 14, the day before Mrs. Minahan departed for a two-day trip to Casco.

George King, a Casco farmer, testified that Mrs. Minahan had left his place on Thursday, March 16, to return to Green Bay.

Attorney Martin seemed pleased by the three men's testimony. But there were plausible questions that not only went unanswered, but no records exist to show whether Mary's attorneys had even raised them. Mary had always stated Mrs. Minahan had been gone from a Thursday to a Saturday. Had the doctor's wife been in Casco twice: once on Wednesday, March 15 through Thursday, March 16, when the temperature had ranged from negative two to twenty-six degrees and the sap was not running—and also the prior week, from Thursday, March 9 through Saturday, March 11, when the high and low temperatures for those three days were perfect for sugaring?

After nearly five years, one might also wonder how both coachmen could have recalled the specific March 14 date that Drissen said he had left the doctor's employment, and Mahoney said he had joined it. If Drissen had departed on March 7 instead, he could have asked the doctor to sign his March 11 reference letter once he had a new job in mind. Mary's attorney should also have asked Henry Drissen why Patrick Mahoney had replaced him in the first place. Was there a chance that Minahan had released Drissen so he could employ a fellow Irishman the day before Mrs. Minahan's Thursday, March 9 departure?

Court adjourned at noon to allow the jurors time to travel home for Christmas Eve. Mary and her two siblings took a coach to Cooperstown to celebrate the holiday with family while Attorney Olin traveled to Milwaukee to spend the weekend with friends. On Christmas day, the Green Bay Christie Hotel proprietor gave new caps to his bus drivers and baggagemen. The policemen gave Chief Tennis a new desk, and the firemen presented Chief Kennedy with a silver water set. But Mary waited for the gift she desired most. Vindication.

ON MONDAY, December 27, before the Cenefelt vs. Minahan trial resumed, Judge Hastings asked the four attorneys to join him in his private chambers to discuss a legal disaster. According to Attorney Martin, one of the impaneled jurors, Joseph DeGreef, the Preble truck gardener, had shared the case's merits with an outside party.

DeGreef had returned home each evening on the Main and Washington electric streetcar line, each night driven by the same motorman. The driver had asked DeGreef about the trial's daily developments, and the truck gardener had frankly answered without any knowledge of wrongdoing. When DeGreef had indicated that the jury would decide against Minahan, the motorman had not kept that sensational news to himself. Minahan's attorney had heard the rumor, secured the motorman's affidavit, and appeared before Judge Hastings that morning.

Inside his chambers, the judge sharply questioned the truck gardener who did not deny the allegations. DeGreef swore he had not heard the judge's injunction not to discuss the case.

Attorney Martin insisted that Dr. Minahan was entitled to a fair trial before twelve unbiased jurors. Olin said he would consider the proposition of proceeding with eleven. Since the civil case was an expensive one to conduct Judge Hastings said he was not ready to call a mistrial. Instead, he would question the rest of the jurors before he made a ruling.

As the bailiff took each juror individually into a little anteroom to speak with the judge and attorneys, Mary huddled at the plaintiff's table with her siblings. At the defendant's table, Dr. Minahan maintained the same unconcerned attitude he had displayed throughout the proceedings, speaking with anyone who stopped to talk. To Mary and her supporters, Minahan was no different than poison hemlock, the toxic white-flowering plant found in the low-lying areas of Wisconsin farmland. It was hard to distinguish from Queen Anne's lace, a completely harmless plant.

As the last rays of sunlight disappeared from the courtroom windows, Judge Hastings, the attorneys, and the final juryman emerged from the anteroom. Hastings had not decided whether to call a mistrial. He admonished the panel to keep silent about the case and adjourned court until morning.

Mary's initial attorney, Charles E. Vroman, spoke to the press that evening. "If the judge holds that it is a mistrial, then the present jury will be dismissed, a new one impaneled, and the case retried from the very beginning. I cannot say just what action will be taken or what the outcome will be, for such a difficulty has never arisen with any case ever tried to this circuit."

At 10:00 a.m. on Tuesday, December 28, after Judge Hastings conducted a two-hour private conference with the attorneys, the judge made his decision. He discharged three jurors and told the attorneys the trial would proceed with nine. In addition to Joseph DeGreef, Edward Gerstner from the town of Eaton and Edmund F. Liebman from the town of Preble were dismissed. Gerstner had expressed to friends that Dr. Minahan was guilty while playing cards inside the courthouse during a trial recess. Like DeGreef, Mr. Gerstner insisted he had not heard the Court's injunction not to talk about the trial to anyone.

Mr. Liebman's dismissal was different. The judge had discharged juror Liebman because Minahan's attorney had noticed Dr. Benjamin Brett, a witness for Mary, walking with the juror. "As for my discussing the case with Mr. Liebman," Dr. Brett said, "not one syllable regarding the matter ever passed between us. It is rather strange that I should be taken to be such a partisan that it would necessitate the discharge of a juror because he passed the time of day with me. The insinuation is a gross reflection and does me an injustice."

It was clear. At least two of the dismissed jurors would have decided in Mary's favor.

A bleak wintry feeling filled her chest. The judge's ruling had sided with Minahan's team rather than hers, a discouraging replay from Mary's first trial.

MRS. EMMA NOLAN, Dr. Minahan's former office lady, could not testify in court due to illness. Perhaps she had contracted diphtheria since the *Gazette* reported that Brown County cases were on the rise. If left untreated the infectious bacteria, which created a throat thickness obstructing the upper airway, could lead to death.

The deposition of Mrs. Nolan would instead be conducted inside her Walnut Street home and read back in the courtroom. Five dining chairs surrounded Mrs. Nolan's sofa where she reclined. A shawl covered her body and pillows propped up her head. Attorney Martin and Dr. Minahan sat to her left, Attorney Olin and Mary to her right, and the court reporter and bailiff in the middle. If Mrs. Nolan had diphtheria, she would have worn a hospital mask. Respiratory droplets could spread the disease if she coughed or sneezed.

Mary attempted to make eye contact with Mrs. Nolan, whom she considered a friend. But Minahan's former office lady only had eyes for the physician. She had worked for him from January of 1892 until April of 1895 and she held Dr. Minahan in high esteem.

Mrs. Nolan testified that she had never missed a day of work at Dr. Minahan's office other than to attend the Chicago World Columbian Exhibition in September of 1893.

"Shortly after you [started to work] there, did you purchase any towels?" asked Attorney Martin, still seated.

"Yes, sir ... The towels that were in use, when I came there, were so poor that we could not use them ... I asked the doctor for some money to get some more, and the old ones I used for window cloths, for rags." She said none of the old ones remained by 1893. She had purchased new towels to replace them, once at Jorgensen & Blesch and another time at Mr. Schuette's store. They had been white and all barred with blue thread, some with plain bars and some with blue and white checks.

Martin handed Mrs. Nolan the small white barber towel with bands of red, that Mary's attorney had submitted into evidence during her direct examination. It was the one she had testified she had saved from her abortion. "Mrs. Nolan, you may state whether or not the doctor ... had any such towels as this in his office."

"I don't remember a towel of that kind." She handed it back.

Attorney Martin smiled and set the towel down.

In rebuttal courtroom testimony, Mr. Schuette, the Savings Store manager, would state that Miss Emma Fifer, Dr. Minahan's office lady before Mrs. Nolan, had bought towels for the doctor's use like the one Mary had.

"Now, Mrs. Nolan," Martin said, "you know this Miss Cenefelt, the plaintiff, do you?"

"Yes, sir." Her eyes finally landed on Mary. "She often visited Dr. Minahan's office." Mrs. Nolan also said that Mary, although uninvited, had called on her in her Walnut Street home.

Mrs. Nolan's voice lacked the warmth she had put on as part of her job at the doctor's office. Her coldness startled Mary. With Dr. Minahan in the room, the tables appeared to have turned. Mrs. Nolan, it seemed, cared more about the physician's approval than Mary's friendship.

Martin asked Mrs. Nolan about the last time Mary had visited her home. She said it was about a month after Mary's first trial, and she had showed her a gold ring she claimed Dr. Minahan had given to her. It was the same ring that Mr. Martin now handed to Mrs. Nolan to examine. She said she had told Mary, the ring looked like the one that had disappeared from the office, the one being held as security for a patient's bill. According to Mrs. Nolan, Mary had said, "Yes, so the doctor said."

As Mrs. Nolan returned the ring to Attorney Martin, he asked her where the ring had been kept in the doctor's office before it went missing.

"[It] used to lay on the [office] desk, and when we got a letter from the woman, I asked the doctor if he wanted to answer it ... He asked me if she had sent the money, and I said no." At that point, Mrs. Nolan said Dr. Minahan had told her the woman was a prostitute so it was doubtful she would ever pay. When that letter had arrived, Mrs. Nolan testified she had looked for the ring and could not locate it. She said the doctor had joined in on the search, and when it had not turned up, he had asked Mrs. Nolan if she had taken it. She had told him she had not.

Later in the courtroom, when Mrs. Nolan's testimony would be read back to the jurors, they would have to wonder why Dr. Minahan had aided in the search for the ring instead of telling his office lady he had taken it to his home where he claimed Mary had subsequently stolen it.

"Where did you usually sit when in the doctor's service?" Martin now asked.

"I was in the waiting room, near to the radiator and near the doctor's private office door." Mrs. Nolan said she could hear when any patients spoke too loudly. "I would go around and let the doctor know of it ... The doctor's words, I never could hear—merely his voice."

"With reference to Holy week, or the week before Easter of 1893, state whether or not you have any recollection of this plaintiff," Martin motioned toward Mary, "coming to the doctor's office on three different occasions ... And then on Monday of the next week, coming back. And while in his private room, screeching out, or crying, or making any noise of any kind?"

"I could not state, exact to the times, that the patient came up there ... and I never heard her cry out. That would have impressed upon me, it seems."

Attorney Martin agreed over the clang and rattle of a passing streetcar. "What kind of a door leads from the doctor's reception room into his private room?" he asked.

"Oh, I don't know, I ain't a carpenter ... They are all warped in every shape and way. They don't fit at all. I was fixing them one day myself and trying to make them shut."

Martin extracted a document from his briefcase. "You may look at this little diagram here." He handed the paper to Mrs. Nolan. "That is supposed to be a curet—something for scraping out, cleaning out the womb. Did Dr. Minahan have any such instrument as that?"

"I don't know of anything like that." She handed the diagram back.

"Thank you, Mrs. Nolan. I have no further questions."

Even though the witness was ill, her slouched back straightened, and her rheumy eyes turned wary as Attorney Olin began. "During all the time you worked for the doctor, he had a good many patients call, I suppose?"

"Yes, a great many, very large, numbering up to fifty a day."

"You heard, I suppose, people crying out in his office at various times?"

"Yes."

"And you became more or less accustomed to hearing that, I suppose?"

"No, it was not so very often ... The doctor did not perform operations there. Of course, sometimes, people go on and on, and they would cry for fear ... I heard a couple of them cry out having teeth pulled."

"You don't want to say whether the plaintiff cried out or not?"

"Why yes, because if I'd heard her, you know, I would have noted it ... If I hadn't known her, probably, I would not have noticed it so much."

"You testified on the former trial, didn't you?"

"Yes, sir."

Olin located the transcript from his briefcase then ran his finger down the page. "Were these questions put to you, and did you make these answers?"

Question: And you have heard ... cries of other people?

Answer: Yes, oh, yes.

Question: And you don't know whether it was this plaintiff or someone else for sure?

Answer: Well, I would know who would go into the room, then out through the waiting room.

Question: But you can't say for sure whether you heard this plaintiff?

Answer: No, sir.

Olin looked up. "Did you testify that way at the trial before?"

Mrs. Nolan squirmed on the sofa. "If I did, it was unbeknownst to me. That is, probably, I overlooked it, because had I—"

"But you don't say that you didn't testify that way?"

"If it is there, I must have."

"And I suppose that oftentimes the doctor let patients out through the side door, who might not want to go through the reception room when he was through with them?"

"If he would let them in that way—"

"I did not say in. I said out."

Mrs. Nolan shrunk against her pillows, and the room's energy shifted. "Of course, when he used to let them in one door, I used to think it was the place to let them out the same door."

"You seem to think that he didn't do that because you would want to know when he got through with one patient, so you could let another in. He could easily let you know that by opening the door afterwards, couldn't he?"

"Yes."

"Did you ever know of the doctor bringing some towels that he had at the house to wash his hands?"

"No ... I don't know of him ever doing that."

"Has the doctor talked with you about ... the towel and the ring recently?"

"He asked me if I—"

"Just answer the question."

"Yes ... The other evening ... On Saturday night."

"I see." Olin curtly nodded. "Did [the doctor] frequently carry about with him any ... instruments ... back and forth from the office to the hospital?"

"He never brought any that I know of. He never carried a satchel like most doctors do ... If he needed anything, he would send me to the hospital for his instruments—"

The brows of Attorney Olin raised in surprise.

"—and I would have to fetch them right back again ... The Sister was very particular."

"Then you did go to the hospital at different times for instruments?"

"Yes."

"And the doctor had a key to [his medical office] rooms, I assume?"

"Yes.

"And he could go in and out without consulting you, when you didn't know anything about it?"

"Certainly."

"Thank you, Mrs. Nolan." Olin smiled.

THE WISCONSIN Teachers Association conference was in session on December 29, 1897, to discuss "mental, moral, and physical ideals" while the Cenefelt vs. Minahan trial grappled with the same issues. The court reporter read Mrs. Nolan's testimony into the record for the judge and jury while the last five witnesses for the defendant awaited their turn to testify.

John Weiner, an ex-saloon keeper and stagecoach driver, was sworn in first. The scent of his slicked down hair filled Mary's nostrils as it had on the numerous rides she had taken with him between Green Bay and Cooperstown.

Attorney Martin established that Mary had been Mr. Weiner's lone stagecoach passenger right before the former trial. "Did you have a conversation with the plaintiff regarding the crime?"

"Yes," Weiner testified. "She told me her troubles with Dr. Minahan ... That she wanted to get even with him."

As a hushed crowd awaited more details, Mary felt betrayed by the man she had trusted, the man who had seemed to have a sympathetic ear, who had commiserated with her over her problems.

"Did she say how she wanted to [get even with him]?" asked Martin.

"By using a gun or by throwing carbolic acid in his face."

Amid the courtroom's uneasy rustling, Mary was stunned by his words. She longed to refute his claims.

"What did you advise her to do?"

"I told her she had better let things go ... to shut up about the matter."

Martin's thin lips curved into a satisfied smile as he sat down and Attorney Olin stood. "Mr. Weiner, did Dr. Minahan come to your home about two months ago to attend to an ill child of yours?"

"Yes."

"Did you have any conversation with him regarding this case?"

"Well ..." he hesitated. "I asked him how it was coming out, and he said the case was all settled."

"Dr. Minahan evidently must have been misinformed," Olin said smoothly. "Did you give him a detailed account of your conversation with the plaintiff?"

Weiner's thumbs slid under the lapels of his suit jacket. "No, I did not."

"You are a particular friend of Dr. Minahan, are you not?"

"Not any more than I'm your friend."

Olin tried to trip the stagecoach driver up about his claims concerning Mary, but Weiner did not back down.

Mary's friend Josephine Bartelme settled onto the witness chair next and fluffed out the skirt of the gown she had undoubtedly sewn. Josephine testified she had written three letters for Mary to Dr. Minahan, one without a signature. "I addressed an envelope and put a stamp on it but did not mail it, although the plaintiff thought I did. Instead, I prepared a 'dummy letter' and dropped it into the mailbox. In this letter, Miss Cenefelt told the doctor that he might have had more taste than to pick out such a wife as he did, a little scrumpy being. She also called him a big goose and expressed the opinion that his wife was too small for him. She also called the doctor a big sport."

A numbness, shock, and loneliness shuddered through Mary. Those private comments had only been spoken when she and Josephine had told fortunes and predicted each other's admirers and enemies. Mary had never meant to share those words beyond her friend's confidence, especially in a letter to Dr. Minahan. In fact, Mary would later state in rebuttal testimony that Nettie was the only Bartelme sister who had written letters for Mary.

While listening to Josephine, Mary's face remained stoic even though she was hurt. She could not comprehend why her friend had betrayed her. Yet Josephine, at age thirty, had to support herself as a seamstress unless she found a husband. If she sided with Mary, Josephine might fear losing clients who socialized with Dr. Minahan.

Mary's attorney stood and approached Josephine. Olin said she had mentioned a letter she had written for Mary, yet he had not seen it admitted into evidence. "Why is that?"

Josephine seemed flustered. "I—I destroyed it."

Olin checked the jury's reaction before sitting down.

The next defendant witness was Josephine's mother, Mrs. John Bartelme. Mary had frequently sat at the Bartelmes' dining room table, enjoying companionable conversation with the family's matriarch. She had cared for Mary's well-being as her mother had.

"Did the plaintiff often visit your home?" Martin asked Mrs. Bartelme.

"Yes. She came there quite frequently and often got into the passion of anger and would rail at Dr. Minahan."

Mary's breathing shallowed. Had Mrs. Bartelme turned on her too?

When Mary had first met Dr. Minahan, Mrs. Bartelme's husband had been the Brown County Sheriff. Now he was the undersheriff. Both positions placed his wife in a Green Bay social tier far closer to Dr. Minahan than Mary. Mary realized, like Josephine, Mrs. Bartelme likely feared she would tarnish her reputation by supporting Mary.

"Several times, I also detected a peculiar odor about the plaintiff," Mrs. Bartelme continued, "and I spoke to my husband about it."

John Bartelme's brief testimony followed his wife's. He told Martin he had detected the odor of iodoform about the plaintiff (an antiseptic dressing used for wounds and sores.) "This was before she had gone to work for Dr. Minahan," he added.

Mary tilted her head, confused, although she would soon understand the iodoform's implications from upcoming testimony.

Mary's uncle, James Loukotka, was the final witness for the defendant. Dressed in his Sunday suit, Mr. Loukotka physically shook while testifying that Mary had frequently visited his home and "she often said she was sick."

"How long is it since these visits ceased?" asked Martin.

"Several months back."

"Did you ... request [the plaintiff] not to come again?"

"Yes."

"Why was this?"

"Because my wife objected." He said Mary's aunt had not known what sort of female diseases Mary might have been bringing into their house.

Mary felt like a windstorm had picked her up and thrown her down. Other than her siblings and Nettie Bartelme, everyone had sided with Dr. Minahan.

On Stage

THE TIME had arrived for Dr. John R. Minahan's testimony. Attired in a white-on-white bow tie and collar beneath a dark suit and vest, the thirty-four-year-old surgeon pleasantly nodded toward the jury panel from the witness stand. He was composed, unruffled, as he had been when presenting his "Injuries to the Knee Joint" paper to the Fox River Valley Medical Society.

Mary could not look at the man who had raped her and ripped out her child. Instead, her eyes focused on the courtroom clock. One click, one breath, one click, one breath.

Minahan testified that Mary had first come to his medical office in January of 1893, two days after he had seen her at the Bartelme courthouse residence.

Dr. John R. Minahan
(Men Who are Making
Green Bay 1897)

"Did you make an examination there?" asked Martin.

As in the former trial, Minahan said, "Yes, and I found her in a bad condition, suffering from a disease of the womb." Minahan said he believed Mary had anemia caused by lack of blood. That was why he had prescribed the emmenagogue pills. He had also prepared an application for her private parts that included iodoform.

Minahan's lies and accusations pelted Mary. She had known they were coming, but it was nearly impossible to bear his abuse again. She glanced at the jurors. The brows of tugboat owner George D. Nau were furrowed, and a fleeting smile crossed the lips of Mr. F.L. Smith, the De Pere Riverside Brick Company owner.

In a row beside the jury box, the brows of Dr. William Fairfield, Dr. Benjamin Brett, and Dr. Fred Brett were also furrowed. Their upcoming rebuttal testimony would state they rarely used iodoform for "private diseases," and a person who had never been in contact with the antiseptic could also carry that odor. Carrie would also testify she had never smelled iodoform on Mary even though they had shared a bed at the Bartelmes' just days before Mary had taken the Minahan job.

Attorney Martin now asked Minahan, "You remember the circumstances of your wife going to Casco?"

"Yes. Mrs. Minahan went to Casco on the morning of [Wednesday], March 15, 1893, and returned the next day at supper time."

"What did she go for, do you know?"

"Maple syrup and butter."

"Was your wife home on the evenings of [Thursday and Friday], March 16 and 17 of 1893?"

"Yes, she was."

Minahan's wife Elizabeth was a ghost in the proceedings, often mentioned but never seen—a missing person in the trial's saga. Her voice was conspicuously absent, but with Minahan there to speak for her, no one in power seemed to notice or mind the omission. She was another silenced woman in the process. But those in the courtroom of Mary's status had to wonder why she had not testified herself, and on her husband's behalf.

The Green Bay Gazette society column had noted that Dr. John R. Minahan had recently entertained his two brothers, Dr. Robert E. Minahan and Dr. William E. Minahan, along with their wives, at his Quincy Street home. There was no mention of Dr. John R. Minahan's wife. In 1893, Minahan had told Mary after her first sexual assault, "If my wife is not satisfied with anything I can give her, she can go where she wants." Wisconsin law gave a husband the "right" to demand his wife consent to sexual intercourse. If she refused, he could use physical force to secure his wishes. Her refusal could also be a husband's grounds for divorce.

No records exist of the couple's divorce, but Minahan's niece would later state: Elizabeth Minahan "died in a mental hospital after their divorce." Husbands could commit their wives, deeming them insane, if they simply expressed contrary opinions or were hard to control.

Earlier in the trial, Dr. John B. Hamilton had testified, "I've had four years of experience handling insane and demented people. There are eleven hundred such patients presently under my care." One of those could have been Elizabeth Minahan.

There is no record of her death, but during the trial it is clear that Elizabeth was still alive. Judge Hastings' upcoming jury charge would shed a faint light on that fact and the reason why she had not taken the stand. Hastings would state, "The wife of the defendant is not in law competent to testify either for or against the defendant, and you should draw no inference unfavorable to the defendant from the fact that his wife was not called as a witness."

That law would have been difficult for the plaintiff's side to swallow. Mrs. Minahan had treated Mary with kindness. Elizabeth's testimony might have helped Mary—if she had been willing to stand up to her husband. The defendant's team had developed their strategy knowing Mrs. Minahan could not refute her husband's claims, a decided advantage.

"Doctor..." Martin continued and placed his hand on the witness rail. "Have you ever had occasion to buy one collar at a time?"

Minahan threw back his curly head and laughed. "I think not for the last fifteen years."

"Did you ever give the plaintiff thirty-five dollars?"

"I never gave her a cent," Minahan testified, looking directly at the jury.

"Did she offer to give you a statement for twenty-five dollars, to the effect that the statement made to Dr. Fairfield was not true?"

"Yes." That tiny word left Minahan's tongue as spectators whispered. That question and answer created an alternate scenario to refute Mary's testimony about the paper Minahan had tricked her into signing. In any case, Minahan's attorney did not offer that coerced document as evidence.

Judge Hastings' gavel and stern voice silenced the crowd.

"Did you ever say anything to her, that made her angry with you?" Martin asked Minahan.

"Yes. I told her she had not followed my instructions regarding her treatment, and she would never get well. I also told her, most of her disease was imaginary, and the best thing she could do was to go home to the farm and go to work."

"Did you tell her she was crazy?"

"Yes, I did."

Martin asked Minahan about the anonymous phone calls he had received, where the individual requesting medical treatment had only given him the address. "Where in the city did you make these [house] calls?"

"Over the East River on Twelfth Street, again at O'Neil's Hotel, and at Oliver Tennis's home." In each case, Minahan said he had discovered Mary had initiated the calls, and he had left without treating her since he believed Mary's ailments were all in her head.

Mary would not dispute those calls, only the impetus for them. She had not been crazy, only desperate for Minahan's help after her womb surgery had failed.

"Did you ever prescribe cold water baths for the plaintiff, or that she throw a pail of cold water down her back?"

"I think I said that."

"What was that for?"

"To rouse her and get her out of bed."

"Is that the usual treatment given a hysterical person?"

"Yes."

Amid whispers, coughs, and creaking seats, Mary sat stiffly in her chair, her eyes focused on the courtroom clock. One click, one breath, one click, one breath.

Martin smiled at Minahan and moved on. "How often have you prescribed these emmenagogue pills?"

"About ten or fifteen times a month."

"Would these pills bring on an abortion?"

"I don't think so."

At Minahan's response, which ran counter to all the medical experts' testimony, the spectators and jury seemed confused, exchanging glances, heads tilted, expressions twisted.

"No further questions," said Martin as Attorney Olin stood.

He first had Dr. Minahan reiterate what Olin would later tell the jury were Minahan's two significant lies. First, he had given Mary emmenagogue pills "to enrich her blood." Second, he did not believe those pills would cause an abortion.

Olin paused to let that testimony sink in. He then peppered Minahan with one question after another.

"Do you know where [your coachman] Patrick Mahoney was on the evening of March 17, 1893?"

"Yes, sir."

"Well, doctor, you didn't know *nor* did Pat on the former trial."

"I did."

"Why didn't you tell the Court where he was?"

"He was off celebrating."

"That is not my question. Why didn't you tell that at the former trial?"

"I didn't know."

Olin smiled, having caught Minahan in another lie.

"You knew the nature of the statement made by the plaintiff to Dr. Fairfield?"

"Only what she told me."

"You told her to be careful, or she and Dr. Fairfield would get into trouble?"

"Yes."

"You never did cause trouble, did you?"

"No."

"When you were called to see Miss Cenefelt at Mrs. Lawe's, you testified she only had a fever and a cold?"

"Yes."

"After that visit, you sent her to the hospital?"

"Upon the request of Mrs. Lawe."

"You knew all the time that [the plaintiff] was a woman of loose character?"

"Yes."

"And you were doctoring her for charity?"

"Yes."

"But did you consider it an act of charity to send her to the hospital when you were aware what the charges would be?"

"The charges there would be as cheap as any [hospital]."

"But a cheaper place could have been found where she could have received treatment just as good?" Olin reminded Minahan that he had just testified that Mary *only* had a fever and a cold.

"Perhaps a cheaper place could have been found," Minahan curtly said.

Olin looked at the jury, drawing their attention to precisely what he was trying to do: to call Minahan's good intentions into question. But Olin had missed a critical opportunity. Between 1893 and 1897, the *Gazette* published at least 225 articles that mentioned the various inpatient ailments and treatments St. Vincent Hospital had provided. None of those described any inpatients treated for an infectious or a venereal disease, which followed the hospital's founding charter.

Olin should have asked Dr. Minahan: Since St. Vincent Hospital refused inpatient services to those with venereal diseases, how could he have admitted Mary on three occasions, totaling nine weeks?

If Mary's attorney had asked that question, Minahan's entire case could have fallen apart.

THE TESTIMONY for the defendant was complete, and Attorney Martin rested Dr. Minahan's case. Attorney Olin could now call rebuttal witnesses. Among those was the servant girl, Miss Helen Doherty. She worked for Reverend J.L. Hewitt and his wife at the Presbyterian Church parsonage next to Dr. Minahan's former Adams Street residence. Attorney Olin asked Helen about St. Patrick's Day of 1893. She testified she had pinned a green ribbon on coachman Patrick Mahoney's coat. In Mary's prior testimony, Minahan's attorney had suggested that Mary had pinned the ribbon on the coachman to prove she had been working for Dr. Minahan on St. Patrick's Day.

Attorney Olin called several other witnesses before Mary. It would be his last-ditch effort to alter her assault date from March 17 to her original March 10 date that Mary had provided in her deposition, first trial, and current trial's direct testimony.

He asked Mary, "Is there anything in particular which would make you remember that Mrs. Minahan was away from home, on the days ... Dr. Minahan was intimate with you?"

"Yes, sir, there is. I had previously asked the doctor for the privilege of going out that evening. When Mrs. Minahan did not come home, I went to Mrs. Bartelme's and met my sister, and she accompanied me over East River to my aunt's."

"Did you get anything over there which your parents had sent?"

"Yes ... some homemade sausage."

But Mary's recollection had not proven a thing. She still had no date. As much as she and Carrie had tried to remember, they could not. Mary's aunt might have worked to do the same if she had not turned on Mary. And Mrs. Lawe might have recalled the date Mary had started to work at her home if only she had not passed away.

The last questions Attorney Olin asked Mary were about the Cooperstown stagecoach driver's testimony. Mary felt relieved that she could tell her side of the story, that she had never told Mr. Weiner she had wanted to get even with Dr. Minahan by throwing carbolic acid in his face or using a revolver.

As Olin sat down, Minahan's attorney approached Mary. He would have been pleased that Olin had called Mary back to the stand. That gave Martin the opportunity to question her again. "Miss Cenefelt," Martin said, "you admit, don't you, that you told Mr. Weiner, when you were riding in his stage to Cooperstown, that you would get even ... with Dr. Minahan?"

"No."

"Didn't you say that you would buy a revolver and do it?"

"No."

"Didn't you have a conversation about shooting?"

"Yes, there was a conversation of that kind."

"Who commenced the conversation about revenge?"

"I don't know exactly, but I think it was myself. Weiner suggested the revolver."

"Didn't you tell Weiner that if you lost this case, you would get even with the doctor by throwing carbolic acid in his face?"

"No, I did not." Mary gazed at the jurymen. She needed them to believe her.

For nearly five years, men had caused Mary pain and tried to keep her quiet. District Attorney Martin, Attorney Vroman, Mr. Weiner, and Dr. Minahan most of all. Even those who had tried to help her like Father O'Brien and Dr. Fairfield had done little to alleviate her suffering or secure justice. But in court that day, the only men that mattered were the nine sitting in the jury box.

"What made you want to get even with the doctor?" asked Martin. "Was it because of your broken health or the alleged occurrences at the doctor's house?"

From the defendant's table, Minahan's pale-blue eyes focused on Mary, intimidating her, frightening her.

Mary's breath shortened. Her hands turned clammy. She looked away and spoke. "It—it was the assault at the house."

Ten years earlier, Paris physician Jean-Martin Charcot first described how a traumatic experience like rape could lead to "hysterical attacks" that could occur years after the trauma. After Mary's extensive testimony, not only in the current trial but in the former one, after being scrutinized for hours on end and sleeping poorly at night, her past trauma could easily have triggered a "hysterical attack" or what is now called a post traumatic flashback.

In the courtroom, there was a cough, then another, and another. Mary's eyes refocused. The sound was coming from juror George D. Nau.

"If you felt so wronged," Martin continued, "why didn't you go out the next morning and swear out a warrant for Dr. Minahan's arrest for criminal assault?"

"Because, at that time, I did not know I could."

Mary, like so many women in the late nineteenth century, had no idea what to do—no idea what she *could* do—after being assaulted and raped. Men had built the judicial system to suppress her voice. Even if a woman reported her rape, Wisconsin law required a high degree of credibility. First, she had to be untarnished. Second, she had to have immediately disclosed the assault to a third party. Third she had to display evidence of physical injury. And fourth, she had to prove she had resisted. Even if a woman passed those tests, justice was often limited.

The year Mary was raped, police caught a Wisconsin man robbing a neighbor's chicken coop. In a nearby town another man was charged with assault with attempt to commit rape. It was not a surprise when the man arrested for chicken stealing—failed chicken stealing at that—was sentenced to eighteen months of hard labor at the state prison in Waupun, while the man who had attempted to rape a woman received only one year in Waupun.

Mary's courage was rare. Without meeting the credibility requirements for her sexual assaults, she had risked everything to expose the truth.

Two Distinct Stories

THE CENEFELT VS. MINAHAN damage suit had reached the two-week mark. The trial was the longest to date in Brown County's history. At least 1,500 people were present inside the courtroom to hear the closing statements. The air vibrated like the Chicago & Northwestern steel railroad tracks seconds before a train's arrival. Prominent physicians, attorneys, businessmen, and farmers were on their feet or had climbed onto the courtroom benches to secure a high perch. Microphones did not exist. Only a fraction of those in attendance would hear directly what was said—but they would be the first to know as whispers rippled through the audience.

Mary gulped down air. She picked at the lace trim on her sleeve. A white pine bough brushed against the courtroom window where a snowy owl perched, free to survey the proceedings without fear.

Mary and her attorneys sat at the plaintiff's table. In the row behind her, those attendees closest to the jury box were three of the four doctors who had testified on her behalf: William Fairfield, Benjamin Brett, and Fred Brett. Next to them were Mary's brother and sister. Both leaned forward as if to protect their big sister.

Seated at the defendant's table, on the center aisle's opposite side, were Dr. J.R. Minahan and his older physician and attorney brother, Robert. Attorney Martin stood directly in front of the jury box. His eyes gleamed, and his thin lips relaxed below his freshly waxed handlebar mustache.

"Gentlemen of the jury," Martin began, "I want to have it understood that the truth will not hurt this defendant. I have never been engaged in a trial where so much weight bears on your verdict. A woman enters into the case and endeavors to prove dishonor against a man of integrity ... She, the plaintiff, asks you to believe that this man of honor, reputation of the best, has committed a heinous crime, and worse than that," Martin's fist slammed the rail, "it outraged her!" Martin laid out Dr. Minahan's defense, how the physician had only treated Mary for a private disease. "And just because she wanted to come to [the defendant's] office, he let her ... [and] he makes an application for her disease ... Who did this?" Martin gestured toward his client. "This big-hearted, generous, good-hearted Dr. Minahan."

Martin's storyline progressed, focused on the absurdity of the idea that Minahan could have assaulted Mary twice, on two different nights, when his neighbors or coachman could have walked in on him. If Mary had been a "virgin," Martin said, "do you not suppose she would have cried out? Why did she not do this?" Martin stepped back. "Because no such thing ever happened. It is a fabrication."

Mary heard rapid footsteps in the courtroom aisle. Minahan's boots. Adrenaline rushed through her. Mary glanced at the defendant's table. The doctor was still there. She took a calming breath, two more...

"Why did this young, innocent girl not leave ... the home of the man who had ruined her?" Martin paced, hands behind his back, the panel's eyes riveted to him. "Some of her relatives lived within a half or three-quarters of a mile from there. Why did she stay and go to bed in the house? Why did she get up and get breakfast for the man who had ruined her? Why did she sit up the next night to let the doctor in when she could have gone to bed? It has been proven by us that Mrs. Minahan was home on the night of March 17, 1893, when the assault was made ... Who shall we believe?" Martin's feet halted.

"[This plaintiff] is rattled. She goes to work at the Lawes'. Eleven days after the alleged assault, she goes to the doctor. She claims she is pregnant ... Now the medical testimony conclusively proves that no person, physician, or otherwise, can, at that length of time, determine that."

Martin talked about the emmenagogue pills and how each ingredient fit Mary's particular ailments. "Take the fact that the doctor gave a prescription. If he wanted to perform a criminal operation, do you suppose he would have written a prescription? No. He would have walked right downstairs into the drug store and obtained the pills ... Then there would have been no evidence."

Sweat formed along Mary's hairline and under her arms. She pictured her tiny bedroom in the Lawes' home, Minahan's prescription clenched in her hand.

Strong wind beat against the courtroom windows.

A flurry of coughs sounded from the jury box.

Mary refocused. George D. Nau, a potentially sympathetic juror, was bent over in a coughing fit.

"The complaint was framed claiming that this abortion was performed on Easter Monday," Martin continued. "Only a thin, warped door was between [Minahan's office lady] and the plaintiff. If she was taken into that little private room, don't you suppose Mrs. Nolan would remember if [the plaintiff] shrieked, screamed, and kicked all the while she was in there? That if she came out crying and bleeding, don't you suppose [Mrs. Nolan] would remember that fact?" Martin placed his hands on the jury rail. "But she does not."

During the witness testimony, Martin had asked each physician, "Tell me, does her condition point toward a private disease or an abortion?" Martin now reminded the jury that every doctor had testified that a "private disease" most likely caused Mary's womb trouble or could have.

"The question of the ring now presents itself." Martin walked over to the evidence table and picked it up. "Why do you suppose the doctor and Mrs. Nolan were looking for this ring when the doctor, as it is claimed, knew he had given it to the plaintiff. Miss Cenefelt testifies that Mrs. Minahan wore the ring. Do you suppose that the doctor would take this ring belonging to a prostitute and give it to his wife?" A dubious expression lined Martin's face. "No... Mrs. Minahan could wear jewelry many times better than that ring." Martin set it back down.

"The defendant in this case was put upon the stand under the most unfavorable conditions ever a human being was. He was called as the first witness in the case. He was taken by surprise. He was presented with this ring, which he knew ought to belong to him, and asked to identify it. But despite these unfavorable conditions, who was it that became rattled? Was it Dr. Minahan or Mr. Olin?" Martin eyed Mary's attorney then turned back toward the jury. "You know which it was."

Martin outlined Mary's interactions with Dr. Fairfield ending with her discovery that the physician had not burned her statement. "What did this doctor want of the original statement?" Martin scowled at Fairfield. "It was unction to his small, shriveled soul. It would answer a purpose ... There has been a suppression of facts by Dr. Fairfield. A fact nursed, nurtured, and kept all these years by him."

Martin stood firmly before the jury to close. "The questions in this case are: Was there a criminal assault? Was there a criminal operation? ... We trust that you will not let your sympathies or your passions interfere with your consideration of the facts. All you have to do, gentlemen of the jury, is to go to that little room and consider the facts ... and we will not fear the result."

The Green Bay Press-Gazette stated, "As a trial lawyer [Patrick Martin] had few equals. He was a formidable antagonist in any legal controversy. He had an unusually keen and searching mind, was a gifted speaker, and a master of English."

Martin had used all those assets to defend Dr. John R. Minahan.

IN THE STIFLING courtroom heat generated by the huge crowd, men surrounded Mary. Sweaty men. Among those were the nine jurymen who would decide her fate. Perspiration ran down Mary's bosom and into her corset. She used a damp handkerchief to blot her face and neck.

At the defendant's table, Minahan laughed, enjoying himself, as if he and his gentlemen friends were simply attending a Washington Park band concert, or a Pavilion Theater performance, or a Turner Hall lecture.

Mary gazed at Attorney Olin as he stood. He believed in her; he was betting his reputation on her. He was a true gentleman who had opened doors for Mary, pulled out her chair, walked on the city's plank sidewalk boards closest to the street, and spoken to her with frank sincerity.

Only his closing statement remained.

"Gentlemen of the jury," Olin said as he positioned himself in front of the panel, his dusty-brown hair neatly parted on the side, his face clean-shaven. "On my honor, as an attorney, ... I have never been engaged in a case where there has been so much merit to render a judgment for my client."

Olin said opposing counsel had endeavored to show that when Mary had not worked on her family's farm, questionable places had employed her. "This is absolutely false ... It must be remembered, to defend her case, counsel must prove that the plaintiff was a prostitute when she went to Dr. Minahan's home to work."

The De Pere Riverside Brick Company owner looked down his nose at Mary. Juror George D. Nau covered a cough with his hand.

Olin was telling Mary's story, detailing the moments that kept her up most nights. He talked about her assaults and how she could not pinpoint their exact dates. How Mary's second assault could just as likely have occurred on Friday, March 10, as Mary had testified to at her deposition, her first trial, and during her current trial's direct testimony. But even if the jury believed the date was March 17, Olin said it was a fact that the defendant's coachman had been out celebrating on St. Patrick's Day. Only Minahan had testified that his wife had been inside the home.

Olin strolled behind the plaintiff's table to reach Mary and gently placed his hands on her shoulders. "Do you accuse this girl of deliberately and intentionally lying? You will find, before the closing of this trial, that the defendant has deliberately lied."

Olin talked about Dr. Minahan's collar. "And he followed this girl into [his bedroom] and then and there committed the [first] assault as claimed by her. Do you suppose that all the facts and details, as have been stated by this girl, have been manufactured?" Olin's determination pulsated through his fingertips, still on Mary's shoulders. He said Minahan's crimes against Mary had not ended with his first assault. They had continued on to his second indecent assault, which had led to her pregnancy and then the criminal operation, which had landed her in St. Vincent Hospital. "It is a fact that the occurrences in this time have been a cause of much sorrow to this girl. It has been burned into her soul."

The story unfolded in Mary's body, her lingering injuries, a daily reminder of Minahan's crimes, and she relived them all in the courtroom.

As Olin walked back toward the jury, he reminded them that after Mary's pretrial deposition Minahan had known she had saved the emmenagogue prescription. That had provided him time to prepare his answer. "[The defendant] testifies ... these pills were used to build up the blood system and did not affect the womb. The trend of the expert-medical testimony has proven that they do have an effect on the womb. The defendant in this case is the only physician who testified he would administer emmenagogue pills to a pregnant woman. He is the only physician involved in the case who testified that he would give these pills to 'enrich the blood.' And this proves that Dr. Minahan did not give those pills for the purpose which he claims."

Olin paused and surveyed each jury member before moving on to the Easter Monday events. Olin stated that Minahan had known Mary was coming. He could have secured the abortion instrument from St. Vincent Hospital and locked it inside his private office on Easter Sunday. When Mary arrived on Monday, to ensure that Mrs. Nolan would not hear Mary's cries as he aborted her child, Minahan could have sent his office lady to the hospital to retrieve an unnecessary instrument. Mary could not recall whether she had exited through the reception room or Minahan's private office side door. The latter, Olin said, was the most probable.

An undercurrent of whispers filled the courtroom, and Judge Hastings' gavel silenced the crowd.

"What did Dr. Fairfield want with [this girl's statement]?" Olin motioned toward the man. "It was to protect himself, as any careful, conservative physician would do. It was not a blackmail scheme to be brought against Dr. Minahan at some future time. Do you think this is another piece of manufactured evidence?

"A point we must touch on is the defense of hysteria ... If you were hysterical and were subject to the crossfire of examination, which this girl has been during this trial, would you not have broken down?"

Every eye was on Mary. She dug her nails into her palms, the pain forcing her to stay in the present.

"I think you would. But she has not. She has born the weariness and trying ordeal with a fortitude, which you all know could not have been done by a hysterical person. She has been dragged in and out of court, day after day, her body reeking with excruciating pain. She has been on the witness stand, time after time, until she could hardly utter a word. So weak that she could hardly hold up her head."

Olin said that the "much-titled Dr. Hamilton of Chicago" had claimed that simply because Mary had trouble sleeping, he believed she was insane. Olin shook his head. "No wonder juries, and people in general, have a bad idea about expert medical testimony."

Olin stood firmly before the panel. "Gentlemen, when you go to your jury room ... let it be your solemn oath to truthfully render a verdict, according to the facts and evidence in the case, those that remain impressed upon your mind."

Wisconsin Supreme Court Justice Burr W. Jones said of Olin, "His great ability, his courage, his earnestness in all good causes, place him in the very highest rank among the distinguished men who have honored the Wisconsin bar."

Olin's earnest courage had shone as he fought for Mary.

Judge and Jury

THE CEΠEFELT VS. MIΠAHAΠ damage case closed at 3:00 p.m. on Saturday, January 1, 1898, while Green Bay Catholic congregations celebrated New Year's Day with thanksgiving sermons inside their parish churches. Only on Christmas and the 4th of July was it illegal to hold court in Brown County.

Through the course of the trial, the opposing attorneys had told two completely different stories. The jury's nine men would need to decide which side had told the truth and which had committed perjury.

In a civil case, Mary, as the plaintiff, had to prove her case by a "preponderance of the evidence," that there was a greater than 50 percent chance her claims were true. In Mary's first trial, the judge had talked about that evidentiary standard, but he had not used concrete examples to help the jury understand. After the jurors awarded Mary a settlement, Minahan's attorney had made a motion to set aside the verdict as "perverse and contrary to the testimony's weight." Martin had believed Mary's attorney had not met the burden of proof, and Judge Hastings had agreed.

To increase the probability of a win for Dr. Minahan in the second trial, his attorney asked Judge Hastings for a "special verdict," which the defendant could request in complex civil cases. Martin's "special verdict" included four written questions that Judge Hastings could instruct the jury to answer: first, whether Mrs. Minahan was home on the nights of March 16 and 17 of 1893; second, whether Mary's criminal assaults occurred on those particular nights; third, whether a pregnancy was the result of those assaults; and fourth, whether Dr. Minahan performed an abortion to destroy the evidence of that pregnancy. If the jurors believed no assaults had occurred on those specific dates, they would absolve Dr. Minahan of any wrongdoing. In other words, Mary would not meet the greater than 50 percent chance her claims were true, and she would receive no settlement.

Olin argued against the "special verdict," and the judge compromised. He said he would use those specific questions only as illustrations rather than in written form during the jury charge.

All the lawyers and doctors crowded up to the rail. Juror George D. Nau coughed while Judge Hastings addressed the panel. "The Court instructs you, at the defendant's request, that the burden of proof is upon the plaintiff to establish the existence of every material fact, to a moral and reasonable certainty, which to base your verdict."

Each juryman listened intently to avoid making a mistake as the three discharged jurors had done.

"To illustrate," Judge Hastings said, "take the question whether or not Mrs. Minahan was home on the nights of March 16 and 17 of 1893." Hastings looked down at his notes. "If the evidence does not establish the fact she was not at home, on said nights ... you must find she was at home ... Again, the question [of] whether or not the defendant had sexual intercourse with the plaintiff, as claimed by her, is one material in this case. And if upon that point, the evidence does not satisfy your minds ... that he did, then you must find that he did not."

Time after time, Minahan's attorney and Judge Hastings had called Mary's sexual assaults sexual intercourse, implying a consensual relationship rather than a violent rape. Those common verbal choices reflected bias against women, both explicit and implicit—and the implications of those words were damaging.

"This is also true," the judge pressed on, "as to whether or not an abortion was committed by the defendant upon the plaintiff ... And unless the evidence ... so satisfies your minds, to a moral and reasonable certainty ... you should find that no abortion was performed."

In Judge Hastings' illustrations, he had used the March 16 and 17 dates for Mrs. Minahan's presence in the home, but he had omitted those specific dates for Mary's assaults, either mistakenly or to give the jury some leeway. In either case, that portion of the judge's charge had boosted Mary's odds of receiving a just verdict.

Judge Hastings continued. He reminded the jurors that Mary had told nobody about her alleged assaults until about a year after they had occurred. "That could be considered suspicious ... tending to discredit the plaintiff's claim. In your deliberations," the judge said, his eyes focused on the panel, "you should not be swayed by passion, sympathy, or prejudice." Yet by using the word "suspicious," Hastings had revealed his prejudice. "Your duty is to give intelligent consideration to the evidence and [to] reach your conclusions, freed from all influences, other than a desire and purpose to ascertain the truth."

Three-fourths of the jury or at least seven members within the nine had to reach the same verdict in a civil suit. If the panel decided in Mary's favor, they would also determine her entitled compensation. First would be her medical and surgical expenses. "From her testimony," Judge Hastings said, "nothing has been shown along that line since she claimed Dr. Minahan paid for nearly all her medical costs." Second, Mary would be entitled to recover past and future compensation for her impaired ability to work, physical pain and suffering, and mental pain, sorrow, shame, regret, and mortification.

The judge informed the attorneys he would receive the jury's verdict up to 10 o'clock that night. If the panel could not agree by then, any verdict reached after that point would not be read until court reconvened on January 2.

The nine jurors stood, one aiding Mr. George D. Nau, who had buckled over into another coughing spasm.

Beaumont House Restaurant
(A Souvenir of Green Bay 1903)

ATTORNEYS OLIN and Stewart invited the three Cenefelt siblings to dinner at the Beaumont House, just blocks from the courthouse. Inside the sophisticated wood-paneled dining room, a waitress in a white mutton-sleeved dress waited on Mary—perhaps the first time someone had ever served her. Attorney Olin said the court bailiff had provided juror George D. Nau a place to lie down owing to his flu-like symptoms. That was not good news. If he was sympathetic toward Mary, his ill-health could impact his ability to argue her case's merits to his fellow jurists.

In the Beaumont House's smoky barroom, men who had attended the trial gathered. They tossed down whiskey, brandy, and pints of beer while rumors and speculation flew on how the jury stood. One found favor with the plaintiff's friends, claiming the first ballot was eight-to-one for Mary. Another story claimed the jurors were divided five-to-three with one abstaining, the majority voting for "No cause of action," since the plaintiff had not provided enough evidence to win. Those sympathizing with Dr. Minahan believed the latter. Mary's backers argued, "What on earth can they disagree about?" and one of the doctor's friends would retort, "For heaven's sake, what can they agree upon? Not upon the plaintiff's testimony, for that was something even she couldn't do."

"It's different this time," one well-known citizen said, bellied up to the bar. "The first trial was short and, prior to it, little was known about the case ... The [jury] leaders took up the matter and quickly argued it to an agreement. But in the second trial, every circumstance and fact has been gone over and over until every juror knows the case by heart. Each member probably made up his mind before entering the jury room, and those jurymen are the sort who will never move a peg once they get their heads set."

The jurors had not reached a decision by 10:00 p.m. on January 1. The only news was that Mr. George D. Nau's condition was no better.

No verdict came in on Sunday, January 2 either.

The Cenefelt siblings had moved to the O'Neil Hotel after the Bartelme family's hostile testimony. Mary curled up under the bedcovers beside Carrie in the dark as they had done as children. Mary had protected her little sister when they were young. Carrie's arm now enfolded Mary.

At 8:00 a.m., on Monday, January 3, the front desk clerk alerted Mary that Attorney Olin had called. She was to return to the courthouse.

JUDGE HASTINGS opened court at 9:00 a.m. Word had gotten out that the jury was returning. Spectators filled the courtroom seats and dozens of men in top hats, derbies, and workman's caps filled the seats and aisles, and leaned against the back wall.

Mary sat beside her two attorneys, dark circles below her eyes. Her hands twisted a handkerchief in her lap while Minahan and his team conferred at the defendant's table.

After forty hours of deliberation, the nine weary jurors shuffled in. The far-left chair in the first row, reserved for the jury's elected foreman, had been filled by the Riverside Brick Company owner Mr. F.L. Smith, who had looked down his nose at Mary for the entire trial. His hair was disheveled, his skin pale. Beside him, juror George D. Nau with a healthy pink sheen on his whiskerless face seemed the best of the lot. The rest of the jurymen sat restlessly on their seats.

The judge addressed foreman Smith. Hastings said that Bailiff Patterson had told him the foreman had an announcement to make.

Mr. Smith nodded and placed his hands on the jury rail to propel him to his feet.

Judge Hastings told him to proceed.

Foreman Smith said the jurors had "failed to agree."

Gasps swirled in the courtroom.

Newspaper reporters scrambled to their feet.

Mary turned to Attorney Olin and asked what the foreman's words meant.

Before Olin could respond, Judge Hastings, a bitter weariness in his voice, asked foreman Smith whether the jurors were deadlocked.

He said they were. No amount of time would allow them to reach the seven juror majority needed for a decision.

Mary's body wilted. Her jaw quivered. She had spent almost two months sitting in the same courtroom, not making a penny, living off her parents' charity. The only thing that had changed was that everyone in Green Bay now knew she had lost her virtue or, far worse, believed she was a blackmailing prostitute. Mary knew she could never walk down Washington Street again without people whispering behind gloved hands. Even if she found a domestic position, Mary could not earn enough to support herself while paying for her ongoing medical costs *and* paying off her attorney fees.

Mary's head dropped to her chest.

She would always be a burden to her family after trying not to disgrace them for so long.

THE JURORS AGREED not to reveal their votes, but someone leaked the results to the press. Mr. George D. Nau, Green Bay's tugboat owner, had been one of the six jurors who had supported Mary. Three jurors had voted for Minahan, including the foreman, Mr. F.L. Smith.

If the three discharged jurors had remained on the panel, where at least two would have voted for Mary, she would have won—for the second time.

THE Socialite

Let her choose ... a MAN in every sense of the word.
Not a mere appendage to a cigarette; not a lounge lizard;
not a perambulating stock-ticker; not an animated booze
receptacle; not a whited sculpture of disease and corruption;
but a man who is physically strong, mentally alert, morally
pure and clean and upright. Without these essentials of
physical health, mental capacity, and moral integrity, a man
is not fitted to make a successful husband and father.

—BERNARR MACFADDEN, *Womanhood and Marriage*,
an early 1900s self-help book

The New Woman

Astor Heights in Green Bay, Wisconsin (Early 1900s Postcard)

STRONG WIND GUSTS buffeted twenty-four-year-old Mollie Bertles on March 23, 1899. The weather did not dim her excitement. In side-buttoned leather boots, she tramped through melting snow on the red brick sidewalk of her family's three-story white frame home at 926 Monroe Avenue. It was known as the Bertles Estate. Mollie was en route to Dr. John R. Minahan's French-mansard-roofed mansion within her own Astor Heights neighborhood. She had heard from a reliable source that the thirty-six-year-old physician's former wife suffered from insanity, so his recent divorce held none of the usual stigma. The well-respected, apparently brilliant, and wealthy surgeon was hosting a dinner party that night to honor the engagement of his colleague Dr. Richard C. Buchanan to Mollie's friend, Miss Jessie Mae Hurlbut.

Jessie had told Mollie the invited guests included five bachelors, four of them physicians. Since Mollie's romance with Sydney A. Benedict, a Shattuck & Babcock salesman, had recently fizzled out after his move to Chicago, she looked forward to the upcoming dinner party all the more.

Under Mollie's warm, woolen cape, she wore that season's fashionable evening attire: a lace-covered bodice, slimmed-down sleeves, and a waist sash to accentuate her trim figure. Some health professionals

Mollie Bertles 1897 Wisconsin State University Yearbook

and social reformers objected to the corset, claiming it restricted breathing and movement. Mollie would have agreed, but like most young ladies of her status, she could not afford to catch an indignant glare for not donning the uncomfortable garment—even if it could impede her progress as a "New Woman."

Mollie had embraced that feminist movement in high school. She had been one of three juniors who had been invited to the Wisconsin state capital with the senior class. The students visited the legislature and inspected the state university. Mollie could see herself on the Madison campus from that moment on, making strides to break through society's imposed limitations on women. She would commit herself to value self-fulfillment over self-sacrifice, to believe in legal and sexual equality, to be well-educated and well-read, and to be physically vigorous. Her goal was to expand the idea that women could not only be society's "moral compass" within the domestic sphere but in the public sphere as well.

Mollie turned north onto Monroe Avenue to walk the five blocks to Dr. Minahan's Quincy Street home. Exercise helped combat her rheumatism, the nomenclature most laity and old-fashioned physicians called rheumatoid arthritis at the time. Mollie's doctor believed her bout with scarlet fever at age nineteen had likely triggered the joint pain in her hands, knees, and feet. It took energy for Mollie's body to fight the inflammation, and she noticed a marked increase in fatigue and tiredness when performing the same activities she had always done easily before.

But Mollie was an optimist. At least her arthritic condition fell into the noninfectious category. Friends and family could not catch her disease. Two doctors, Benjamin P. Riley and F.E. Smith, had recently classified arthritis into two categories, which would later be disputed. The noninfectious included Rheumatoid, Callous, Osteoarthritis, and Gout. The infectious category included those diseases like Tuberculous, Syphilis, Gonorrhea, and Still's Disease that created arthritic-like symptoms in the patient.

No cures existed for either category. Yet Mollie kept her hopes up. After all, she could now achieve symptomatic relief from aspirin, recently discovered by the German Bayer Company. More scientific advancements could be on the horizon meaning she would no longer need to count on quack "miracle remedies" advertised in the *Gazette* like Severeign's Rheumatism Cure or Broncho's Rheumatism Remedy.

As Mollie walked through Astor Heights, to her left was St. James Park. Soggy leaves covered the lawn tennis court and a moldy scent whirled in the air. Adjacent to the park was Attorney Patrick H. Martin's three-story Madison Street turret mansion, currently under construction to replace his old home which had sat on that spot. He and his wife Mary were Mollie's personal friends. This is, of course, the same Mr. Martin who had represented Dr. Minahan in the Cenefelt vs. Minahan trials that had ended in January of the prior year.

Mollie had followed the proceedings; everyone had. Mr. and Mrs. Dorr Clark's home was next door to the Bertles Estate, and Mary Cenefelt had been their on-and-off maid, though she obviously was no longer employed there. Mollie had read Mr. Martin's impassioned closing argument printed in the press. Because Martin believed in Dr. Minahan's innocence and virtues, Mollie believed in them too.

A carriage rolled past, its wheels spraying dirty slush from puddles. Mollie eyed the six empty lots her papa, John F. Bertles, had purchased as a real estate investment. He believed affluent Green Bay residents would soon be clamoring for those desirable river view lots on "The Hill."

Volunteer Firemen—John F. Bertles seated first on the left (Courtesy of the Neville Public Museum of Brown County)

Mollie's papa was a self-made man. He had arrived from Creemore, Canada, at age twenty-one with practically no funds. He worked as a laborer until he saved enough to open the Bertles Sewing Machine and Supplies store where repairing equipment had been her papa's specialty. Currently, he supervised the Green Bay Water Works and sat on the Kellogg National Bank board. He had been a volunteer fireman, a legal safecracker, a city alderman, and a board of education member. He and Mollie's mother, the former Eliza Switzer, had instilled the importance of education in their four daughters and two remaining sons. After the tragic death of Mollie's eleven-year-old brother, she had become the eldest sibling, a paragon of her parents' ideals.

At Cass Street, Mollie waited as an electric streetcar passed before she crossed Monroe Avenue and traveled east. Seven years earlier, she had graduated from Green Bay High School, where she had been her Class of 1892's salutatorian. Before attending university, Mollie had taken a year's sabbatical to participate in the Woman's Christian Temperance Union (WCTU), founded in 1874. The organization's initial purpose was to make home life safer for women and children by promoting alcohol abstinence in men. By 1890, the WCTU was the world's largest women's organization. Mollie had been the press reporter for Green Bay's 1892 WCTU convention. She had distributed Union leaflets to homes of the poor, primarily those containing children, and she had handed out alcohol abstinence pledge cards to Green Bay High School students.

OLD HOWE SCHOOL

Howe School (Courtesy of the Neville Public Museum of Brown County)

Propelled by her motto, "Knowledge ... is Power," Mollie headed off to the Wisconsin State University (the current University of Wisconsin) in September of 1893 and joined the Gamma Phi Beta Sorority, chartered to promote social development and higher literary culture. Four years later, Mollie earned a Bachelor of Arts degree. As the Green Bay High School alumni president, she had given a speech that closed with, "I shall rise again ... to broader fields of work, a potency in school and city!" When Mollie secured a fourth-grade teaching position at Howe

School, about three blocks from her current route, she set out to make good on that promise.

Mollie and her former beau Sydney had attended the wedding of Dr. John R. Minahan's sister Mary to John H. McCormick, an Ohio Coal Company agent reputed to drink as hard as he worked. Nobody had mentioned the bride, a teacher friend of Mollie's, had been in the "family way." The wedding reception had been held at Dr. Minahan's home, which Mollie could now see in the fading light as she turned north onto Quincy Street.

Another Minahan sister, nineteen-year-old Daisy, taught third grade at Howe School. She had introduced Sydney and Mollie to her physician brother at the reception. Mollie already knew who Dr. J.R. Minahan was. Everybody in Green Bay did. At that point, St. Vincent was still the only hospital that served the city's residents. As its attending physician and surgeon, Dr. Minahan and his medical successes were constantly mentioned in the press. At his sister's wedding reception, Dr. Minahan's considerable charm and keen sense of humor had enthralled Mollie. While she conversed with Sydney and Dr. Minahan, a match to the men in conversation, she perhaps noticed the possessive gleam already burning in the surgeon's eyes.

A maid answered Dr. Minahan's front door and relieved Mollie of her cloak. The physician had transformed the former St. Vincent Hospital into a home befitting a *Ladies Home Journal* fashion plate. The front room's Art Nouveau furnishings upholstered in opulent velvet, tapestry, and leather fabrics provided ample seating. Massive pocket doors opened into a wallpapered dining room. But the prime attraction was the host, elegant in a black tailcoat, a white bib button-down shirt, wingtip collar, bow tie, and U-neck vest.

Dr. Minahan welcomed Mollie, his pale-blue eyes taking her in. She was not a traditional beauty, but her finely chiseled features were striking, and her thick lashes exquisitely framed her dark, flashing eyes. She wore her raven hair swooped up into a mass of neat curls to give her petite frame a few extra inches of height.

The dining room's grand chandelier and black walnut table were decorated with "charmingly arranged roses, carnations, smilax, palms, and ferns." A place card stood by each setting of fine China and sterling silver like that at a wedding banquet. Mollie had been seated close to Dr. Minahan. Per his request, she called him J.R., as did all guests in attendance.

As the four-course meal, catered by W.J. Rupp's restaurant, was served, the two guests of honor, Dr. Buchanan and Jessie Hurlbut, shared their July wedding plans, deemed by the press to be "the society event of the summer season." Dr. Minahan then monopolized the conversation, philosophizing on current topics and sharing anecdotes about his hunting and fishing adventures. "Everyone who knew [Dr. Minahan] well," one of his surgery nurses stated, "also knew that no story ever lost anything by his telling it."

Mollie had been on her high school debate team. In her senior year, she supported the affirmative side of "Resolved: Women should have equal rights with men." At Dr. Minahan's dinner party, Mollie would have had no qualms in sharing anecdotes about her fourth-grade students, her bicycle adventures, and the Girls Whist Card Club she had organized. But whether she got a word in edgewise amidst the host's self-satisfied storytelling is unknown.

While Mollie perhaps sipped on a single glass of wine, Minahan abstained. The same went for tobacco. Those socially accepted vices did not define him. But a new medical diagnosis likely did. The personality disorder, narcissism, had been designated the prior year by British physician Havelock Ellis, indicating "an inflated sense of their own importance, a deep need for excessive attention and admiration, troubled relationships, and a lack of empathy for others."

The dinner guests thanked Dr. Minahan in the foyer at the evening's end.

A chilly wind blew in from the opened front door as Mollie took her leave.

The Courtship

WHITE ORCHESTRA members positioned their violins, clarinets, flutes, and trombones. Two weeks had passed since Dr. Minahan's dinner party. Mollie and her eighteen-year-old sister Kitten arrived at Maccabee Hall on April 15, 1899, for the Assembly Club's final dance of the season, a social event that Green Bay's elite could not miss.

Mollie's gown featured a fashionable low neckline and a modest train that would not interfere if a gentleman asked her to dance. Her eyes surveyed the gaslit hall filled with the city's most eligible young women and men who primarily lived on "The Hill." She was startled to see her former sweetheart, Sydney Benedict.

The orchestra's first number began and Sydney advanced toward Mollie. He told her he was visiting for the weekend and asked her to dance. In Sydney's arms, Mollie watched as Dr. Minahan entered the hall. She missed a step on the polished plank floor as J.R.'s eyes fixed on hers, that possessive gleam making his eyes into shiny new dimes.

The music selection finished and Sydney thanked Mollie for the waltz. He made her promise to look him up when she traveled to the Windy City. Sydney departed as Dr. Minahan approached. J.R. gave Mollie a bow and asked her to dance while out of the corner of his eye, he watched her former beau's retreating figure. Mollie later testified that J.R. had "a suspicious and jealous disposition."

Dance after dance, Dr. Minahan kept Mollie to himself. On the small of her back, she felt his palm's light touch as they glided over the floor.

In between numbers, their conversation did not lag, a positive quality in Mollie's eyes. He told her their mutual friend, Mr. P.H. Martin, had recently held a gathering that J.R. attended in honor of Bishop Mesmer. Dr. Minahan also talked about his clergy friend, Abbot Bernard Pennings, who J.R. said often took over for him after he had exhausted all his medical resources on a patient. Although J.R. told Mollie he did not belong to any church, she believed his friendships showed an open-mindedness to religion, which was important to her.

Before Sydney, Mollie had dated Ed Carroll, a Beaumont Hotel clerk, during her university summer breaks. But after she returned to Madison for her senior year, another young lady won his affection. First, Ed had disappeared from Mollie's life, then Sydney. In the late nineteenth century, a woman usually married in her early to mid-twenties. The groom was typically at least five years older, reinforcing the Victorian age's strict hierarchy of the husband over his wife. That age difference also provided the groom time to accumulate the financial means to support his new bride and their potential children.

At age twenty-four, Mollie perhaps felt she was running out of time.

She gazed up into Dr. Minahan's eyes. Could he be the right man? He had been married before and had shared a bed with his wife. He had sexual experience and she did not. Those thoughts made Mollie blush. She did not consider whether there had been any other sexual partners in Dr. Minahan's life.

Mollie knew a man's lack of purity prior to marriage was considered socially acceptable, although a woman's lack of purity was certainly not. "Young men must sow their wild oats," was almost universally conceded. Indeed, the majority of Mollie's friends believed that "a reformed rake made the best husband." After his flings, he would be "a master in the art of charming the feminine heart." The woman to whom he brought his final and lasting devotion was looked upon as a "fortunate creature."

Four months later, Mollie became that "fortunate creature" when her parents announced their eldest daughter's engagement to Dr. John R. Minahan and Mollie resigned from her Howe School teaching position. It looked like a perfect match: The brilliant Dr. Minahan was one of Green Bay's wealthiest men, and Mollie came from a highly respected Astor Heights family.

TWO WEEKS BEFORE Mollie's November 22, 1899 wedding date, J.R. blew into the Bertles home, his eyes dark and dangerous. In the wainscotted foyer, he shoved two letters into Mollie's hands. He said they had arrived at his house with Green Bay postmarks. Neither contained a return address or signature.

"They did not directly reflect upon my honor," Mollie later testified, "but accused me of being easy." One of the letters focused on Mollie's "doings in the city of Chicago ... with one Sydney Benedict." The author stated for such a "noble man" as Minahan to marry a woman of such "bad character" was deplorable.

J.R. asked Mollie whether she had seen Sydney behind his back.

Mollie admitted she had met him the prior week, but only for lunch, when she and her mother had taken a train down to Chicago's Marshall Fields & Company to shop its ready-made fashions.

J.R. snatched the letters back and accused Mollie of not being truthful about her Chicago trip. Was she certain she had only had lunch with Sydney? And what would her mother have to say?

Mollie grabbed J.R.'s arm but he tore it away. He strode into the front parlor and Mollie sped after him. Mrs. Bertles was reading in a chair, her graying hair secured inside a white-filigree snood.

Before Mollie could stop J.R., he handed the letter referencing Sydney to her mother. J.R. ordered Mrs. Bertles to read it. Mollie implored her mother not to do so, but it was too late. Her mother's eyes were already darting across the page, her brow creased. Gasping, she lifted her head and asked who had written those dreadful lies.

J.R. did not answer. Instead, he interrogated Mrs. Bertles about the Chicago shopping trip.

Mollie's mother had raised her daughter with love and quiet discipline, but Mrs. Bertles was also a force to deal with whenever she smelled an injustice, particularly one involving her children. Mrs. Bertles stood up to J.R., defending Mollie. The mother's story matching her daughter's in every detail.

J.R. was quiet and flustered. He apologized to Mollie for overreacting. He said it was wrong of him to doubt her. His work had overtired him. That year, he said, he had already conducted more than 350 operations.

J.R.'s jealousy should have been a warning sign for Mollie, but his repentant words swayed her emotions. In the parlor's familiar warmth, Mollie relaxed. The stressful situation resolved. The sheet music she had been playing rested on the Steinway piano's music stand. Mollie's knitting basket sat by a chair. "I believed [J.R.'s] protestations, that he did not believe a word of what was stated in [those] letters ... That the author was some malicious and jealous person, intent upon preventing our marriage."

The Wedding

A WHIRLWIND OF activities kept Mollie's mind off the letters: wedding showers, catering decisions, gown alterations, and seating arrangements. Nothing could damper her marriage plans to Dr. John R. Minahan, whom many considered Green Bay's most eligible bachelor.

At 8:00 p.m. on November 22, 1899, Mollie's wedding got underway in her parents' parlor, large enough to hold the 150 seated guests. Mollie's six dearest female friends entered bearing ribbons for the wedding aisle. Among them were Daisy Minahan and Mollie's high school friend, Mayme Comstock. Mollie's sister, Kitten, led the bridal procession. Their twenty-year-old sister Annie, the maid of honor, followed with a bouquet of pink roses and maidenhair ferns. Mollie's two younger sisters had returned from college for the occasion. There was no doubt that the three were related. All shared the Bertles' petite frame, dark curls, and finely sculpted facial features.

Bedecked in their finest silks, satins, tweeds, and furs, the guests stood. Mollie glanced down through her tulle veil at her bodice's emerald-cut diamond pin, J.R.'s wedding gift to her. Clutched in her hands was a hyacinth bouquet. Mollie's French lace wedding gown draped perfectly over her trim hips as she and her papa proceeded down the aisle toward the bay window. From that vantage point, under an arch of brakes and palms, Mollie gazed back at her guests as J.R. and his groomsman, Dr. Lenfesty, brought up the rear. Mollie's papa stepped away, and J.R.'s imposing figure took his place.

The Congregational Church's Reverend E.H. Smith performed the wedding ceremony. After Mollie and J.R.'s wedding supper, the newlyweds climbed aboard the midnight train heading south toward Milwaukee. Mollie rested her head against her new husband's shoulder as they embarked on the first leg of their six-month European honeymoon. That travel length was possible since J.R.'s brother, Dr. Robert E. Minahan, would handle J.R.'s patients during his absence. Dr. Robert had given up his Kewaunee law and medical work to move to Green Bay the prior year to join J.R.'s practice as an equal partner.

At about 3:00 a.m., Mollie held her new husband's hand as they climbed off the train in Milwaukee and took a horse-drawn taxi to the Pfister Hotel dubbed "The Grand Hotel of the West." All rooms featured electricity and an individual thermostat.

Mollie stepped into their lavish room. Her stomach knotted as she gazed at the brass bed where she and J.R. would consummate their marriage. Velvet drapes covered the windows like a theater stage before the performance. A maid had lit the fireplace and shadows played across the walls.

Pfister Hotel in Milwaukee – circa 1900 (Library of Congress)

The Victorian Age that Mollie had grown up in frowned upon females who were too forward, "displaying a worrisome sexual appetite." Most men believed that a wife only submitted to her husband's embraces to gratify him or to conceive a child. But with the "New Woman" movement, novel ideas had emerged about a women's emotional and sexual satisfaction. Yet most women "of quality" like Mollie, even those who thought of themselves as "New Women," had not been exposed to uncouth talk about bedroom activities or basic knowledge about their bodies.

Two wall sconces lit the Minahans' private bathroom. Behind its locked door, Mollie drew a bath and cleansed herself with French-milled soap. She stepped out and toweled herself off. Her cheeks flush from the heat, she slipped into her ivory peignoir and removed the pins from her dark hair that cascaded over her shoulders.

Mollie turned off the bathroom light, took a deep breath, and opened the door.

Into the darkened room, she stepped.

The sheets rustled.

Dr. J.R. Minahan waited.

THE DESK CLERK asked J.R. and Mollie how their short stay had been. J.R. said a perfunctory "Fine," and Mollie blushed. The clerk handed J.R. their bill and a letter postmarked from Green Bay. He read the latter, his face stoic, and showed it to Mollie.

She gazed down at the anonymous letter. In substance, it said: J.R. had to realize he was a "sucker" to have married Mollie, though again, the allegations did not directly reflect upon her "chastity and honor."

J.R. removed the letter from Mollie's shaking hands and slipped it into his coat pocket. He told her not to worry. He held no stock in that letter or the prior ones.

The Minahans took a train to Chicago and transferred to the Limited Express. They settled in for their twenty-hour journey to New York City inside a Pullman Palace car. Its grand interior featured plush seats, sleeping berths, and porters for their every need. But through the entire journey, Mollie could think only of the letters. J.R. had said the

author had to be some "malicious and jealous person intent on stopping their marriage." But the new letter proved the author was aware they had wed. Had that person been one of their wedding guests? Mollie had assumed the author was a male, but maybe the letter writer was a female who had set her eyes on marrying J.R.

When the Minahans arrived at New York's Grand Central Station, the air was alive with movement. Streetcars charged along Manhattan thoroughfares

Astoria – circa 1900
(Library of Congress)

amid dense traffic of carriages and drays. Mollie and J.R. eased out of their livery coach at the Astoria and a doorman welcomed them into its majestic lobby. John Jacob Astor's seventeen-story hotel, completed in 1897, catered to the wealthy upper crust's needs. The scent of massive floral arrangements camouflaged the smell of ever-present tobacco smoke. On the low octave keys, the lobby pianist played Edvard Grieg's famous tension-building masterpiece, "In the Hall of the Mountain King."

The reception clerk handed J.R. another anonymous letter from Green Bay. His face hardened as he read it. "J.R. assured me that he knew the accusations ... made against my honor to be absolutely false. And that in the future, he would burn ... all letters of a similar nature ... unread."

But his words did not curb Mollie's angst.

MOLLIE ATTEMPTED to enjoy the Manhattan sights with J.R. They took a carriage ride through Central Park, a tour of the Metropolitan Museum of Art, and a stroll through the Herald Square District, where theaters, music halls, and vaudeville amusements lined the streets. But her thoughts kept reverting back to the letters.

The Minahans returned to the Astoria and took the elevator to their floor. Two women desk clerks and a force of bellboys greeted them. J.R. used a key to open the door to their room and the two stepped inside. Fireplace logs had been lit during their absence and created an intimate setting. Two chandeliers hung from a twelve-foot stenciled ceiling surrounded by ornamental plaster. Flock wallpaper, soft to the touch, covered the walls. Rich drapery hung over the headboard of their bed, its duvet turned down for the evening exposing crisp white sheets.

J.R. closed the door, and his eyes met Mollie's. "He requested ... to permit him to make a slight physical examination of my person. I asked why he should make or desire to make such an examination. He answered evasively and insinuatingly, and I became justly indignant at the reflection cast upon my honor and threatened to return home."

J.R. backtracked, apologizing. He claimed his request was unjustified, and he gave no credence to the letters.

But as Mollie gazed at her husband's impassive face in the firelight, questions about the letters and J.R.'s reaction to them alarmed and confused her.

J.R. HEADED to the lobby to pay their bill on December 1, 1899. Under Mollie's supervision, a pair of bellboys loaded the Minahans' four steamer trunks onto two carts. They told Mollie they would meet her in the lobby. She took the passenger elevator down to the ground floor. Dozens of guests milled around speaking all sorts of languages. Two hotel attendants roamed through the lobby, placards held high, designating the correct door to catch an omnibus to the Port of New York or Grand Central Station. In his dark traveling suit, J.R. stood beside a floral arrangement. "[He was] reading a letter of like nature after his promise to burn [them] unread. I told him his asserted belief in the accusations [was] an insult to me."

In the Astoria's gilded lobby, everyone would have admired the wealthy and handsome Green Bay newlyweds: the petite young bride, slim and dark, now twenty-five, her diamond wedding pin attached to her traveling suit's bodice; her thirty-six-year-old husband, debonair in his calf-skin gloves and black derby. But the crowd could not see beneath the surface.

"J.R. again protested that he did not have even an accusing thought of me ... He was reading [the letters] for the sole purpose of finding, if he could, the author."

The two bellboys arrived, Mollie's trunks on one cart, J.R.'s on the other. The lobby attendant passed with a Grand Central Station sign— Mollie's train route to home. The Port of New York hotel attendant followed—her steamship route to Europe.

Mollie weighed her options.

SCENTS OF GARBAGE, sewage, and industrial fumes swirled in the air. A southwesterly wind blew freezing rain onto Mollie's cheeks. Under a green-striped awning, she walked up the Aller steamship gangway, her arm linked into J.R.'s. Mollie had promised to "have and hold J.R. for better, for worse..." Only one week into her marriage, Mollie could not accept defeat.

She convinced herself, once they steamed out to sea where no letters could reach them, everything would get better.

Strange Lands

THE MINAHANS' week-long trans-Atlantic crossing neared its end, and every moment had been perfect, just as Mollie had hoped. J.R. had been attentive to her needs and there had been no mention of the letters. In addition to fine dining and musical entertainment, the two had enjoyed playing bridge and reading in the library.

That morning, Mollie strode around the Aller steamship promenade deck in the brisk air, calling out a jaunty hello to anyone she passed. Mollie felt ultra-awake. Adrenaline pumped through her veins as if she had drunk four cups of tea. She stopped at the rail, drew in a breath, and looked down at the cobalt ocean. Her period was ten days overdue, and she was never late. She had to be pregnant. Not the best timing, perhaps, yet wondrous news.

Eight years earlier, Mollie had helped her mother give a "charming lawn party" for her youngest siblings Alma and Willie. About fifty other "lads and lassies" had attended. Their spirit and childish wonder had warmed Mollie's heart, prompting her desire to become a teacher. Now, as a young married woman, instead of helping to mold the minds of schoolchildren, she would actually have a little boy or girl of her own. Mollie was thrilled, and J.R. would certainly be since his first wife had been barren.

At that evening's dinner, the dark-mustached Captain Wilhelmi, dressed in a double-breasted uniform and cap, welcomed each guest as they arrived in the dining salon. It was a spacious room, 50 by 40 feet, and lit by an open well from the upper deck's ladies' salon. Mollie and J.R. were seated in swivel chairs across from another couple at one of the dining room's communal tables. Mollie could hardly wait to talk privately to J.R. about her surprise as waiters in white aprons and rolled-back cuffs served each course. After their meal, Mollie and J.R. stepped out onto the promenade deck. She grabbed his hands and beamed up at him. Mollie told J.R. about her pregnancy news, but his response was like nothing she had imagined.

J.R. gazed at her in stunned silence. Finally, he said her condition would ruin their honeymoon. As a doctor, he knew she would be miserable. "He tried to induce me to take some medicine that would relive me [of my pregnancy]. I was greatly aggrieved ... at his assumption, wholly unwarranted and unjustified, that I would participate and cooperate with him to that end. And I refused."

THE ROCK OF GIBRALTAR came into view from the Aller steamship deck, the limestone promontory located on the narrow gap between Spain and Africa. The Minahans sent a ship cablegram to Mollie's papa on December 8, 1899, that stated, "We reached Gibraltar safely. Due to the fact that neither one of us was sick, we had a delightful voyage."

That was far from the truth. Ever since Mollie had shared her pregnancy news with J.R., she had hoped to receive an apology for his callous request, but by the time they disembarked in Genoa, Italy, Mollie had yet to hear J.R.'s repentant words. Instead, he kept insisting that the decision to relieve Mollie of her pregnancy was just as much his as hers. Like a child, J.R. had gone to great lengths, attempting to get his way, cajoling Mollie, giving her the silent treatment, and pouting.

They departed on a train with connections to Rome. Although the landscape was unlike anything Mollie had ever seen with its villas, picturesque villages, and cliffs dropping into the sea, she could only think about J.R.'s shocking request and continued wish to destroy the life growing inside her.

The Minahans stepped off the train into Italy's sprawling capital city. Mollie's gloved hand held onto J.R.'s arm as if they were the perfect American newlywed couple. Porters hauled their trunks from the baggage car into one of the carriages lining the street. Amid ancient ruins and not far from Sistine Chapel's chiming bells, the Minahans' carriage took off, its horses clattering on the stone piazza as bicycles whooshed past. The stench of human sewage mingled with the scent of roasted coffee. The driver dropped the Minahans off at The Grand Hotel, Italy's first to have electricity and private bathrooms.

Inside their suite, J.R. browsed through a Baedeker travel guide with foldout maps and leveled his eyes on Mollie. J.R.'s first suggestion to abort Mollie's child with medicine had failed as had all his other tactics. He tried another approach. "He assured me, that my condition and inevitable ill health would spoil the pleasure of our visit. Under this pretense for excuse, he proposed to me that I permit him to relieve me of my pregnancy by means of an operation. I was greatly aggrieved and shocked at his proposal and willingness to thus [destroy], by means I believed criminal, the object of our marriage."

J.R. insisted Mollie was not carrying a child, just an embryo. It had not quickened yet. "He assured me that because of his skill, he could perform such operation as was necessary, without peril to me."

Mollie backed away and said she would never do as he asked.

J.R. stomped out, and the door slammed behind him.

Mollie's fingers fumbled as she removed her traveling clothes. She curled up under the bedcovers with the unshakable desire to protect her child as disturbing thoughts attacked Mollie's mind. When she was ten and her parents' firstborn Joseph was eleven, the two siblings had been in the backyard stable after their papa had given his horse a workout. Mr. Bertles walked out as Joey sat on an upside-down pail, rubbing the horse's hind legs with liniment to cool any swollen areas. The bucket tipped over, and Joey fell under the animal, spooking it. Mollie screamed, her feet frozen to the dirt floor, as the horse's hooves trampled her brother's head. Their papa heard Mollie's cries and rushed in. He yanked the horse away from her brother's mangled skull, blood pooling beneath it, and instructed Mollie to go for help. Although a doctor had removed two-dozen bone pieces from Joey's injury and her parents had consulted numerous other physicians to keep him alive for weeks, he had never regained consciousness and eventually succumbed to the terrible injury.

Mollie's tears dampened the feather pillow in the unfamiliar Italian hotel room. She still faulted herself for not reacting, not grabbing the horse's harness, not saving her brother. But maybe she could finally seek redemption by saving her own child from its father.

Mollie shivered and pulled the bedclothes tight to her neck, struggling to believe the transformation in her husband. She had read *The Strange*

Case of Dr. Jekyll and Mr. Hyde by Robert Louis Stevenson. Mollie would not yet accept that her Dr. Jekyll had transformed into an evil Mr. Hyde.

THE MINAHANS traveled from Rome to Venice with its Grand Canal, Renaissance and Gothic palaces, renowned casinos, and thoroughbred horse racing venues. Two of J.R.'s passions were poker and horses. Gambling was legal in Europe. All games of chance were illegal in America, although secretly conducted in private clubs or the privacy of one's home. But Mollie enjoyed little of the city's sites. "While I was, in fact, suffering such [pregnancy] ills and effects, J.R., night after night, under pretext of curiosity to see the 'underworld,' left me alone in strange lands ... without companionship, until the early morning hours—greatly to my distress."

On January 1, 1900, the Minahans arrived in Monte Carlo, situated at the base of the Maritime Alps along the French Riviera. Inside the Hotel de Paris casino, J.R. mingled with the international elite. A nauseous and homesick Mollie stayed in the hotel room. She imagined her family's excitement while attending Mr. and Mrs. P.H. Martin's gala open house to celebrate the new century and the Martins' newly constructed home.

When the Minahans arrived in Paris, Mollie's nausea subsided. She put on a good face as they visited sites like the Eiffel Tower, the Arc de Triomphe, the Louvre, and Notre Dame Cathedral. But J.R. later alleged that Mollie had asked him to take her to the Moulin-Rouge in the Jardin de Paris. He testified he had "refused to go or permitted Mollie to go" due to that cabaret's titillating nature, where women's undergarments were indecently exposed while dancing the Can-Can.

The Minahans curtailed their six-month honeymoon to less than three months. On February 16, 1900, Mollie and J.R. stepped onto the porch of his Quincy Street home, now her residence as well. Across the street was Attorney and Mrs. C.E. Vroman's house. Before Mollie had departed for university in 1893, the Vromans had invited her to their cultural fundraising event. Mollie had recited Tennyson's poem "Dora," about the self-sacrificing heroine who had given up everything to protect a child's well-being: *Dora said again, "Do with me as you will, but take the child, and bless him."*

Mollie placed a hand on her belly and crossed the threshold of her new home.

Lost Soul

MOLLIE QUIETLY played classical piano selections inside the front room of the Minahans' twenty-three-room mansion. She and J.R. had been back from their honeymoon for about two weeks. Mollie had managed to lock away her concerns about the letters. She was determined to forget about J.R.'s requests to abort their child and his heartless behavior. She desperately wanted their marriage to work for their future baby's sake.

Mollie's eyes drifted over to J.R.'s sixty-six-year-old mother, dozing in a wheelchair, tired out after Father Ricklin's visit. Her mother-in-law had recently suffered two strokes. She and J.R.'s twenty-one-year-old sister Daisy lived in the house as did the coachman, a housekeeper, and a cook. Scrub women, hairdressers, and dress-makers arrived at different times— "quite a crowd," J.R. complained. He told Mollie, with all that hired help, he expected her to keep his home and dining table in "first-

Rev. Leo Ricklin (Men Who Are Making Green Bay 1897)

class shape" so he could invite a guest over at any time and "not feel ashamed." He also expected Mollie to be the primary caregiver for his mother since Daisy taught third grade, and J.R.'s medical and surgery practice consumed him.

J.R.'s mother, the former Mary O'Shaughnessy, had married his father, William Burke Minahan, in 1857 in Almond, New York. William had arrived in America with his parents at age fourteen from North Inishkae Island, Mayo County, Ireland. Shortly after the birth of their first child,

Robert Emmet, they migrated to Wisconsin where J.R.'s father earned a living as a shoemaker. The couple purchased 160 acres of land in Calumet County, a mile west of Chilton, and their farm prospered.

While J.R.'s mother gave birth to twelve more children, her husband taught school before serving as the Calumet County superintendent of schools for twenty years. Three of J.R.'s siblings had died in infancy, and one brother, James, had passed away while in his freshman year at Wisconsin State University. According to one of his father's poems, James had died in an asylum, "bereft of reason."

Mollie knew J.R.'s father was a demanding and "outspoken Irishman," traits her husband had inherited. A female cousin of J.R.'s revealed that when she had been a little girl living on her parents' farm just west of the Minahans', J.R.'s father had resided at her house rather than his. "None of his children could live with him ... He was a devil ... And my father used to wait on him as if he was a king. Uncle William would say, 'John get my horse,' and he would give the same order to my father when he came home."

J.R.'s father had not changed over the years. After his wife's strokes, he had wiped his hands of her care and only visited Green Bay on brief occasions, choosing to live on their Chilton farm—choosing to give his new daughter-in-law the daunting responsibility of caring for his ailing wife.

Minahan family – Standing: James, Dr. Robert E., Dr. John R., Dr. William E., Grace (Philleo), Hugh. Seated: Daisy, mother Mary O'Shaughnessy, Ellen (Jaeger), Victor I., father William Burke Minahan, Mary (McCormick) (Roger Minahan Papers)

That night after Father Ricklin's visit, the four Minahans were seated around the black walnut dining table while the cook served their meal. J.R.'s mother turned to her son and told him that Mollie had "violently protested" when St. John's Catholic priest had visited the home that morning. Instead of sitting with Father Ricklin and the senior Mrs. Minahan, J.R.'s mother said Mollie had "played hilarious airs upon the piano." Even though Mollie told J.R. she had welcomed the priest and played uplifting tunes for their enjoyment, J.R. refused to believe her.

Daisy gave her sister-in-law a sympathetic look and squeezed Mollie's hand under the table.

Elks Club included a ballroom
(A Souvenir of Green Bay 1903)

ONE THING THAT Mollie and J.R. did have in common was the love of cards, and they were both skilled players. They joined the Bohemian Club, a club comprised of married couples within their social circle whose members took turns hosting dances and themed parties at venues like the Elks Club or playing cards in their homes.

Three weeks after their honeymoon return, on March 9, 1900, the Minahans entered the home of Mr. and Mrs. W.E. Kellogg, where eight Bohemian Club couples chatted before being seated at a dining table draped in white linen. Maternity dresses with features such as boxy jackets and gathered center bodice panels were both artful and comfortable and allowed a pregnant woman like Mollie to engage in social activities.

During the light supper, J.R. charmed the group with stories of the Minahans' European travels, though this version was told through his Lazarus & Morris rose-tinted glasses.

Mollie listened silently. She felt isolated from the conversation. She could not reveal her distressing version of their honeymoon to friends and family.

A partnership Hearts card game followed where the gentlemen found their female partners from childhood photographs of the ladies. Mollie enjoyed herself that evening, sitting across from her engaging male partner while J.R. sat at another table, his eyes focused on Mollie rather than his cards.

J.R. never said a cross word to Mollie in front of friends. But on the carriage ride home that night, he did a private knifing of anything he perceived she had done wrong. In particular, J.R. accused her of being too friendly with her gentleman card partner.

Mollie had only been in her marriage for four months, yet she knew it was failing. First was her dreadful honeymoon. Now her disenchanting domestic life. The signs she had seen in her parents' marriage were missing: her papa's interest in her mother's daily activities, his hand on her shoulder when he gazed down to admire her cross-stitch work, and her papa's offer to help with her mother's church projects.

J.R. *did* have his exhausting medical practice and surgical schedule, which he expounded upon at length when he arrived home for dinner. Even though Mollie gave him her undivided attention, he never thought to ask about her day, only his mother's and sister's.

Each morning, a sense of melancholy infused Mollie. But then she would think about the dear child growing inside her, and Mollie's spirits would lift. She would visit the second-floor nursery she had lovingly outfitted with a crib, rocking chair, stuffed animals, and shelves lined with books. A baby of her own would bring Mollie the joy that she fiercely craved in her joyless marriage.

MOLLIE'S RHEUMATISM FLARED in April, likely from the rainy weather and her marital stress. She had selected J.R.'s oldest brother, Dr. Robert E. Minahan, as her primary care physician. She also consulted with a Chicago physician, Dr. Frank Billings, who treated Chicago's rich and famous, including a Mr. Armour, the millionaire meatpacker. Billings' ongoing arthritis research was perhaps why Mollie had selected him.

Both physicians discussed Mollie's rheumatism and weakened immune system with her. They said her disease placed her at an increased infection risk, which could impact her developing child. But Mollie pushed those warnings aside as she impatiently counted the days until her baby's August arrival—the event that would change her life.

On June 24, Mollie was picnicking with female friends in De Pere Park when the sound of a massive explosion nearly broke her eardrums. She later discovered that the Turner Society's German musical festival, called the Saengerfest, had opened in Green Bay and a Fond du Lac-Oshkosh nine-coach excursion train, filled with attendees, had crashed into a freight train being sidetracked at the West De Pere station. Authorities had removed the dead and injured one-by-one while Mollie's husband had performed surgeries on many victims that day and in the days to come. On about July 2, he was interrupted amid one.

At about six and a half months pregnant, Mollie climbed out of the bathtub and her abdomen seized. She reached for a towel and another spasm cut through her belly. Mollie gazed down, petrified to see blood trickling down her inner thighs. She cried out, and her Belgium housekeeper, Julia Marique, rushed in. While Mollie slipped into a loose maternity dress, Julia contacted Dr. Robert and J.R.

A wheelchair awaited Mollie at the entrance to St. Vincent Hospital. When she saw the bright red stain on her dress, Mollie prayed. She could not lose her baby.

Inside a private room, a Sister helped Mollie undress and slip into a hospital gown as her abdominal pain increased in spaced contractions. Dr. Robert arrived and checked her condition. Two Sisters wheeled Mollie's bed into a surgery suite, then one placed a mask over Mollie's face. As the scent of chloroform filled her nostrils, the hazy figures of her husband and his brother appeared, both dressed in white scrubs and surgical bonnets.

MOLLIE AWOKE in a shadow-filled room. She slid her hand over her stomach and moaned. Its mound was softer and lower than before. Yet her child could still be alive. A Sister entered and told Mollie how sorry she was for her loss. Mollie stared at her, not comprehending. How could her innocent child, the tiny being she craved to hold, craved to kiss, craved to cuddle, be dead.

The Sister departed when J.R. entered. He had also lost his baby, but no compassionate words came out of his mouth. He gazed down at Mollie from the foot of the bed, his arms crossed over his chest. He said her miscarriage was all her fault. "I could never bear children because I was syphilitic." J.R. said he knew those letters were true.

Mollie could not absorb his shocking and heartless words. "J.R. said that [our] child, thus prematurely born, had been examined by him and found [to be] syphilitic. And that such disease was always inherited from the mother."

Mollie sagged against the pillows. How could J.R. be so cruel? How could he hurt her so? Why could he display concern for his patients but never for her? He bewitched men and women with his charm, yet never felt bound to the truth.

Although despairing, Mollie found the strength to speak out. She said he was lying. She was not to blame for their child's death. J.R.'s only intent was to "wound and insult" her by implying she had "contracted the disease through illicit sexual relations." Mollie charged J.R. with hiring someone to write and mail those letters.

For months, she had considered that disturbing possibility. She accused J.R. of providing their honeymoon itinerary to the letters' author. How else would those letters have arrived in Milwaukee and New York on those exact dates?

J.R. denied her accusations outright and said, if he had "ascertained the truth" concerning Mollie, "he would not have married her."

Gaslighting

THE GREEN BAY July 4th celebrations were underway with Hagemeister Park picnics, scenic steamboat excursions to Sturgeon Bay, and the Oneida Indian Reservation baseball game. But Mollie had nothing to celebrate. She keened in her Quincy Street home, grieving the loss of her child while J.R. continued to blame Mollie for their baby's premature delivery.

Mollie realized that J.R. had tortured her throughout their short marriage, and even before, with the letters. Her engagement had been too brief. Those three months had not provided Mollie the opportunity to discover J.R.'s personality defects. Or, she admitted, she had chosen to ignore them. Mollie had initially thought J.R. was fascinating and handsome, a thrilling dancer, one who spoke to her as an intellectual peer. But his true personality had now been revealed. Her husband had no ability to empathize with Mollie over her miscarriage, over her medical issues, over the trying times Mollie experienced with his mother. J.R. was selfish and self-involved. He could never understand what she was feeling and he rarely apologized or was remorseful for the way he acted. Yet he seemed highly attuned to imagined threats concerning Mollie's involvement with other men.

J.R.'s cruel behavior was more than Mollie could handle, and her rheumatism flared, making every joint in her body swell. He attributed Mollie's condition to syphilis. In its second and tertiary stages, he said the disease could attack her bones and joints. He assaulted Mollie with those words until she wondered whether she did have that dreaded disease. Yet she knew she could only have gotten it from one person: him.

Mollie had heard rumors that J.R.'s brother-in-law, John McCormick, frequented Green Bay's houses of "ill-repute." Maybe J.R. had done the same prior to their marriage. Maybe he had contracted syphilis or believed he had through his association with women of "another type." Maybe her husband was secretly treating himself with mercury.

Before taking her wedding vows, Mollie now realized she should have considered those suppositions. But she had been too enamored by the idea of being Mrs. John R. Minahan to have perceived that the city's famous surgeon, who had asked for her hand in marriage, could have been "morally corrupt."

Mollie had every right to be worried. A Wisconsin Legislature report in 1914 would state: "The most startling fact regarding venereal disease ... is the large number of married men who frequent houses of prostitution in various cities of [Wisconsin]. Several prostitutes or 'madams' have stated that not less than fifty per cent of their customers are married men." The report also found that it was practically impossible for any woman to have long periods of promiscuous sexual intercourse without contracting either gonorrhea or syphilis or both. "Having once contracted a venereal disease, the prostitute very soon infects her patrons, and they in turn infect other people, many of whom are absolutely innocent of any immoral act."

Whatever the reason behind J.R.'s accusations that she had syphilis, Mollie knew his belief was destroying her life. Other than J.R.'s word, she had no evidence that she had that disease. But Mollie was more than shrewd enough to question his diagnosis.

Although she knew little about syphilis, Mollie had a way to find out. On the first floor of the Minahans' home was J.R.'s library. In addition to shelves filled with medical books, his sanctuary housed a desk, gun collection, billiard table, trophies, and a scale model Civil War battle scene. While J.R. spent his days at his Parmentier Block medical office and St. Vincent Hospital, Mollie had ample time to peruse his medical books.

She first located a study conducted by France's noted professor, Alfred Fournier. He had consulted with 887 women afflicted with syphilis. Of those, 220 were married. Fournier determined that 164 of them had caught syphilis from their husbands.

Mollie sat back, shaking with anger. Had she joined these other women who had naively caught the "unmentionable disease" from their husbands? At age twenty-five, she had already contracted rheumatism. Could she have syphilis too? Her cheeks flushed even thinking about that word which was never spoken out loud.

Mollie continued to read how the first stage of syphilis was usually contracted through sexual intercourse with an infected party. A small red spot like a pimple or ulcer could form on the sex organs within the first two weeks. But the site could increase to the size of a five-cent piece.

In the Minahans' New York hotel room, only a few days after their wedding, J.R. had wanted to make a "slight physical examination" of Mollie's person. She realized he had likely been seeking proof that she had contracted syphilis from another man rather than him.

As Mollie read on, she learned how the disease's second stage, the most contagious, occurred six weeks to four months later with symptoms such as headaches, bone pain, mouth fever sores, skin rashes, or swelling of the glands. That stage normally lasted for about two to three months, but it could last up to one year.

In March and April of 1900, Mollie had attributed her joint pain and headaches to rheumatism. Maybe she had been wrong. If so, she realized she most likely was in what the medical book called the "latent syphilis stage," where there was no evidence of the disease in or on her body, yet she could still be contagious. That stage could last for years, and if the infected person never sought syphilis treatment, the disease could move into the third or tertiary stage and damage the brain, nerves, eyes, heart, liver, bones, joints, and cause death.

But what disturbed Mollie the most was that a pregnant woman in the first, second, or latent stages of syphilis could pass the disease onto her developing baby, resulting in a miscarriage, a stillbirth, or a birth to a child infected with syphilis.

Mollie held back a sob. Could she have unknowingly caused her miscarriage? But in J.R.'s medical books she also discovered that about 10 to 20 percent of all known pregnancies ended in miscarriage, nature's way of aborting any abnormally developing fetus.

What was the truth? Had Mollie contracted syphilis from J.R.? He had said their premature child had that disease. But the medical books stated that no test existed to determine that fact. Maybe the syphilis research had advanced since the publication dates of those books.

To prove to herself *and* J.R. that she did not have that disease, Mollie had to see a doctor, but not her husband's brother. Her Chicago physician would be the best choice.

J.R. and some of his gentlemen friends had plans to depart on August 25, 1900, for a five-day sailing cruise to the Detroit Harbor. His absence would allow Mollie the opportunity to see Dr. Billings without J.R.'s knowledge.

But as her husband's departure approached, Mollie realized she had waited too long. Her period was two weeks overdue. Less than two months had passed since her miscarriage, and not even J.R.'s claim that Mollie had syphilis had halted his rights inside their marital bed. In Mollie's mind, that elevated her fear. Why would any man purposely have sexual relations with a woman he believed had syphilis unless he had it, too? Mollie knew she should be thrilled about her pregnancy. But how could she be when she might have placed her new child at risk.

UNDER THE SHADE of Monroe Avenue elm trees, Mollie strolled beside her sister Annie. Whiffs of fresh-cut grass sweetened the air. The two sisters had always been close, sharing similar "New Woman" views and spiritual convictions. Although they had been raised Catholic, both sisters had joined the Congregational Church, feeling more comfortable with its protestant beliefs. Annie had just graduated from the Rockford, Illinois Female Seminary and lived with their parents in the Bertles Estate while searching for a teaching job. Like Mollie, Annie had joined the debate team in high school and supported the affirmative side of "Resolved: The intellect of woman is equal to that of man." The judges had awarded Annie's three-girl team the decision, besting the three most intelligent boys in their class.

The two sisters entered St. James Park and sat on a bench near the bandshell. Mollie turned to her sibling and shared her pregnancy news. It pained Mollie to watch the joy on Annie's face transform into horror as Mollie revealed her marriage details: her suspicions about the anonymous letters; J.R.'s requests to abort her first pregnancy; his claims that Mollie had contracted syphilis before their marriage; that she had passed that disease onto the baby she had lost; and Mollie's fear that J.R. had given her that shameful disease.

Throughout her agonizing disclosure, Annie squeezed Mollie's hand and offered a handkerchief when tears got the best of Mollie. Annie also added her voice to Mollie's curses, all directed at J.R., and agreed that Mollie should see her Chicago physician as soon as possible.

MOLLIE'S MEDICAL examination showed "no evidence of syphilis." But Dr. Billings confirmed that no test could conclusively prove she did not have the disease. He also confirmed the grim possibilities: If Mollie was a syphilis carrier and an active stage occurred, a miscarriage was probable; if the disease remained dormant, her child with inherited syphilis could go full term and be born dead or die shortly after; but if her syphilitic child survived, symptoms like peculiar snuffling and difficulty breathing usually developed within a few weeks of birth. Sometimes, however, the disease's significant developments occurred later in life, generally around puberty, when her child's eyes, bones, brain, and nervous system would suffer.

Dr. Frank Billings
(Digital Resource Library of Illinois History)

Billings told Mollie that a mercury compound was the standard syphilis treatment. But since she was pregnant and showed no signs of the disease, he would not prescribe that remedy. Mercury was a poison that could harm Mollie's developing child.

Mollie told Dr. Billings that if she did have the disease, she could only have gotten it from her husband. Yet, throughout her engagement and marriage, J.R. had seemed perfectly healthy.

Billings explained that if her husband did have syphilis, he was likely in the disease's latent stage which meant he might not be contagious.

The doctor's last words gave Mollie hope.

After J.R. returned from the sailing trip, Mollie told him about her syphilis examination. Even though her Chicago physician had found no signs of the disease on Mollie, she figured J.R. would still claim she had syphilis. Mollie was not wrong. When she also told J.R. about her pregnancy, she later testified, "He caused me great distress by telling and insinuating that because of syphilis, I never could bear children."

In the autumn of 1900, inflammation spread throughout Mollie's joints in the cold and damp weather. She questioned whether her pain was caused by the "unmentionable disease," as J.R. continued to claim, instead of rheumatism. She also questioned why, as an intelligent woman, she stayed with an abusive man. But like most women of that era, Mollie considered divorce an "unmitigated evil," a confession of failure. Mothers taught their daughters to question themselves rather than their husbands, to understand, as a wife, how she might have caused their marital difficulties and to develop a plan to repair their problems. But how could Mollie fix J.R.'s belief that she had been immoral prior to their marriage and contracted syphilis? That falsehood had poisoned his mind. Mollie could not prove he was wrong, and so his word would always win over hers.

A brilliant mind with few options, Mollie chose to stay in hopes that J.R.'s accusations would halt once she delivered a healthy child.

ON DECEMBER 6, 1900, Mollie and J.R. dressed for the Charity Ball. All proceeds would be donated to the Associated Charities to help the community's poor.

Before departing, Mollie started to cramp and bleed. She sobbed as their coach delivered her to St. Vincent Hospital. A repeat tragedy to Mollie's July miscarriage occurred.

Mollie's mother held her daughter's hand in the recovery room as J.R. entered dressed in his evening attire. "He professed to my mother his regret ... that because of syphilis ... I could not bear children."

Mrs. Bertles stood up to J.R. and defended Mollie. "He was told by [my mother] that if he would permit me to regain my normal health and would treat me kindly, there was no reason why I could not bear children."

In the weeks that followed, Mollie felt an overwhelming sadness. She wrestled with the reason for her second miscarriage. During her pregnancy, she had been attentive to her safety: not lifting anything too heavy, not reaching for items up on shelves, and avoiding all jolts, particularly from a fall. Maybe she did have syphilis or maybe her rheumatism was responsible for her premature deliveries. Mollie feared she might never bring a healthy child to full term.

The Bohemian Club held a private masquerade on February 9, 1901, at the Knights of Pythias Hall. Couples danced to the Trombone Orchestra in costumes such as Dolly Dimple, Sitting Bull, Uncle Sam, and Minnehaha. The club awarded prizes to Mollie for the "finest costume" and J.R. for the "best comic" one. Perhaps dressed as a geisha, this being a time long before attentiveness was paid to inappropriate cultural appropriation, Mollie hid her anguish behind a paper fan while J.R. pranced around like a king's jester. Only Mollie saw his true personality hidden behind his mask.

Turner Hall (A Souvenir of Green Bay 1903)

On their ride home, the Minahans passed Turner Hall where Mollie had attended a phrenology lecture with her papa on "Good and Bad Heads." Many scientists considered phrenology a reputable theory at the turn of the nineteenth century, which stated the shape and size of the cranium indicated a person's character and mental abilities. But in actuality, phrenology was a pseudoscience with no real basis in fact and was used to support the eugenics and racist thinking of the time.

Professor W.G. Alexander from New York's Fowler and Well's Institute had discussed a series of notable and notorious men's cranium pictures, such as those from railway founder George Stephenson, inventor Elias Howe, American Dictionary creator Noah Webster, and Kansas serial killer "Bloody" John Bender. Public examinations had taken place at the lecture's close. Professor Alexander had asked for volunteers, and when no willing subjects appeared, he called upon four. Among them was Mollie's papa. The professor measured each of their heads. Mr. Bertles achieved the best results in the "Good Head" category.

Mollie had to have wondered what her husband's measurements would have indicated since his treatment toward her continued to be "cruel, brutal, and inhuman, with only rare intervals of kindness."

Mollie often hiked along the Fox River adjacent to her childhood home. Surrounded by the comforting sounds of croaking frogs and chirping crickets, she began to think "further cohabitation and life with J.R. [was] impossible." He had crushed her optimistic spirit. She hated who she had become. But when Mollie confirmed she was expecting again, less than four months after her second miscarriage, she felt she had no option but to remain in her marriage.

ONE JOY IN Mollie's life was her sister-in-law Daisy, who still resided in the Minahans' home. At nearly five feet nine inches tall, Daisy towered over Mollie. J.R.'s sister had graduated from a Wisconsin Normal School before teaching at Howe Elementary. She was not as attractive as her sister Mary, but Daisy's expressive pale blue eyes offered Mollie comfort and compassion. Like all the Minahan siblings, Daisy was intelligent, gifted, and perceptive. She continued to notice how her brother treated Mollie. Daisy's presence in the home frequently provided Mollie a buffer against J.R.'s cruelty, alleviating some of her pain.

Daisy Minahan (Roger Minahan Papers)

Daisy won *The Green Bay Gazette's* "Most Popular Teacher" contest and was awarded a six-seat theater box for the performance of "She Stoops to Conquer," featuring America's foremost comedian Stuart Robson. Daisy included Mollie in her party of six on Friday, May 10, 1901. Most of The Green Bay Theater audience, dressed in their finery, took seats in the mezzanine that could seat nearly 1000 guests. Women's perfume and men's cigar smoke trapped in suits mingled in the theater's hot rising air.

The gaslights dimmed and the performance began. While Daisy and others in the theater box laughed at the humorous antics on stage, Mollie's worries and hopes about her pregnancy distracted her. From her readings, she knew she should remain "serene and well-poised in spirit," the most conducive for her developing child. But how could Mollie follow those instructions with a husband like J.R.? And what about the recommendation that a husband should abstain from sexual relations with his pregnant wife to prevent a miscarriage?

But Mollie's chief fear continued to be whether she had syphilis.

ON FRIDAY, SEPTEMBER 6, 1901, as Mollie reached her pregnancy's fifth month, she and the nation were stunned when the anarchist, Leon Czolgosz, shot President McKinley. The president died seven days later and Chief Justice McKenna swore Vice President Theodore Roosevelt into the presidential office. While the nation mourned McKinley's death, and New York prison officials executed the anarchist by electric chair, the Brown County Circuit Court added the third Mary Cenefelt vs. Dr. John R. Minahan civil case to its November 1901 calendar.

Final Judgment

GREEN BAY FAMILIES prepared their Thanksgiving meals on Thursday, November 28, 1901. J.R. left his Quincy Street home in his best suit to attend his third trial against Mary Cenefelt. Most businesses had closed to give their workers a holiday, but the Brown County Courthouse was open. Four years had passed since the last Cenefelt vs. Minahan trial, and J.R.'s luck remained intact. The syphilis bacterium was still a mystery, and Judge Hastings, who had seemed prejudiced against Mary in her first two trials, would preside at her third. Hastings had beaten Judge Calkins in April to keep his seat on the Fourteenth Judicial Circuit Court bench.

If the current trial called a similar number of witnesses to the second one, it would last three weeks. J.R. had not booked any surgeries. He had no plans to hold any Washington Street medical office hours. His life was on hold, which meant Mollie's was too.

She had reached the eighth month of her third pregnancy and had not miscarried. Mollie now worried whether her child would be stillborn, or if it lived, would it display symptoms of syphilis inherited from her. In addition, the trial cast a pall over her child's birth. Would her baby have a father with a clear name? Or would its papa's alleged criminal acts be draped over her child's future?

Mollie had to notice the parallels between her history and Mary Cenefelt's. J.R. had wanted to abort Mollie's baby with medicine, and Mary claimed J.R. had given her a prescription to do so. When Mollie refused to take J.R.'s suggested medicine, he had proposed a criminal operation, just as Mary said he had conducted on her. And J.R. still believed Mollie had syphilis, as he claimed Mary did. Mary's accusations against Minahan and Mollie's lived experience were nearly the same. Even if Mollie had wanted to testify to those parallels, because of J.R.'s "marriage privilege," she could not have done so. She was a silenced wife like the first Mrs. Minahan.

MARY CENEFELT, now thirty-four, sat in the same seat at the plaintiff's table. Her haggard body, drab hair, and bent-over frame made her look more like her sixty-seven-year-old mother. At the defendant's table, thirty-nine-year-old Dr. John R. Minahan projected a sense of good health and prosperity, sitting tall, his cheeks clean-shaven, his curly ginger hair still full but variegated with strands of white.

For Mary's third civil trial, Carrie would be the only Cenefelt sibling testifying on her behalf. Their youngest brother, John, who had supported Mary in her former trials, had fatally shot himself inside the Wanish saloon. Mary's little brother had left no suicide note. The family believed his dental studies had unbalanced his mind. Or a girl he had kept company with could have been the reason for the suicide. The couple had reportedly argued that night. The morning Mary's brother-in-law had discovered John, he had immediately sent for Mary knowing how close the two had been. John had looked up to her, supported her, and danced with her at Zeddie's Hall. Now his courtroom seat was empty.

Attorney Patrick H. Martin and J.R.'s attorney and physician brother, Robert E. Minahan, represented J.R. once again. An eager new attorney, twenty-six-year-old Henry F. Cochems, represented Mary. No records provide insight into why her former attorneys had stepped down. Perhaps because she had been unable to pay their attorney fees.

Mary's young lawyer, a Sturgeon Bay, Wisconsin native, had earned a literary degree at the University of Wisconsin, where he had been a talented football halfback. Cochems obtained a Harvard law degree and opened a Milwaukee firm with his best friend C.A. McGee. Clients admired the two attorneys' brilliance and oratory skills, but their cases were often unprofitable. Cochems, with his beak-like nose and bushy eyebrows, perhaps felt Mary's case might change that trend. He

Attorney Henry E. Cochems
(The Project Guttenberg)

sat beside her in a three-piece suit, although a football uniform would have fit his large physique far better.

Austere in black robes, Judge Hastings took his seat behind the bench centered between the American and Wisconsin flags. A ten-member jury was selected. Both attorneys gave their opening statements, then Mr. P.H. Martin "sprung a surprise," by entering an accusation of "champerty and maintenance." His goal was to have the judge throw out the entire proceedings before the witness testimony began. Martin argued that a party other than Mary's past or present attorneys had offered to pay her trial costs and that party had no legitimate interest in the case. If Mary's attorney won the case, Martin alleged that party would receive a portion of the awarded damages. Martin targeted his charge at Dr. William E. Fairfield. In Mary's prior trial, Martin had claimed that Fairfield had kept Mary's original statement as "unction to his small, shriveled soul. It would answer a purpose." Mary's former attorney Mr. Olin had countered that Fairfield's action was to protect himself: "It was not a blackmail scheme to be brought against Dr. Minahan at some future time."

In the years following the second trial, Minahan had continued to exclude Dr. Fairfield from St. Vincent's operating room. That could have been one of the reasons why Fairfield had asked the Montreal Order of Misericorde Nuns to consider opening a second Catholic hospital in Green Bay. That Order had already established a home for destitute infants and unwed mothers inside the city's abandoned St. Joseph Orphanage. St. Mary's Hospital, the answer to Fairfield's request, would open in the next eighteen months at 411 N. Webster.

Minahan's attorney made his case against Dr. Fairfield for nearly a week. Judge Hastings finally ruled: "Champerty and maintenance has not been shown."

J.R. returned home in a sour mood. Unless he and his attorneys came up with a new tactic, there was a good chance the upcoming trial would end like the last, with no conclusion—or this time, Mary might even win.

During the trial, the same witnesses testified for both sides. Mary was still unable to provide evidence to establish her exact 1893 assault dates. Because of that, as in the second trial, March 16 and 17 were used.

Minahan's case depended on the jury believing he had only treated Mary for her "unmentionable disease." Even so, Attorney Cochems, like his predecessors, never questioned Minahan on how he could have admitted Mary into St. Vincent three times against hospital policy if she had a venereal disease.

On December 12, J.R.'s sister, Daisy, attended her brother's trial to provide J.R. support during his testimony. As Green Bay Historian Jack Rudolph stated, "You might hate a Minahan or love him, but you never ignored one ... Being what they were, they couldn't have avoided controversy if they had tried—and nobody ever accused a Minahan of backing away from a fight ... They were a closely-knit lot, as many a misguided outsider discovered ... Anyone else, who stuck in an oar ... was quickly overwhelmed by waves of Minahans swarming in from all directions."

After four weeks of testimony, the jury received the case on December 21, 1901.

"While there is no certainty about the outcome," *The Green Bay Gazette* reported, "it is generally believed the jury will fail to agree on a verdict. The testimony introduced has been very conflicting and, as the Court said, the decision is on which party told the truth—and which committed perjury."

The jury reached a unanimous verdict at 5:00 p.m. on December 22, 1901. Those in the community wondered how the jurors in the prior trial had deliberated for forty hours without reaching a decision when, in the current one, they had arrived at a verdict in only seven hours. On the other hand, why would the jurors need to deliberate any longer when their only job was to answer five questions? As in the prior trial, Judge Hastings' jury charge had included the defendant's request for a "special verdict." But instead of verbal illustrations, the judge had provided the jurors with an official form containing the unaltered questions submitted by Dr. J.R. Minahan's team.

Mary sat beside her attorney in the courtroom awaiting her fate for the third time. She had not found work since her second trial. She had lived on her parents' Cooperstown farm, where they had fed her, clothed her, and paid for her medicine. The verdict had to go her way, otherwise, she would be a burden to her family for the rest of her life.

The jury foreman handed the "special verdict" document to Judge Hastings. With a poker face, he read it and handed it to the clerk of courts to read the five questions and their answers aloud.

The clerk of courts cleared his throat and said the first question asked: *Did the defendant, on March 17, 1893, assault the plaintiff and have sexual intercourse with her?*

The clerk of courts looked up and said the jurors' answer was "No."

The weight of that tiny word hung in the courtroom as the clerk read the second question: *Was Mrs. Minahan, the defendant's wife, at home on March 17, 1893?*

The clerk said the answer was "Yes."

Everyone held their collective breath as the clerk read the third question: *If your answer to the first question should be "Yes," then answer this: Did such intercourse result in the plaintiff becoming pregnant?* Since the first question's answer was "No," the clerk said the jurors had not answered the third question.

Mary and her supporters sunk back against their seats. They were scattered around the gallery: her sister and most likely Nettie Bartelme, Leo Lawe, Mrs. Reis from the hotel by that name, the doctors who had testified on Mary's behalf, the jurors who had supported Mary in her first and second trial, and Miss Nye, who still felt guilty for helping Mary secure a job at the Minahans' in the first place. They knew the questions were unfair. Even if the jurors believed Mary's assaults, which caused her pregnancy, had occurred on a date other than March 17, 1893, the panel could not designate that in the "special verdict." Attorney Martin, J.R., and his brother smiled at the defendant's table. They had undoubtedly known that when they had carefully constructed the questions.

The clerk said the fourth question asked: *If your answers to the first and second questions should be "Yes," then answer this: Did the defendant perform an abortion upon the plaintiff by force and against her will at his office on April 3, 1893?* Again, the clerk said, the jurors did not answer since they had only answered "Yes" to the second question.

The courtroom's heavy silence elevated the tension as all awaited the final question, the most crucial to Mary's future. The clerk read: *If your answer to the fourth question is "Yes," then answer this: At what amount do you assess the plaintiff's damages as a direct and proximate result of such treatment?* The clerk said the jurors had not answered since the fourth question had not been "Yes."

Cries of outrage from Mary's supporters filled the courtroom while Minahan's backers cheered. Judge Hastings banged his gavel repeatedly until the crowd noise dwindled.

Mary covered her face with her hands as Hastings ruled: Miss Cenefelt would receive no settlement. In addition, she would be responsible for Dr. Minahan's trial expenses.

The uproar unleashed again. J.R. basked in the limelight. The city hero who had protected his medical profession from a blackmail scheme, an illegitimate malpractice suit, and the lies of a prostitute with syphilis.

Spectators surged to their feet. Carrie pushed through the throng and sat down next to Mary. But what could Carrie say? The verdict had destroyed Mary's reputation beyond repair. In effect, the decision had banned her from Green Bay for life. Mary could not work there or live there. To pay her attorney fees and those of Minahan would be impossible. No attorney in their right mind would take on her subsequent appeal. For Mary, all hope was gone. She fell helplessly into Carrie's arms.

Outside the courthouse, reporters surrounded J.R. and his attorneys. Mr. P.H. Martin said, "The case is ended, and the verdict is a just one. There are no grounds for a new trial, and I am confident an appeal will not be taken. I am confident this will settle the case for good. It is a decided victory for Dr. Minahan."

The result was final. While many believed justice was served, there was much to suggest that no such aim was even possible given the limited understanding of syphilis, but more powerfully, the gross inequity between Minahan, a rich man, and Mary, a poor woman. In the *Allen v. Farrow* 2021 documentary, exploring Woody Allen's alleged sexual abuse of his daughter, her attorney said, "To prosecute a person, with no allegiance to the truth, who is powerful, rich, and a local celebrity, is nearly impossible." That proved abundantly true for Dr. Minahan, to the great detriment of Mary.

The Birth

SCENTS OF CINNAMON, nutmeg, and fir filled the Minahans' home as the birth of Mollie and J.R.'s child neared. The holiday season had taken the community's attention away from the Cenefelt vs. Minahan trial's outcome. No matter what Mollie thought about it, she had put the ordeal behind her to remain "serene and well-poised in spirit" for the sake of the child growing inside her, the one Mollie had never imagined she could carry to full term.

Yet Mollie could not forget her Chicago doctor's warning: If she was indeed a syphilis carrier, her child could be born dead or die shortly after. Mollie could not bear those thoughts after all she had lost and all she hoped for. She had whispered and sung to her child. She had played piano lullabies for her baby. Her child's midnight kicks had woken Mollie and made her smile. Her baby had to survive.

Mollie's sister-in-law Daisy departed for the Wisconsin Teachers' Conference on Saturday, December 28, leaving Mollie without a helpful female relative in the home. The senior Mrs. Minahan had suffered a third stroke and slept most of each day. On Sunday, the Union Congregational Church minister titled his sermon "The Good New Days," signaling the hopefulness of the times, the hope Mollie yearned for in the years to come.

That night, J.R. put on his overcoat to go out. He knew as well as Mollie that their baby could come at any moment. "I begged J.R. to spend the evening at home with me and forego a game of poker. He became greatly enraged and accused me of always interfering with his pleasures and said, 'I hate the very sight of you and your damned sniveling and complaining!'"

J.R. pushed past Mollie and stormed out. "The Good New Days," it seemed, would never come to the Minahans' house.

J.R. returned after midnight, and Mollie's labor started soon after. Most women delivered their babies at home. Since Mollie had experienced two miscarriages and had the financial means to pay, J.R. contacted his brother, Dr. R.E. Minahan, who admitted Mollie into St. Vincent Hospital. As she struggled through contractions for nearly twenty-four hours, her mind, body, and breathing were in a state of panic. Would her child be stillborn, or would it die shortly after?

On Tuesday, December 31, 1901, when her eight-pound son emerged from her body, his robust cries filled the room.

Mollie sobbed in relief as he was cleaned off and placed into her arms. She gazed down at the tiny being she had carried for nine months, John Bertles Minahan, marveling at her baby's soft and sweet breathing. There were no signs of snuffling or gasping, yet Mollie knew those symptoms might not reveal themselves for a few weeks.

She refused to consider that possibility.

J.R. entered the room, a look of pride on his face as if he had done all the work himself. He said his physician brother had told him the baby promised to be "a strong child." But then J.R. shifted his stance, and his stoic features returned. He warned Mollie that only time would tell since they both knew Mollie had syphilis, and she could have passed that disease onto their son.

Mollie's same fears lurked, but J.R. could not dispel her joy. She did not honor his comment with a response. J.R.'s vicious accusations had not stopped her from delivering a healthy child.

During Mollie's six weeks of postpartum confinement, her little boy flourished. Quickly, however, the novelty of having a son wore off for J.R. In his limited free time, he hunted, ice-fished, played billiards or poker, or anything to be away from home. That provided more time for Mollie to dote on her "miracle son," the one who had arrived after two miscarriages, the one who was thriving, who displayed no signs of being a child with syphilis.

THE SENIOR Mrs. Minahan died in July. Although she had not been an easy mother-in-law, Mollie mourned her passing alongside J.R. and his siblings.

Mrs. Minahan's death provided Mollie new freedom. In October, she and ten-month-old John traveled by train to Ironwood, Michigan with her mother to visit Mollie's sisters. The city of nearly 15,000 residents was where Annie and Kitten had secured elementary school teaching jobs. It was in the Gogebic Iron Range in Michigan's Upper Peninsula, about eighteen miles south of Lake Superior. Several mines were in production, attracting European immigrants.

The foliage was at its peak as the three sisters and their mother took walks each day along the plank sidewalks. Scents of chocolate from the Ironwood Candy Kitchen and yeast from breweries filled the air. Trolley cars passed on the iron-red, dusty streets while Mollie pushed John's buggy. The four women laughed and reminisced about childhood memories. For those few days, Mollie forgot about her terrible marriage, forgot about her fears, and only felt her family's warmth, love, and stability—the things she intended to provide for her son.

Kitten and Annie were disappointed when Mollie could not stay to attend a dance that week in Ironwood. But Mollie had already scheduled a rheumatism appointment in Chicago with Dr. Billings. Her mother accompanied Mollie back on the train. Mrs. Bertles got off in Green Bay with her grandson, whom she would watch until her daughter's return, while Mollie continued on to Chicago.

When Mollie's train returned to Green Bay late the next day, water-slicked carriages waited outside the station, the horses' flanks shaking off the rain. Protected by the carriage driver's umbrella, Mollie stepped into the coach. She first asked the driver to stop at the Bertles Estate so she could pick up her son, then the three continued on to the Minahans' Quincy Street home. The driver carried Mollie's luggage into the front foyer where J.R. was waiting. Instead of giving his wife and son a welcoming smile, he interrogated Mollie about the Michigan trip and her day in Chicago. J.R. also asked about John's health, as if hoping to hear bad news, to prove that his syphilis prediction about their little boy was true.

All the positive energy Mollie had gained from her trip dissipated as the walls of her home closed in around her.

THE 1902 Christmas season arrived. Daisy, who had been away in Milwaukee since September to take classes on how to teach the "deaf and dumb," returned to Green Bay. After her mother's passing, Daisy had moved into her sister Mary Minahan McCormick's home, and Mollie sorely missed Daisy's company.

Attorney William Lincoln Evans (Men Who are Making Green Bay 1897)

Mollie's sister, Annie, arrived from Ironwood for a few weeks. At Mollie's invitation, Annie and her beau Attorney William Lincoln Evans, a respected lawyer in the Evans and Merrill Green Bay firm, attended dinner at the Minahan home. Coincidentally, Evans had been the notary public to witness and validate Mary Cenefelt's first trial "complaint" authored by Attorney J. Calvin Stewart against the man now seated across the dining table from Evans.

When J.R. entertained company he was usually at his best, but he did not consider Annie to be company. Like Mollie's mother, Annie annoyed and irritated J.R. Both women often stood up to him and put him in his place. The dinner was awkward. The two men had no common interests. While J.R. perhaps talked about his Gentlemen Driving and Riding Club friends and his horse, Jimmie Lawrence, who had won several races that fall, Evans, with his boyish face, listened politely. But when Evans discussed the articles he had written in the history and churchmanship fields, J.R. expressed his distaste for religion.

Hagemeister Park where J.R. raced his horses (A Souvenir of Green Bay 1903)

After Mollie's sister and Evans left around midnight, J.R. exploded. He asked Mollie how she had allowed the two to stay so long. "He said he believed, and had good reason to believe, that my sister ... was immoral and that he would not permit the presence of my sister at his home ever again."

Ugly words flew back and forth, J.R.'s barrage of insults about Annie bouncing off their bedroom walls, while Mollie defended her sister. In high school, it had been easy for Mollie to eloquently express her arguments to an intelligent debate opponent who could understand the logic of her words. But the man she had married was anything but logical. As their marriage had worn on, it had become clearer: J.R. was an accomplished bully who always got his way. He felt he was superior to Mollie and her sister, and he could and should save the world from immoral women like them.

A weary Mollie finally relented to J.R.'s mandate that Annie not set foot in their house again. Mollie despised herself for allowing J.R. to strip away her determination to stand up for her sister. But as Mollie lay in bed that night, unable to sleep, playing back her painful defeat, a thought made her eyes open: Could her husband be the immoral one? Maybe his claims about Mollie and Annie were simply a cover for J.R.'s extramarital affairs.

Immoral Accusations

MOLLIE KEPT watchful eyes on J.R.'s outside activities during the first two months of 1903. If he was having an affair, it was not evident unless he was involved with his surgical nurse. The two had traveled to Escanaba, Michigan, on January 6, where J.R. had been called to perform an appendicitis operation. He and his nurse had also taken a train on February 19, to Campbellsport, Wisconsin to attend to an engineer who had been badly injured in a railroad wreck. Still, Mollie had no proof of an affair with his nurse. Until Mollie had concrete evidence of immoral conduct on J.R.'s part, she decided she would keep her suspicions to herself.

Two months later, she and J.R. left by train to visit Hot Springs, Arkansas, in the picturesque Ouachita Mountains. The March trip was the first time Mollie had left fifteen-month-old John in the care of their housekeeper Julia. But Mollie had no qualms in doing so. Her little boy was very attached to Julia.

Hot Springs was a prime location for "medical tourism." Popular atlases like *King's Handbook of the United States* described Hot Springs' waters as "beneficial in cases of diseases of the skin … and for rheumatism and syphilis." Named for the natural spring water that flowed from the ground at 147 degrees Fahrenheit, the city contained twenty-five hotels, numerous boarding houses, and half a dozen bathhouses. Inside the latter, in addition to the soaking tubs there were beauty shops, gymnasiums, and mechanotherapy machines such as electrical massages, vapor cabinets, and needle showers to promote healing.

Hot Springs Arkansas 1900 (Library of Congress)

About half of the Hot Springs health seekers were wealthy people like J.R. who only claimed to be victims of overwork and over-feeding and simply utilized the bathhouses to feel and look healthier. The other half of the city's visitors hoped to find a cure or temporary respite from their ailments, like Mollie. During the Minahans' three-week stay, she soaked daily in the bathhouse tubs, drank medicinal water, and sweated out her body's alleged poisons. She rested in a cooling chamber afterward then returned to the hotel's veranda to take a nap, read, and write letters to Julia to check on her son.

In mid-April, Mollie and J.R.'s train returned to Green Bay. Her rheumatism aches and pains had subsided, and she felt stronger. But J.R. continued to torment her, insisting their trip had only helped Mollie's syphilis symptoms. Since she refused mercury treatment, J.R. claimed the disease would permanently injure her bones and joints.

Soon after their return, J.R. refused to speak to Mollie "without any apparent cause." Over the next three weeks, he treated her as if she was invisible. When Mollie missed her period, and J.R.'s physician brother confirmed she was pregnant again, she felt overwhelmed. How could she give birth to another child when her husband acted as if she did not exist? "I told J.R. of [my pregnancy], to which he replied, 'If you are, I know nothing about it. It is no child of mine.'"

Mollie hid the truth of her miserable marriage from her best female friends, including Mayme Comstock who had placed ribbons on Mollie's wedding aisle. Now Mayme's turn had arrived to marry Attorney Edgar B. Warren. Mollie entered the home of the groom's mother for a kitchen shower hosted in Mayme's honor. An original poem accompanied each guest's gift. Mollie's poem was a tongue-in-cheek ditty on a potato "masher," playing on the word's second meaning which described a male sexual harasser.

Mollie peered over at Mayme, who was giggling like the others over Mollie's poem. She ached to share her problems with Mayme in the heartfelt, unrestrained way they had in high school. But Mollie's impulse—even in the strictest confidence—would have been a dangerous endeavor. If word got back to J.R., there would be no telling what he would do to her.

Mayme Comstock Warren's wedding photo and the poem Mollie B. Minahan wrote for her friend's wedding shower. (Courtesy of Beverly Hart Branson)

The day after Mayme's wedding, Mollie removed old clothing from the master bedroom armoire to donate to the poor. From one of J.R.'s suit coat pockets, she noticed an envelope containing a letter from her sister, Annie. The Ironwood, Michigan postmark was six weeks old, about the date when J.R. had stopped talking to Mollie.

She sat down on the bed to read Annie's letter, its envelope already slit open. Her sister wrote about a male friend of Mollie's from her college years, who had expressed disappointment that Mollie was not at last fall's Ironwood dance. Annie said she had told him that Mollie and her mother had left Ironwood that day so that Mollie could travel to Chicago for a doctor's appointment.

Mollie confronted J.R. that night. She held out the letter and asked why he had stolen it from the mailbox.

He said Mollie had done far worse. "He charged me with having gone to Chicago in the fall of 1902 to meet the man mentioned in the letter for illicit sexual relations. And J.R. persisted in his accusation, though

I pointed out to him how utterly impossible it was for [that man] to be at the dance in Ironwood and to meet me in Chicago."

But J.R. would not let up. He told Mollie he knew she was secretly seeing that man whenever she went to Chicago for her doctor's appointments. He said the child Mollie was carrying was that man's, not J.R.'s, and he stormed out.

Mollie stood there, her sister's letter shaking in her hand. She had yet to discover any sort of evidence that J.R. was having an affair. Now he had accused her of having one.

In late July, Mollie's pregnancy nausea subsided, and she took her toddler on excursions to Bay View Beach and the Green Bay harbor. Mollie's child dazzled her. John was a bright and determined little boy who showed no signs of syphilis. He would point at seagulls, steamers, and trains, his sweet voice attempting to utter each name. On his sturdy little legs, he would dash along the shoreline to beat a tugboat hauling a coal barge. John would crouch down to pick up an acorn, a goose feather, or a shiny pebble to add to his treasures at home. Any one-on-one time Mollie could spend with her son provided her a welcome reprieve from her marriage turmoil.

UNDER A SAPPHIRE SKY, the pungent cider scent of fallen apples filled the Minahans' side-yard. Mollie played in the fallen leaves with John, her growing stomach hidden below the maternity dress she wore.

J.R. strode up the sidewalk and caught sight of Mollie. He told her she was a disgrace, carrying that child. "That he had made one woman get out ... as was the fact ... and that he would get rid of me too. [He] would divorce me ... that no woman was any good after she'd had children." J.R. also reminded Mollie, since she had syphilis, the new baby would likely have it too.

Mollie gathered John into her arms, pressing his head to her chest. She told J.R. he was lying. John was thriving. Her new baby would thrive as well.

BY JANUARY OF 1904, Green Bay's population surpassed 25,000 citizens. That number increased by one when Mollie delivered her second son, Robert Bertles Minahan, on February 13. Mollie had brought two healthy little boys into the world. Neither showed any signs of syphilis.

During Mollie's six-weeks of postpartum confinement, she suffered a rheumatism flare. "J.R.'s treatment toward me," Mollie later testified, "was markedly neglectful and cruel, to such an extent, as to seriously endanger my life."

Mollie rocked her newborn in the nursery as John stacked wooden blocks by her feet. She so wished she and her sons could move up to Ironwood, Michigan, to live near her sisters, to start a new life without J.R.'s daily abuse. But if Mollie attempted to leave with the boys, she feared J.R. would file a suit to strip her of her parental rights by claiming she had contracted syphilis due to immoral behavior. And Mollie could not disprove his accusations. In addition, she still had no evidence of any immoral behavior on his part.

If J.R. retained custody, what would become of her boys? Especially Robert. Mollie gazed down at his dear little face. J.R. still maintained that Robert was not his. Yet Mollie knew for public appearances, and to spite her, J.R. would not dispute his parental rights in front of a judge.

John tugged on Mollie's skirt to show her the tower he had built. As she praised her son's ingenuity, she recognized she had to stay in her marriage. She had no other choice. She had to sacrifice her own physical and mental health for her little boys' welfare.

SHORTLY AFTER Mollie's confinement ended, her mother became gravely ill. "J.R. showed me no sympathy whatsoever. On the contrary, he manifested an utter indifference to my mother's welfare. Though fully conscious that her death was momentarily expected, he went to a poker party." Just before daybreak, the Minahans' phone rang.

Mollie rolled over in bed and discovered J.R.'s side was empty. The phone stopped ringing, and there was a knock on the bedroom door. Mollie opened it and her housekeeper Julia said that Mollie's father had been on the phone. Mollie was to come to her parents' home immediately. He had also sent word to her sisters. Their mother's condition had deteriorated.

The entire Bertles family was present when Mrs. Bertles passed away later that day. Mollie would never forget how her mother had stood up to J.R. on Mollie's behalf. She would also never forget that "J.R. had not returned home at five a.m. when I was called to the deathbed of my mother."

The Other Victims

MOLLIE SLIPPED INTO a floral silk and linen dress in April of 1904 to attend her brother-in-law's swearing-in ceremony. Green Bay had elected Dr. Robert E. Minahan as its twenty-fourth mayor for a two-year term that provided no salary. While still performing his physician role, Dr. Robert felt it was his civic duty to serve and provide "social uplift" to the community after the former mayor had stepped down due to a city council bribery scandal.

Mollie believed a scandal could also be brewing inside her marriage. Two weeks had passed since the funeral of Mollie's mother, and J.R. had never given Mollie a credible reason for his absence from their home when she had been called to her mother's deathbed. On top of that, when Mollie opened her jewelry box that afternoon to attach her wedding pin to her bodice for the ceremony, she discovered the brooch was missing. Mollie felt certain that J.R. had taken it as he had done to some of her other valuable jewelry "simply to irritate" her, only to return the pieces later. She marched into his dressing room, leveled her eyes on him, and asked him about her wedding pin.

He gave her a beguiling smile and said she must have misplaced it.

Mollie had no recourse but to walk away.

The new mayor and his wife Nellie held a reception inside their Georgian Colonial at 840 S. Monroe Avenue. Their only child Eben, working on his university law degree, was in attendance, as was Daisy Minahan, now living on the third floor of Robert's home.

Eben Minahan (Roger Minahan Papers)

Daisy showed Mollie the emerald-cut diamond ring J.R. had given her for her birthday. "I examined said diamond," Mollie later testified, "and was convinced that it was the same that had been in my pin."

Mollie cornered J.R. about her supposition. He played the innocent, claiming the accusation was an affront to his integrity. But that suspicion was minor compared to a rumor Mollie overheard that night: that J.R. had been paying attention to his surgery nurse of "shady reputation."

Mollie's face flamed at hearing those words. Behind J.R.'s claims that Mollie was immoral, she had finally uncovered her own evidence to challenge J.R.

Clouds gathered, the sky purpled, and a cold wind blew from the northeast as the Minahans' coachman drove Mollie and J.R. back to their home. Inside the master bedroom, Mollie confronted J.R. about his surgery nurse.

According to Mollie's later testimony, she said her husband retorted, "You had better get out before you are kicked out! You are nothing but a damn dirty prostitute!"

Mollie had suffered enough. Aided by her housekeeper, Mollie packed up her two little boys and the Minahans' driver dropped the three off at her papa's house. Mollie planned to get his advice and remain there until she figured out her next move. But upon her arrival, Mollie found her papa in bed, attended by a private nurse. He was so ill that Mollie felt she could not burden him with her problems. "Though suffering great pain and humiliation, I returned home. J.R. professed to me that he did not mean what he had said. That I had irritated him into saying it." He denied that he and his nurse were involved, but J.R. said he would fire her to satisfy Mollie.

J.R.'s unexpected expression of remorse and kindness gave Mollie a sense of hope. His words made her believe that things might get better. Trapped in her circumstances, she chose to have hope, no matter how small.

But Mollie's accusations were probably true. Years later, J.R.'s niece wrote, "Gladys Kraynick is, or was one of ... J.R. Minahan's sweeties. She is the nurse whom he had so blackened all over the region that when he fired her, she was unable to get work anywhere in this county. He said she was immoral. The thing that got him sore was she went out with a dentist afterward, and since she belonged to J.R., he thought she had no business cheating."

BY 1904, nearly half of the Minahan family had settled in Green Bay, including J.R., Dr. Robert, Mary Minahan McCormick, Daisy, and their youngest sibling Victor Ivan Minahan, better known as V.I. After he had attended Oshkosh Normal, where the college had allegedly expelled V.I. for carving his initials into the auditorium's woodwork, he had graduated from Stevens Point Normal and earned a law degree at the Wisconsin State University.

Daisy & V.I. Minahan in Florida.
(Roger Minahan Papers)

V.I. had established his Green Bay law firm inside the same Parmentier Block building that housed his two eldest brothers' medical practice. To support V.I.'s new firm, J.R. had moved his legal business from Mr. P.H. Martin to his brother. Mayor R.E. Minahan had also named V.I. "special graft case prosecutor" for the city's bribery scandals. The twenty-three-year-old attorney had indicted half of the city council for accepting construction contract bribes and protecting prostitution houses in exchange for diamond rings, office desks, and pianos.

Three years had passed since the third Cenefelt vs. Minahan trial. In mid-October of 1904, J.R.'s feet thundered into his Quincy Street home. He picked up the telephone receiver and called his attorney brother. Within Mollie's hearing, J.R. told V.I. that his former maid, Mary Cenefelt, had dashed toward him on Washington Street. If he did not give her money or free treatment, J.R. claimed she had threatened to blind him by throwing acid in his face. He told his brother he wanted Mary arrested.

Mollie's brother-in-law contacted his Irish friend Nicholas J. Monahan, Brown County's newly elected municipal judge. Based on J.R.'s affidavit, Judge Monahan signed a warrant for Mary's arrest, charging her with blackmail. Deputy Sheriff John Gauerke tracked Mary down at her parents' Cooperstown farm. She was transported to the Brown County jail and placed into a cell with a steel bedstead, horsehair mattress, thread-worn blanket, washstand, and toilet bucket. Two other women were in Mary's cell block, the first arrested during a Jefferson Street disorderly house raid, the second serving three months after her husband caught her inside a southside hotel with another man.

Unable to secure legal assistance, Mary stood in the courtroom alone and pleaded not guilty. Judge Monahan set her bail at $500, far more than she could produce, and Mary returned to her jail cell. A few days later, Mary's parents secured her bail, and she was released into their care.

On December 5, 1904, Judge Monahan held Mary's preliminary examination. She had secured the firm of Calkins & McGruer to represent her. They filed an affidavit against Judge Monahan for prejudice, and the Court transferred Mary's case to Judge Hastings, no less prejudicial in Mary's eyes. But she finally caught a break before heading to trial. District Attorney Cady nolled her case, stating there was insufficient evidence to prosecute Mary.

Mollie perhaps felt a connection to Mary who had narrowly escaped a criminal trial, albeit with considerable trauma and expense, all because of J.R.'s allegations. Mollie knew only too well what sort of misery her husband could levy on the women in his life.

The Breaking Point

MOLLIE SUFFERED a severe inflammatory rheumatism attack in August of 1905, and J.R. once again claimed her untreated syphilis had caused her condition. Crippled with pain, Mollie required advanced treatment at Mount Clemens, Michigan. J.R. accompanied Mollie there by train, and she checked into the exclusive Park Bath House and Hotel with spacious verandas, promenade halls, elevators, and private bathrooms.

During the Civil War, the city's local businessman, Charles Steffen, sank his first oil well in Mount Clemens, hoping to hit the jackpot. Instead, sulfur-perfumed brine spewed out, an alternate windfall once doctors discovered the liquid's so-called medicinal properties. According to advertisements similar to those for Hot Springs, Arkansas, individuals could seek Mount Clemens' cures for rheumatism, syphilis, jaundice, obesity, polio, and liver problems.

J.R. left Mollie in Michigan and returned to Green Bay, promising to write daily letters to alleviate her worry about their children. It was the first time sixteen-month-old Robert and three-year-old John would be in their father's care without Mollie's presence in the home.

Each day an attendant pushed Mollie's wheelchair from the Park Hotel through a marble-floored hallway to the attached bathhouse. In her private bathing area, Mollie soaked in a tub of dark, rotten-egg-smelling mineral water heated to about 98 degrees. The

Park Hotel in Mount Clemens (Postcard)

water allegedly released toxins from her opened pores to soothe her pain. A vigorous massage followed before she was wrapped in heated towels and sent to the hotel's solarium to relax or nap. The entire course included three weeks of daily treatments.

By the two-week mark, J.R. had only sent Mollie two letters. Her worry about her children negated any benefit from the treatments. Mollie's condition became so critical that an assistant physician telegraphed J.R. Her husband traveled fifteen hours to get there by train. "By the time he reached [Mount Clemens], I was somewhat improved, and J.R. expressed and manifested ... great annoyance at being called."

J.R. later testified, "No serious or alarming symptoms ever developed, threatening Mollie's life while she was at Mount Clemens, but I allege that through a mistake of an assistant physician, such a report was made."

Mollie told J.R. to speak to her doctor. The Mount Clemens physician had deemed that four additional weeks of therapy were necessary to treat Mollie's rheumatism. Even after J.R. talked to Mollie's doctor, "J.R. professed to believe that my trouble was syphilis."

J.R. returned to Green Bay. Over the next two weeks, Mollie received no letters from him. Her sister, Annie, had moved back to Green Bay. Even though J.R. continued to prohibit Annie from entering their home, Mollie wrote her sister and asked her to check on John and Robert to keep her apprised of their health and welfare. Per Annie's letters, Mollie believed her children were safe.

During Mollie's last week in Mount Clemens, her doctor met with her to discuss the rheumatism therapy regimen she should follow upon her return to Green Bay. That included exercise, heat treatments, and deep breathing techniques to relax her nerves. Her doctor said he knew, however, that Mollie's physician husband believed her health problems were syphilis-related. To help Mollie deal with that difficult situation, he wanted her to know about a major breakthrough related to the syphilis disease.

Protozoologist Fritz Schaudinn and Dermatologist Erich Hoffman (National Library of Medicine/ Digital Collections)

German protozoologist Dr. Fritz Schaudinn and dermatologist Erich Hoffman had discovered an identical tiny corkscrew-shaped bacterium within their patients' syphilis chancre sores and lymph node samples. To do so, they had stained the samples with a variant of methylene blue, a dye used for clothing, and under a microscope, the invisible syphilis infectious agent suddenly appeared. It was hard to believe that this tiny bacterium, named Treponema Pallidum Spirochete, had caused millions of people to suffer and die over the past 400 years.

Mollie's doctor said worldwide research teams were now focused on developing a blood test to determine whether an individual was a syphilis carrier—knowledge Mollie had wanted to know ever since her first miscarriage five years before.

Her doctor promised to write Mollie once a syphilis blood test was discovered.

With that encouraging news, Mollie finally took time to inventory her life. J.R. alleged she had syphilis and that she had passed that disease on to their sons. Mollie reflected on J.R.'s other assertions: that he had not hired someone to write those anonymous letters; that J.R. had examined their first premature child and claimed it had syphilis; that J.R. had not taken her jewelry; that he had not cheated on Mollie with his nurse; that Mollie's sister was immoral; that Mollie was too. In each example, J.R. had deemed he was the only one who knew the truth. He had kept Mollie in a constant state of insecurity, doubt, and fear as means to control her.

But no longer.

She believed her Mount Clemens doctor's diagnosis. She had rheumatism, not syphilis. That meant her boys could not have the disease either. And she and her sons should soon have scientific blood test results to prove Mollie right.

Even so, Mollie now realized how difficult it would be for her to leave her marriage with her boys, given her financial condition. She had studied the work of the feminist Victoria Woodhull, who stated, "A woman's ability to earn money is better protection against the tyranny and brutality of men than her ability to vote." Mollie knew those words were true. Before marrying J.R., she had the protection of financial stability from her family and her teaching job. It had vanished once she had taken her wedding vows. Only unmarried women could teach. What little money Mollie had saved from teaching at Howe School she had long ago spent. Her only income was what J.R. provided to her. Mollie could ask her ailing father for financial support, but she would only do so as her last resort.

Still, although Mollie felt trapped, she had finally recognized J.R.'s lies once and for all.

WHEN MOLLIE returned to Green Bay, she continued to see Dr. Robert for her rheumatism which angered J.R. He remonstrated her for refusing to believe she had syphilis. "[He] demanded that I permit him to treat me for [that disease], threatening that he would forbid [his brother from] making any further professional visits to me ... I told him I had no syphilitic trouble, and I refused to ... permit treatment for [that] disease."

Mollie defied J.R. and continued to see Dr. Robert for her rheumatism. She also began to confide in him, believing J.R.'s brother to be a man of character and resolve.

Green Bay City Hall
(Souvenir of Green Bay 1903)

Earlier that year, Mollie had watched Dr. Robert, as mayor, wield a sharp ax to chop wood on the Green Bay City Hall's snow-covered front lawn. He had poured kerosene over the pile and used a match to ignite a large bonfire. Horse-drawn drays had pulled up filled with roulette wheels, slot machines, and other gambling devices seized from overnight raids. Under the mayor's direction, policemen had pitched the expensive paraphernalia into the flames as the owners looked on in disbelief. "In the words of Sir Walter Raleigh," Mayor Minahan's voice had boomed, "the ax is a sharp medicine, but it cures all disease."

Mollie had sharpened her own ax to destroy J.R.'s lies.

Probability of Error

TWO MONTHS AFTER Mollie's return from Mount Clemens, J.R. called her into his library where the sweet-alcohol scent of firearm cleaning solution permeated the air. He tipped back on his leather chair and instructed Mollie to sit. J.R.'s desk between them, his eyes peered down at her like those from the five-point buck mounted on the wall behind him.

His money, J.R. said, was "going out every which way, like water out of a bucket that sits in the sun for six months." He slid a piece of paper toward Mollie and said the document contained his monthly liabilities on the nearly one hundred land and rental property mortgages he held. J.R. then delved into their personal expenses. Mollie's, he said, were out of control while his expenditures were "curbed down pretty well."

As a successful physician, Mollie believed J.R. made at least $16,000 annually (about $542,000 in current valuation). She asked him about his $2000 Toledo touring car. Automobiles were still considered playthings of Green Bay's wealthy with only about a dozen in the city. J.R.'s brother, Dr. Robert, also owned one. J.R. volleyed back that his vehicle was necessary for his profession, then quickly turned the conversation back on Mollie. "To tighten up the leaks," J.R. said he would give her an $800 annual allowance. That would be her "pin money" for whatever she pleased. He would still pay her drug, dentist, and livery bills, but only if they stayed in the proper range. He would also provide her with a $200 monthly household allowance to run *his* home.

Mollie hated to feel like hired help, beholden to J.R. for every penny she spent, but she had no other choice. She soon realized the monthly household allowance was not enough. When Mollie ran out of her designated funds, she charged goods, planning to pay them off with her next month's allowance. J.R. stormed in one night and said he was being "dunned on every corner" for what she had charged. They argued back and forth, "uphill and downhill."

In late November of 1905, Mollie visited her papa, his pallor gray, a blanket covering his knees, and a medicinal smell in the air. He told Mollie her husband had recently stopped over and alleged she had verbally abused J.R. by telling him, "Damn you, I'll bankrupt you; I'll spend every dollar that you've got. I'll break you." J.R. had asked her papa to prevent Mollie from incurring obligations in J.R.'s name.

That information angered and humiliated Mollie. She sat down beside her papa and held his frail hand. She denied she had ever said those words to J.R.

Her papa assured Mollie that he believed her. He said he had told her husband he would not interfere in their marriage. That she and J.R. had to work out their money problems together.

Mollie knew her parents' finances had been handled very differently than hers. Mollie's papa believed her mother's support for his endeavors, her intuition, and her creative suggestions had helped him succeed. But most of all he credited his wife with being a source of strength and admiration to their six offspring, teaching each child to be honest, forgiving, generous, and patient. Therefore, the money her papa made was his wife's income as much as his. In Mollie's eyes, J.R. was a far smaller man than her papa, not willing to give Mollie any credit for her contribution to their marriage for fear his words would detract from his own achievements.

Mollie gazed at the spot in front of the bay window inside her papa's parlor. Six years had passed since she and J.R. had stood there under an arch of brakes and palms and exchanged their wedding vows. J.R. had promised to have and hold her for better, for worse, for richer, for poorer, in sickness and health, to love and cherish, from that day forward, till death us do part.

Mollie had tenderly gazed up at J.R. on her wedding day and believed his words.

She returned to her Quincy Street home and located J.R. in his library. She told him he should never talk to her father about their private matters again. Mollie then added, "I have denied myself many things that I have fairly and reasonably been entitled to, that I might aid and further your ambition to accumulate money, which you have done very successfully." To be "pinched down" to $200 a month, Mollie said, was unreasonable. She demanded a household allowance increase. J.R. finally agreed to "open the floodgates and let the money go."

THE PUBLIC RARELY referred to syphilis by its name, even in the confines of their homes. Such euphemisms as "a rare blood disease" were used. When the *Ladies' Home Journal* published articles about venereal diseases, the magazine lost 75,000 subscribers. That could be why the May 10, 1906, medical paper, published by German bacteriologist August Paul von Wassermann and two other scientists, had drawn little public press. However, the three men's discovery of a blood test to detect that elusive pathogen of syphilis was astounding news within the medical community. Mollie's Mount Clemens doctor wrote her about that wonderful development, although he said it would be many more months before a syphilis blood test could be conducted in the U.S.

In the meantime, Mollie was dealing with J.R.'s ongoing jealousy. She sat beside him in his touring car as they drove away from a Bohemian Club party in June. Over the noisy engine's sound, J.R. accused Mollie of being far too interested in Mr. Frederic Hall, the Beaumont House proprietor. Five months earlier, the Halls and Minahans had attended a Green Bay Theater box party performance of "The Pit." But rather than watching the play, J.R.'s eyes had kept stealing glances at Mollie and Frederic. J.R. said Hall was a "notorious libertine" and remonstrated Mollie, telling her, "A woman might be seen once with Hall, but if ever seen a second time, that her reputation would be shattered." The windows steamed up from J.R.'s heated breath, even more so when Mollie did not respond.

German bacteriologist August Paul von Wasserman (Wikimedia)

A month later, Mollie and several lady friends, including Frederic's wife, spent a week at the Ellis Cabin near Red Banks. A boardwalk descended from the cliff to the beach below, where reflected light and wind constantly changed the bay's texture and hue. For generations, that area, twenty miles north of Green Bay, had been a popular summer colony for residents. But it was also a romantic day trip location.

Mollie and her sweetheart during college had motored a naphtha launch to that picnic spot with another young couple for Mollie's nineteenth birthday. That nostalgic memory tugged at Mollie's heart when J.R. let her down once again. "It was understood and agreed that the husbands of these ladies should come [to the Ellis Cabin] and spend the Sunday," Mollie later testified. "Though J.R. had agreed to the plan, he failed to come. Upon my return home, he charged me with tagging, [being an unwanted third-wheel] ... making me a laughing-stock of the party in my desire to be with Mr. Hall."

The next week, Wisconsin Fish Company owners Mr. and Mrs. George Saunders entertained about thirty friends on their large boat called the *Anti*. Among the guests were the Minahans and the Halls. While enjoying a ride on the

Red Banks area (A Souvenir Book of Green Bay 1903)

waters of Green Bay, a band played until the host announced that guests should be seated for dinner. A lady member of the party placed Mollie next to Mr. Hall and seated J.R. next to herself. When the Minahans reached home, in front of their housekeeper, J.R. accused Mollie of having "sexual relations with Mr. Hall." J.R. told Mollie that the lady who had seated her next to Mr. Hall had "aided and abetted in the accomplishment" of their "illicit relations."

To be insulted by J.R. in their bedroom's privacy was one thing. In front of their housekeeper was another. Mollie left the house, fuming, after she checked on her sleeping children. The night was foggy, and streetlamps summoned mosquitoes. Mollie strode three blocks to the home of J.R.'s brother, Dr. Robert, who had been reelected mayor for his second two-year term. The front porch light came on after Mollie knocked. A maid escorted her into Dr. Robert's mahogany-paneled library.

Without even taking a seat, Mollie told him, "On several occasions, and wholly without reason, J.R. has grossly insulted me and caused me great pain and suffering by intimating and charging me with illicit sexual relations with [Mr. Frederic] Hall." Mollie asked Dr. Robert to talk to J.R.

That request would test Dr. Robert's allegiance to Mollie over his brother, a rarity in the close-knit Minahan clan, especially given the brothers' history. Mollie knew J.R.'s father could only afford to send one of his two eldest sons to college, so Robert had devised a plan. While he attended Rush Medical College, J.R. taught school and sent R.E. money to fund half of his studies. Their father's money provided the remainder. When J.R. entered medical school, R.E.'s physician income plus their father's contribution financed J.R.'s education. The two brothers were now partners in a joint medical practice founded on professional trust.

But Dr. Robert also trusted Mollie's earnest words.

He told her he would telephone J.R. and admonish him for his unwarranted jealousy.

J.R. sat in his dim library when Mollie arrived home. He looked up, his icy stare and silence more threatening than words. As payback, he treated Mollie to a "long course of neglect, insult, and indignity," culminating in an action in late August of 1906 that J.R. knew would cause Mollie "more pain and suffering than any other."

Mollie had arrived home from visiting her ailing father and looked for the boys. Julia told her Dr. Minahan had taken them on a journey, but he had not disclosed their destination.

Two days passed without any contact from J.R. That emotional stress triggered a rheumatism flare in Mollie's joints. She entered Dr. Robert's Washington Street consultation room to seek treatment and told him, "I hate and despise [your brother]." Mollie explained how J.R. had taken their sons, and she asked Dr. Robert for help to locate the boys.

Once again, Robert came through for Mollie. He made calls and drove to locations without telephones, including a small cottage J.R. owned across the bay from Red Banks. That was perhaps where Robert had found his brother and the boys. Wherever he found them, Robert succeeded in bringing Mollie's sons home.

After Mollie tucked her boys safely into their Quincy Street beds that night, she entered J.R.'s library. He glared at her and claimed he had exercised his parental right to remove his sons from Mollie's "immoral influence," and her current syphilis symptoms proved his claim.

As the years had passed, J.R. had seemed to dismiss the idea that Robert was not his. But he had not eased on his assertions about Mollie's health. Yet, ever since her return from Mount Clemens, she realized that J.R. had stopped insisting the boys had inherited syphilis from her—rather surprising, but a huge relief to Mollie.

IN THE FALL OF 1906, Mollie's Chicago physician told her about the Wassermann test's availability in the U.S. and its eye-opening results. Doctors had used the test to analyze the blood of 262 insane patients at the Mount Hope Institution near Baltimore. The test had proved that 86 percent of the population were infected even though doctors up to that point had only diagnosed eight cases. In Europe, physicians had utilized the Wasserman test on 100 "immoral women." Only one had displayed outward symptoms of syphilis, yet the results revealed that about 85 percent were infected.

Even given that unsettling information, Mollie had no fear. She knew she did not have syphilis. She was composed when her blood was drawn and sent to a lab. When the doctor told Mollie he was pleased to inform her that her test was "negative," which meant there was a 90 to 95 percent probability she did not have the syphilis disease, Mollie felt a surge of power and vindication. After being dragged down for six years by J.R.'s false claims, she finally had her proof.

Mollie returned home and entered J.R.'s library. She stood tall as she told him about her blood test results.

He huffed and said she undoubtedly fell into the range of error probability, and the Wasserman test had not proven a thing.

Mollie had expected her husband's contentious words. No matter what J.R. chose to believe, Mollie knew the truth.

She did not have syphilis.

Neither did her sons.

Protecting His Image

J.R.'S FINANCIAL FIXATION, Mollie discovered, was due to a new project. *The Green Bay Gazette* reported that the Minahan Building Company, newly incorporated by J.R. and his two brothers, Attorney V.I. Minahan and Mayor R.E. Minahan, had purchased the American House and its property. The three-story hotel sat on the prime northeast corner of Washington and Walnut, where two streetcar lines intersected.

On January 30, 1907, a blast jarred Washington Street. Phase one

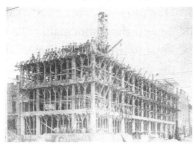

Minahan Building Construction
(Courtesy of the Neville Public
Museum of Brown County)

of J.R.'s plan was to tear down the American House and erect a modern six-story office building. Workers razed the hotel and used ten pounds of dynamite to blast a well. Construction had begun on the Minahan property. The plan included eighty offices, first-floor retail space, two elevators, and an innovative letter chute where building occupants could drop mail from any floor to a central ground-level box. The best grade of St. Louis pressed cream-color brick would encase the exterior adorned with fancy cut stone and terra-cotta trimmings. The Minahan Building would be the finest and most imposing in the city and cost $150,000 (about $4.8 million in current valuation).

For generations, marriage had given the husband the right to demand a physical relationship with his wife. But the "New Woman" movement advocated for a wife's privilege to choose whether she would consent to her husband's desires. In the Minahans' seemingly irreparable relationship, however, not even J.R.'s continued claim that Mollie had syphilis had stopped him from enforcing his legal rights inside their marital bed. "I informed him I was pregnant, and he tried to prevail upon me to submit to an operation to avoid [my] condition."

More than seven years had passed since their honeymoon when J.R. had uttered similar words. Once again, holding back tears, thirty-two-year-old Mollie stood up to her husband, aided by the proof she was not a syphilis carrier. "At all times, since my marriage, I have been willing to bear children and become the mother of a family. I was greatly aggrieved and shocked at [J.R.'s] proposal ... and I refused."

The Minahan Building Company's second phase was in motion. J.R. stood beside his brother, Mayor Robert E. Minahan, and addressed the city council. J.R. asked the members to consider a franchise proposal that would save the city substantial money. J.R. said the Minahan Building's basement had room to house boilers and dynamos to furnish light and power to Green Bay's business district. The franchise, which required the installation of new street and city conduits, would not exceed eight cents per kilowatt and would deliver savings of $800 per year ($25,000 in current valuation).

Knowing that Green Bay's mayor backed the proposal, the city council agreed that utility company rivalry could benefit the municipality. The council approved the Minahan Building Company franchise for a period of twenty years. Mayor Minahan signed the ordinance in July of 1907 with no details provided to the public, a break from the city council's standard operating procedures.

THE MINAHAN BOYS, now ages six and four, were as excited about their sibling's forthcoming birth as Mollie. They helped pick out names and redecorate the nursery. Mollie assured herself the child inside her womb would be as healthy as her boys. But in Mollie's fifth month of pregnancy, tragedy struck again. Her active infant became eerily still, and Dr. Robert confirmed there was no fetal heartbeat. At St. Vincent Hospital, he induced labor and used instruments to help remove Mollie's stillborn child.

To cope with her grievous loss, Mollie kept John and Robert close, while J.R. reiterated, since she refused to treat her syphilitic condition, she had no one to blame but herself.

More than ever, Mollie wanted to escape from her marriage with her boys, but she, like so many other women of that era who lacked financial resources, felt helpless to do so against a powerful husband. And J.R. was gaining more power and prestige by the minute. His surgery practice was thriving, his skyscraper was nearing completion, and his franchise electric and power work would soon begin. J.R. would never allow Mollie to damage his public image by taking *his* sons away from him.

Bird's Eye View of Green Bay 1908 (Postcard)

THE GREEN BAY GAZETTE'S February 27, 1908, society column reported that Mr. and Mrs. Frederick G. Hall, of the Beaumont Hotel, had left on the Chicago & Northwestern railroad for a three-week trip to Hot Springs. Mollie and J.R. boarded the train one week later to join the couple. Even though J.R. had claimed illicit relations existed between Mollie and Frederick, Mollie believed J.R. had put those unfounded accusations behind him, otherwise he would never have agreed to the trip.

The Minahans made an overnight stop in Chicago and checked into the Sherman House known for its "first-class customer service, top-flight evening entertainment, and famed College Inn restaurant."

The next morning, Mollie told J.R. she would meet him at the train depot after she shopped on State Street. A few hours later, Mollie stepped into the Grand Central Station marble-floored waiting room and located J.R. He stood next to a Corinthian column looking like a Roman warrior ready for battle, the light from the stained-glass windows turning his starched white collar green. He bent over and sniffed Mollie's breath. J.R. accused her of meeting another man and becoming intoxicated. His cheeks turned the color of boiled beets as his accusations rang loudly.

The shocked gazes of two women travelers landed on Mollie. Mortified, she defended herself and told J.R. she had only purchased clothing for the boys at Marshall Fields. Mollie held out a shopping bag as proof.

J.R. shoved it away and said she was lying. He claimed to have overheard Mollie on the phone back in Green Bay making an appointment to meet some party in Chicago. He alleged she had said the two had better go down on separate trains to avert suspicion; that Mollie would stay at the Sherman House while the other party should stay at the Palmer House.

"I specifically deny," Mollie later testified, "that in March 1908, or at any other time or place, I ever became intoxicated, or that I was ever, in any degree, under the influence of liquor. [Or that] J.R. ever heard me telephoning to some party making an appointment to meet [that] party in Chicago."

She told J.R. the same inside the train station. Yet as they boarded a Pullman Observation car, Mollie knew her words had been futile, having had no effect on her husband. She dreaded the trip ahead, which she had so looked forward to after her miscarriage. Mollie now feared, in addition to J.R.'s most recent accusations, those former ones about Frederick Hall would resurface, ruining the vacation not only for Mollie but for her friends.

A porter escorted the Minahans to their seats. Mollie sat down beside her self-righteous husband on the plush swivel chairs. She knew she had to escape her abusive marriage, but how?

DR. ROBERT E. MINAHAN decided not to run for a third mayoral term. The candidate R.E. backed was Winford Abrams, the city council president. The two men spoke at a campaign rally at Heynen's Music Hall. Abrams presented his platform while the mayor defended the Minahan Building Company franchise, which had become a heated issue. *The Green Bay Gazette* had finally published the entire franchise ordinance that had passed ten months earlier. Due to a heavy loss of business center subscribers, Wisconsin Public Service, the current light and heat provider, would need to levy higher rates in the outlying city sections. In response to the price increase, many Green Bay residents had lined up against the franchise, and J.R. was worried. So was his sister, Daisy. She had stepped away from her teaching job to become the Minahan Building office manager.

Daisy's first duties were to lease the office and retail space. Behind the 160 feet of sidewalk prism windows, she secured Mae's Haberdasher, which offered custom and ready-to-wear men's clothing, and Kathryn O'Malley's Beauty Parlor, where "hairdressing and removing moles, warts, and superfluous hair" were her specialties. Additional first-floor tenants included a drugstore, a buffet, and the weather bureau, which would utilize the Minahan Building's six-floor roof height for sending flag and light warnings to water vessels.

Minahan Building with J.R.'s office on sixth floor (Postcard)

On April 10, Dr. Robert E. Minahan's candidate, Winford Abrams, became Green Bay's twenty-fifth mayor. Seven days later, Mollie's sixty-three-year-old papa died at his home of heart failure. Mollie felt the loss heavily. He had always been a loving and considerate father and a wonderful grandfather to her boys.

Mollie and her siblings all gathered in the law office of Attorney William Lincoln Evans, the new husband to Mollie's sister, Annie. Evans read Mr. John F. Bertles will out loud. He had evenly divided his property between his six children. Once probate settled their father's debts, Evans said each sibling would inherit about $13,000 (around $421,000 in current valuation).

That incredible news startled Mollie. It was wholly unexpected. Her papa had equally split his inheritance rather than providing a greater portion to his sons, which was often the case. That large sum would be more than enough for Mollie to finally secure both her freedom and that of her boys from J.R.

But Mollie's hopeful plans were soon clouded with worry. Wisconsin Public Service brought an action against the Minahan Building Company to stop furnishing power and light to the downtown commercial district.

The complaint charged that Dr. Robert E. Minahan, Green Bay's former mayor, had been a stockholder when the city council had granted the franchise, and he had influenced the decision. The rollout of the Minahan Building Company power and light franchise halted.

In addition to that disastrous news, the number of surgeries J.R. had conducted that year had not met his projected milestones. Another city surgeon was the reason.

Dr. Julius Bellin, born into a Belgian immigrant farming family,

had graduated from Iowa State with degrees in medicine and dentistry. When he arrived in Green Bay in 1904, the Minahan brothers excluded him from St. Vincent Hospital's surgery facilities. But Bellin found a way around that. In addition to Green Bay's two Catholic hospitals, St. Vincent and St. Mary's, Alex Hume and his two sisters Mildred and Ellen had opened the fifteen-bed non-sectarian General Hospital in 1899. Dr. Fred Brett, one of the physicians who

Dr. Julius Bellin
(Courtesy of Bellin Health)

had sided with Mary Cenefelt during the Cenefelt vs. Minahan trials, purchased that hospital in 1902 from the Hume family. Five years later, Dr. Bellin purchased it from Dr. Brett and the competition between Bellin and J.R. commenced.

Dr. Bellin had outgrown the General Hospital on Adams Street and had recently purchased the D.W. Britton home on the corner of Webster and Lawe to expand. The physician was renovating it into the thirty-bed Deaconess Sanitarium and Training School for Nurses (the initial foothold for the current Bellin Hospital within the Bellin Health System). And the two surgeons' rivalry would

General Hospital
(A Souvenir of Green Bay 1903)

not end there. Dr. Bellin would soon construct a seven-story office building caddy-corner to J.R.'s six-story Minahan Building. The Bellin-Buchanan Building would be the tallest and most modern in Green Bay, supplanting the Minahan Building's title.

Mollie's home atmosphere was at its worst, doors slamming, constant shouting, and J.R.'s grievances spoken in front of their sons. J.R. owned 137 shares of the Minahan Building stock worth $137,000 (about $4.4 million in current valuation), but the bank would not pay dividends until the office building had active tenants. Plus, the building had cost more than planned, and the stockholders had secured approximately $35,000 in loans. If the Minahan Building Company lost the franchise litigation, J.R. claimed the bank would reduce his stock value to "twenty-five cents on the dollar."

J.R.'s words chilled Mollie's blood.

If his conjecture came to pass, she feared his sights would target her inheritance. If J.R. were willing to take her sons without telling her where they were going, he would not bat an eye at taking her money— Mollie's escape route out of her marriage.

True Intentions

FIVE MONTHS HAD PASSED since the franchise litigation had begun with little progress on either side, and Mollie was still anxiously awaiting her inheritance, tied up in probate. It was February 9, 1909, and Mollie ate breakfast at the dining room table, listening to her sons' banter as scents of coffee, waffles, and buttery syrup filled the room. Snow fell outside, obstructing the view from the windows, as J.R. departed for St. Vincent Hospital without saying goodbye.

The front bell rang. Moments later, Julia entered the dining room in her standard gray dress and white pinafore. She told Mollie that J.R.'s brother, Attorney V.I. Minahan, was at the door and wished to speak to Mollie.

Surprised at his early morning interruption, she stepped into the cold foyer with a questioning tilt to her head. Powdery snow covered the shoulders of her brother-in-law's wool coat and the small brim of his black derby. V.I. frowned below his pencil-thin mustache. He said he had a message from J.R.: "If I did not submit to an immediate separation, on the grounds of cruelty, J.R. would bring an action for divorce, charging me with adultery ... He would ruin my reputation and that of ... my family."

Mollie was stunned.

Her speculation had been wrong.

J.R. did not want her inheritance. He wanted more.

This was his ultimate threat, to try to coerce her into filing for a separation or divorce. That action would be financially advantageous for J.R. at this moment. As the injured spouse, he could claim his funds were at their lowest ebb because of the franchise litigation, while Mollie would soon receive her papa's inheritance. Therefore, J.R. would argue that he should not be required to provide Mollie any alimony, especially since she had initiated the action.

In a moment, she saw through his scheme.

Mollie told V.I. to tell his brother he could not bully her. She knew J.R.'s adultery claims were unfounded. They did not scare Mollie. After fending off her husband's lies for a decade, she was prepared to fight back.

"For the sake of our children, ... though I was suffering greatly in health, mind, and body from ... J.R.'s cruel and wanton treatment and neglect, I refused to be driven into bringing an action for divorce." Yet Mollie now understood J.R.'s true intentions. He wanted out of their marriage, as did she. However, to receive what was rightfully hers, Mollie needed to be patient, to wait until her husband initiated his own divorce action.

That night, J.R. returned home as if his threat had never occurred.

Mollie erected a permanent glass wall between them—a wall that would protect her—but where she could watch his every move.

MOLLIE'S SONS, Robert in first grade and John in third, both attended a full day of classes at Howe School. That allowed her to reengage in social activities. She entertained the Euchre club, participated in a Ridge Point women's outing, and attended the monthly Women's Club meeting where a member presented the Women's Suffrage Petition. Before submitting it to the Wisconsin state legislators, prominent Green Bay women affixed their names to it. Mollie added her own, fortified by the suffrage movement and its "New Woman" tenants. The petition took her back to her roots and gave her the strength to face the fight ahead.

That was until September when J.R. took away Mollie's allowance. Her inheritance was still in probate, so she had no funds at her disposal. J.R. also barred Mollie from using credit at any retail stores, even for their children's food and hers. In essence, he enslaved her. He was forcing her to either live under his tyranny for her survival and the boys' or destroy her future, just to get away from him.

At that point, all of Mollie's social activities ceased.

ON OCTOBER 25, 1909, jack-o'-lanterns flickered on neighborhood porches when J.R. finally served Mollie his official divorce complaint charging her with "cruel and inhuman treatment."

The unmitigated evil of divorce, the confession of their collective failure, had arrived at Mollie's door. She could not climb that slippery hill alone. Mollie and her sister, Annie, huddled inside the Evans' front room, J.R.'s divorce complaint in Mollie's hand. Annie was one of the few who knew how Mollie had suffered. Both agreed it was a blessing that J.R. had not charged Mollie with adultery.

In J.R.'s complaint, he cited examples of Mollie's inhuman behaviors toward him. How she complained about his work hours, late arrival to dinner, and that his work interfered with her "society duties." How she had "falsely and wickedly" told his brother Robert slanderous and untruthful things about J.R. He claimed Mollie had always neglected their home. After J.R. had remonstrated her for its conduct and care, he alleged she had retorted, "I don't give a god damn for the home. I have consulted Lawyer Greene, and he says, if you don't catch me in adultery, I can have the children, and you'll have to give us all the money we want, and the home can go to hell!"

Mollie knew J.R.'s prime purpose in life was to be recognized as one of Green Bay's wealthiest and successful men. If the court awarded her a significant settlement, that action would wound her husband more than anything else. But for that scenario to happen, J.R.'s further accusations could not sway the Court. He alleged that during their children's infancy, Mollie "evinced an aversion toward them, claiming they annoyed and bothered her;" that she "persistently deserted them for selfish purposes," such as attending parties, where she became intoxicated. But J.R.'s final statement hit Mollie the hardest. He alleged she was an "unfit and improper mother," and he prayed that the Court would dissolve his bonds of matrimony and give him custody of their children.

A neighborhood dog barked. The mail dropped through the chute onto the Evans' foyer floor. Life was going on around Mollie, but she knew her world could be about to end.

Mollie could not lose her boys.

Grace Warren, John Minahan (8), unknown, and Robert Minahan (6) (Roger Minahan Papers)

Annie apprised her husband of Mollie's situation, and Evans recommended that his sister-in-law contact Attorney Patrick H. Martin. Evans knew there had been a falling out between Martin and J.R. No records provide the reason. But the last reported connection between the two men was in a *Green Bay Gazette* article on December 23, 1901 titled "A Verdict Returned for the Defendant." That was when Mr. P.H. Martin had successfully represented Dr. J.R. Minahan in the third and final Cenefelt vs. Minahan trial.

THE MINAHAN BUILDING now housed Attorney Martin's law office. He agreed to meet Mollie at his Madison Street home to protect her from running into J.R. Inside Martin's wood-paneled library, a fire burned and crackled. Mollie handed him J.R.'s divorce complaint, and she watched him read it.

Martin's thin lips tightened as he raised his curly head. When he said he would be honored to represent her, hope surged through Mollie. She had not only engaged an attorney who knew J.R. better than any other in Green Bay, with the exception of his attorney brothers, but she had secured another confidant, an ally she desperately needed.

As the sounds of a passing train filtered into the room, Mollie told Martin all about her loveless relationship with J.R. She argued that his constant abuse had to be harming her sons' developing minds. Rather than simply responding to J.R.'s divorce action, Mollie wanted to join it, claiming "cruel and inhuman treatment" as well. She believed she had more ammunition than J.R. to win the battle. Though, as of yet, Mollie told Martin she was not ready to disclose all of her marriage's humiliating details to him and the Court. She first planned to leverage that information with J.R., to attempt to negotiate the boys' custody prior to their trial date.

Two weeks later, Brown County Circuit Court added the Minahans' divorce trial to its May 1910 calendar. That would give Attorney Martin about six months to prepare. He subpoenaed J.R. to attend a pretrial deposition where Martin would only ask him financial questions. Both Mollie and her attorney believed J.R. was "concealing and covering up his property and interests" to reduce her alimony or separate maintenance financial awards. In Court Commissioner Davis's fifth-floor Minahan Building office, the week before Thanksgiving of 1909, light poured in from the windows facing Washington Street. J.R. and his attorney brother, V.I., stood beside Commissioner Davis as he swore J.R. in. Then the three men and Attorney Martin took seats around a rectangular table. The radiator clicked as heated water moved through the pipes.

Martin eyed his former friend. "Doctor, we want to get at your worth."

"You can get at that pretty quick," J.R. quipped back as the commissioner's shorthand noted his words.

"What amount of property or money were you worth at the time you married Mollie?"

"About ninety thousand dollars." ($2.9 million in current valuation.) J.R. said that consisted of real estate, mortgages, and horses. But because of Mollie's "wasteful spending," that figure had dropped by nearly 25 percent.

J.R. said his Quincy Street home, situated on four lots, was valued at about $8000. "I sold the rest of my real estate property to provide capital for the Minahan Building project." J.R. agreed that his office building would be worth what it cost once tenants fully occupied the six floors and when the electric light and heat plant operated to maximum capacity. In addition, the building and franchise would provide an annual 6 percent return on investment. However, J.R. added, there was a good chance he could lose nearly everything due to the unresolved franchise litigation.

For six months, J.R. had repeated that mantra—that he would face financial ruin—ingraining that possibility into the minds of those in the city, including the judges who might preside at the Minahans' divorce trial. J.R. said he also owed about $55,000 between his bank and individual loans.

When Martin asked J.R. about his surgical and medical yearly earnings, he said, "Since my brother joined my practice in 1898, we have equally split our total annual professional income." As close as J.R. could figure it, his prior year's earnings were about $8,000. Kellogg National Bank was his primary institution, but he and Robert had also opened a Bank of Green Bay joint account within the last two years. "We thought it would be handy to have that banked by Doctors Minahan."

Martin had been making notes and frowned. "Haven't you repeatedly stated your annual professional income was twenty-five thousand dollars?"

"I certainly have not! That would be too foolish. All the doctors in town are not making that much. Out of five burials, in the last three or four years, four of them were buried through charity."

"That is right. You and Robert were making all [the money]."

"If they worked as hard as I did, they would make some too."

Attorney Martin leveled his eyes on J.R. "I am still surprised at your annual professional income."

"Well, on the street, it would feel laughable, knowing the man. I heard folks say a while ago that you, Mr. Martin, took in seventy-five thousand dollars a year."

"Me?"

"Yes, and that is in comparison."

"I do, but I don't keep it."

"I would keep it if I could get it." According to J.R., he and his brother only collected about 30 to 40 percent of the amount they billed for medical services.

"Isn't it generally recognized that surgery is the height of ambition for most practitioners because it is more lucrative?" Martin cocked his head.

"Maybe, with some. I done an operation this morning ... We took out his stomach and practically gave him a new one ... I should have got three hundred dollars for it, and what do you suppose I got?" Minahan crossed his arms over his chest.

"I don't know."

"Thirty-five dollars and it will cost me every dollar of it before he leaves the hospital."

"But you expect to get more of it?"

"I don't expect to get more out of him ... but I could not turn him down."

"That is not the rule?"

"That is the rule ... We get it if we can. We wouldn't get one dollar from this man if we didn't pound at him and tell him his friends would have to come to his help."

"But you still do more lucrative work?"

"We do if we can get the fellow who has the lucrative funds. But our expenses have increased enormously." J.R. said his combined office rent and salaries for a pathologist, stomach content expert, and surgical nurse totaled $3,700 a year. Then there were surgical instruments, catgut, and ligatures. The Minahan brothers had also put $4,000 into their operating room.

"Was that a gift to the hospital?"

"It was a gift to ourselves. We wanted certain things the hospital could not afford, and we bought them. We are the only ones who can operate in that room."

The deposition had not achieved Martin's goal: to uncover Minahan's total assets and property interests, particularly his annual salary.

Martin assured Mollie he would get a judge's order to subpoena J.R.'s bank records.

Even so, Mollie feared her husband would find a way to combat a court request, to hide the truth from the woman he hated, to do all he could to destroy Mollie's financial future.

Secret Treatments

J.R. PERSISTED in living in the house during the Minahans' divorce proceedings, ridiculing Mollie at every turn. He would laugh when her stiff fingers dropped a coffee cup, rebuke her when he noticed a dust ball behind his library's leather chair, and make fun of her when she recited a poetry piece to the boys. In addition to the hallway phone, J.R. had installed a second one in his office. Whenever Mollie made a call, if she heard a slight click, she would know J.R. was eavesdropping. His presence was "a constant source of worry" to Mollie, impairing her health. She told her sister, Kitten, she feared J.R. might make additional false accusations against her at their divorce trial.

J.R. was also suspicious of Mollie. He later testified that at Mollie's request, Mr. Fredric Hall had played "Tom the Peeper." Hall had gone up to the Minahan Building's sixth floor and raised the letter slide to peer into J.R.'s private office. After a "wild chase," J.R. had caught Hall, who confessed he was "attempting to get evidence against J.R."

Mollie did not deny that allegation. To combat her husband from doing the same, Kitten agreed to move into the Minahan residence in December of 1909. After her engagement announcement to Willard Fish Harris, a Colorado School of Mines graduate, Kitten had moved back to Green Bay from Ironwood, Michigan. She promised Mollie she would remain in the Minahan home until Mollie's divorce trial was concluded in late May. Kitten felt it was her duty even though, while awaiting her June wedding, she would have preferred to live with her sister, Annie.

Mollie attempted to make the 1909 Christmas season joyful for seven-year-old John and five-year-old Robert. Their dark eyes gleamed as they helped Kitten and Mollie decorate a freshly cut evergreen with pinecones, crocheted ornaments, and popcorn strings. Then on Christmas morning, the two boys raced downstairs to find beautifully wrapped presents under the boughs.

A month later, after Mollie tucked her boys into bed and kissed their foreheads, she descended the stairs and passed the library. Its door was closed and J.R. was inside. Wind thumped the windows as Mollie sat down across from her sister on an upholstered armchair by the front room's hearth.

Kitten looked up from her stitchery and told Mollie she could see why the boys were "attached to Mollie." She was a "devoted and considerate mother," and her sons were "dutiful and obedient" unless J.R. provoked them.

He had recently told the boys, "You won't go in your mother's old launch next summer. You will go with Pap in his nice Thomas Flyer." J.R. had just ordered a five-passenger Thomas Flyer automobile from the Lucia Bros. Motor Car company on Adams Street. Mollie knew that J.R. was using that new vehicle to entice the boys into spending more time with him instead of her after their divorce. Mollie's old launch was a rowboat that J.R. had bought some time before and determined to sell, to deprive Mollie of the pleasure of using it with her sons. To retain the boat, J.R. had made Mollie buy it from him.

She had watched the boys' response to J.R.'s news about his fancy new car. Of course, they were excited, but young John's guilty eyes had also landed back on Mollie, realizing he had hurt her feelings. She knew that no parents should place their children in such a position.

Kitten glanced toward her brother-in-law's library to verify the door was still closed. Until the divorce action, Kitten said, J.R. had seemed to pay "little or no attention" to the boys. But ever since, she had noticed how "conspicuously attentive" he had been to them whenever the public could observe his conduct. She believed J.R.'s recent affection was only a pretense to influence the court. Kitten believed J.R. had never loved the boys or anyone else since he was incapable of developing emotional attachments.

Mollie sadly agreed.

The library door creaked open. J.R. walked past the front room and scowled at the two sisters.

Kitten raised her head in defiance. She told Mollie she knew what Annie had gone through with J.R. and his vile accusations. Kitten would give him no reason to sully her name. But Kitten admitted it gave her pleasure to know her presence in the home was offensive to J.R.

MOLLIE HAD SUFFERED for two years from painful hemorrhoids and uterine lacerations caused by her third miscarriage. The latter had created hematomas, which had become life-threatening. Operations to deal with both problems were deemed necessary by her Oshkosh physician, Dr. C.W. Oviatt. Mollie made out her last will and testament, separate from J.R.'s. In the event of her death, she wanted to make certain her sons would be the primary benefactors of her inheritance.

Mollie left her children in Kitten's care and took the train down to Oshkosh. At St. Mary's Hospital, Mollie talked to the Sister behind the admission desk. "I was much humiliated to learn that J.R. had written to the doctor and Sisters in charge, stating ... he was no longer paying [my] expenses."

Mollie still went ahead with her hemorrhoid and uterus surgeries, planning to use her eventual inheritance to pay the bills. But Mollie shortened her hospital convalescing stay due to her financial condition.

Dr. Oviatt insisted that once Mollie arrived back in Green Bay she would need absolute rest, nourishing food, and freedom from aggravating and trying conditions. "Any harsh treatment or conduct," the doctor told Mollie, "likely to cause her [to] worry, would retard her recovery."

When Mollie arrived back in Green Bay, J.R. demanded that Kitten leave their home. But, per Mollie's request, her sister refused. That night, Kitten brought Mollie dinner in bed and told her she did not want to worry Mollie, but she had to relay what had occurred while Mollie was away. She said she had been humiliated to discover that J.R. had barred grocers and butchers from utilizing J.R.'s credit to sell Kitten the necessities for Mollie's home and children. To feed the boys, Kitten said she had bought items at her own expense.

Kitten's distressing report upset Mollie, but there was nothing she could do. She knew that J.R. controlled their money, and merchants could not afford to lose his business by not following his wishes.

While Mollie slowly recovered from her surgeries, she "occasioned much distress of mind," owing to her great strain and worry. Her condition was called "melancholia," a sweet-sounding word for depression. Mollie's meager appetite waned further. Her hands constantly quivered. She could not sleep at night. She had tried to negotiate with J.R., to settle their children's custody before trial. Those negotiations had failed. Even though Wisconsin's "Tender Years Doctrine" presumed a mother was usually the best parent to care for a couple's young children, Mollie knew there were caveats. If the court deemed the mother was mentally or morally unfit, the court could award the children's custody to the father.

The Brown County Medical Society met in Dr. A.W. Slaughter's office on January 20, 1910, where members elected Dr. John R. Minahan to "the office of censor." In that capacity, he would examine any material about to be released by society members, such as books, journals, or medical articles. Minahan would suppress anything he considered to be politically unacceptable or obscene.

J.R. wielded that same power inside his home. Eight-year-old John reported to Mollie that Pap had told John his mother was a "bad woman." That she was "breaking up their home." In tears, John said Pap had compared Mollie to a well-known woman who Mollie knew had committed adultery. Pap had told John that the woman was "bad," and her little boy chose to go with his papa, "and the court followed the little boy's wishes."

Mollie hugged her son, consoling him. She refused to fall as low as J.R. She knew he was deliberately upsetting the children and using them to hurt her. But she would not join in.

Yet Mollie wondered whether that decision was a mistake as she walked to her attorney's home. A maid escorted Mollie into Mr. Martin's library. Once Mollie settled onto a chair, she expressed her fear of losing her sons unless she shared the humiliating truth about her marriage with Martin and the Court. Before J.R. decided to amend his "cruel and inhuman treatment" divorce petition to add adultery or her mental health issues, Mollie wanted to amend hers. With a constricted voice mixed with tears, she told Martin about her appalling decade of marital abuse, leaving nothing out—not even J.R.'s claims that she had syphilis.

When Mollie finished, she could not look at Attorney Martin.

In an empathetic voice, Martin told her he'd had no idea what she had been through, and Mollie lifted her head.

Martin agreed that J.R. was wholly unfit to care and provide for their children's welfare. He said he would amend Mollie's divorce petition to include her new revelations and submit it to the court. In the meantime, Martin suggested they make four pretrial requests to the Brown County Circuit Court: first, to secure a restraining order to keep J.R. out of the house; second, to provide Mollie exclusive custody of their children; third, to require J.R. to pay her temporary alimony and Martin's fees; and fourth, to restrain J.R. from hiding the total value of his assets.

Martin's earlier subpoena had requested that J.R. provide access to *all* his bank accounts and bank books. As Mollie had expected, her husband had dodged that request by only producing a transaction list from Kellogg National Bank and a cash book.

BEFORE JUDGE E.B. BELDEⁿ, on April 4, 1910, Attorney P.H. Martin made arguments for Mollie's pretrial requests while Attorney V.I. Minahan argued against them. To take Mollie's mind off the courtroom proceedings, she attended a Women's Club meeting inside the Kellogg Library where the members discussed the city's "no-license" saloon campaign. If the drinking establishment did not follow the law to close on Sundays, exclude minors and women, and refuse to sell to habitual drunkards, the club agreed the city should revoke the saloon owner's license.

After the Women's Club members signed the petition, Mollie returned home, and her telephone rang. She grabbed the receiver and heard Attorney Martin's voice. He said the judge had granted Mollie's four pretrial requests.

That amazing news was too much for Mollie to absorb.

Martin said that J.R. had been at the courthouse and he had been livid. He had intended to kick Mollie out of the house. Now, while awaiting their divorce proceedings, the reverse was happening. Although J.R. had to follow the court order, Martin cautioned Mollie not to celebrate just yet. Her husband planned to appeal the judge's decision.

Mollie's home atmosphere immediately changed without J.R.'s daunting presence in the house. There was laughter, music, and easy conversation. He could no longer "intrude himself into the living room" and talk to the children, saying things calculated to insult her. He could no longer interfere with her boys' discipline, which had been markedly more difficult since the divorce action began. From the comments J.R. had made to their sons, she knew he had been "persistently working to alienate the children's love for her, to destroy their respect for her ... and her authority over them." To incite hatred for her sisters, whom J.R. frequently spoke falsely about to poison the boys' minds with contempt and disrespect.

Mollie's peace, however, was short-lived. Two days after her husband's departure from their Quincy Street home, his attorney brother filed J.R.'s appeal to reverse the judge's decision on Mollie's pretrial requests. Once again, Mollie and Attorney Martin met. He sat across from her at the Minahans' dining room table now that J.R. had moved out.

Mollie shook her head when Martin said that J.R. denied his conduct and treatment of Mollie could be a constant source of suffering to her. He claimed a change of address would seriously injure his business because he had a known phone number. Since Mollie's father's death, her family's Monroe Avenue home had been vacant. There was no reason, J.R. argued, why Mollie could not move there. He also alleged her recent hospital surgeries were "totally unnecessary." That she had gone to St. Mary's "solely to excite the court's pity and sympathy."

J.R. claimed that Mollie could pay her litigation expenses and support. Even though her father's inheritance was still in probate, J.R. said the bank had provided Mollie credit until the court released her money. Conversely, J.R. claimed he had no means to pay Mollie's temporary alimony or attorney fees "to satisfy her extravagant and greedy notions," since his combined Minahan Building loan and life insurance premium payments exceeded $14,000 annually.

Martin looked up from the document. That figure was far more than the $8,000 medical practice earnings J.R. claimed he had made the prior year. Even including the income from the Minahan Building, Martin told Mollie that information made J.R.'s earnings look suspect, and she agreed.

When J.R. alleged it would be bad for the children if she gained temporary custody, since she had never cared for the boys or had any control over them because she gave society engagements more attention, Mollie's hackles rose. Even more so when J.R. claimed he had "perfect control" whenever he took care of their sons.

It was no surprise that J.R. was fighting back, but his vicious allegations still stung Mollie.

She and Martin came up with a plan. Martin would secure affidavits from Mollie's Oshkosh physician, housekeeper, and sister, Kitten.

The morning after the Minahans' housekeeper provided her affidavit, Mollie apologized to Julia for putting her in the middle of the divorce action. Julia said after being with the family for seven years, she had figured it might come to this. Julia told Mollie not to worry. Her affidavit stated that Mollie had "practically been the boys' sole caregiver, and they were very much attached to her." And it was "wholly untrue" that Mollie had ever neglected them or her home due to society engagements. In fact, Julia said, Mollie had been so preoccupied with the care of her children, home, and health that she could give little time to anything else.

Two days later, to Mollie's great relief, the judge denied J.R.'s appeal. During the Minahans' pending divorce action, Mollie would continue to be awarded the sole use of their home and the custody of their children, while J.R. would be ordered to pay Mollie temporary alimony and her attorney fees. In addition, he was to provide the proper records to disclose his total financial worth.

Mollie had beaten J.R. in the first round, but she could not relax. She watched as he removed his personal items from their home, a dangerous glint in his eyes. He tromped off the porch, climbed into his automobile, and sped away. Mollie settled onto the front porch swing, the tightness in her chest dissipating.

Her attorney had recently asked Mollie, if the judge awarded her a divorce, whether she would like to request the Minahans' Quincy Street home as part of her settlement. "Mr. Martin suggested that I might ... reconstruct the home into a flat for rental purposes ... I expressed [my] belief that there was no money in that, and I did not feel that I would care to undertake the burden." Mr. Martin had offered Mollie an alternative. He told her he planned to build rental houses on lots adjacent to his home and one of those might interest her. "I proposed to Mr. Martin that should he conclude to build a house, one suitable to my means and needs, I would be glad to take a lease ... and would probably occupy it continually."

Mollie stepped inside the house that she and J.R. had shared since their honeymoon. In every room, Mollie could picture painful memories. She would be glad to leave those raw moments behind when she started a new life, in a new home, with her sons.

That scenario had to happen.

J.R. AND HIS ATTORNEY brother finally replied to Mollie's marital abuse counterclaim allegations on April 7, 1910, one month before the trial date. Martin walked the four blocks to Mollie's home to discuss the document, and the two sat down at the dining room table. He said J.R. had denied nearly all of Mollie's marital abuse accusations, then twisted them into contrived comebacks to make him look like the hero. But there was one particular paragraph Mollie needed to hear, although it would be difficult.

Attorney Martin looked down and read: J.R. was "firmly convinced" Mollie had contracted syphilis before their marriage, and she still had that disease.

Even though Mollie was appalled at the idea of talking about J.R.'s syphilis accusations in court, she had expected her husband's words. But she had not expected those that Martin read next—although she should have.

J.R. said, because of Mollie's syphilis, he had treated his sons to relieve them of "any taint that may be in their blood ... which they may have contracted from their mother."

Mollie recoiled in horror.

How foolish she had been. Ever since her Mount Clemens six-week stay, J.R. had lulled her into trusting he no longer believed their boys had inherited syphilis from her. J.R. had tricked her. Apparently, over those five years, his syphilis obsession had only grown stronger. So much so that he claimed to have secretly treated their boys for syphilis—a disease they most certainly did not suffer from—with dangerous and damaging drugs.

Mr. Martin said the document gave no details.

Mollie could only imagine the worst.

Games and Stipulations

WORRY CONSUMED MOLLIE. She would watch her six- and eight-year-old sons leave for school in their short trousers, jackets, knee-socks, and leather shoes. Mollie could see nothing in their eyes, their skin, their gait, their demeanor which would indicate that J.R.'s claim about treating them for syphilis was true. Since the boys' births, neither John nor Robert had required medical attention "except on two or three occasions of a very trivial nature." Her boys slept and ate well. Both of them loved to play in the fresh air.

J.R. had filled his divorce counterclaim with lies. Mollie prayed his statement about utilizing syphilis drugs on the boys was false too. Yet her thoughts reeled back to when she had left them in J.R.'s care: the month and a half she had been at Mount Clemens; the three days J.R. had disappeared with John and Robert; and the week Mollie had spent at Red Banks with her women friends. J.R. could easily have treated the boys at any or all of those times. As a physician, Mollie knew her husband could walk into a pharmacy, talk to a chemist over the marble-topped counter, and purchase a mercury syphilis treatment whenever he chose. J.R. had perhaps told John and Robert the medicine was an iron tonic that would make their bodies strong. Mollie had heard stories about "chocolate drinks laced with mercury" that infected husbands used to treat their wives and children without their knowledge.

Mollie knew that many physicians questioned the effectiveness of mercury treatments due to the "profound side effects" such as oral ulcers, excessive salivation, tooth loss, nerve damage, and kidney failure. Those thoughts made her breath quicken, especially knowing that some patients even died from "mercury toxicity during or shortly after treatment."

Mollie did not want to scare John and Robert by interrogating them. It was not as if she had to prove that J.R. had treated them. He had already admitted he had. As a medical student, J.R. had taken the Hippocratic Oath. One of its promises was: "First, do no harm."

If he had indeed treated their sons with dangerous syphilis drugs, J.R. had broken his oath.

Mollie had to gain custody of the boys now more than ever.

No other outcome was acceptable.

TWO WEEKS BEFORE the Minahans' divorce trial, Mollie's attorney received a call from J.R.'s attorney brother. He said his client had requested a meeting between both parties.

On a dreary gray day, Mollie and Martin sat across from her husband and V.I. Minahan inside J.R.'s sixth-floor, wood-paneled office in the Minahan Building. J.R. had tastefully furnished it with comfortable armchairs and a sofa. His massive walnut desk was

Washington Street with Minahan Building (Postcard)

to Mollie's left as if waiting for the king to take his seat. It was the domain of a successful man. A wealthy man.

It was a location probably chosen to intimidate Mollie.

Her eyes would not meet J.R.'s. Mollie gazed at his brother instead. V.I. announced his client, with certain conditions, was prepared to withdraw his divorce complaint and counterclaim reply.

Mollie was stunned. Yet she knew J.R.'s community appearance was of the utmost importance to him. He likely feared that when his dirty laundry was paraded in the courtroom, as it had been in the Cenefelt vs. Minahan trials, the community might ridicule and reject him. Back then, J.R. had been a young surgeon, making his mark. Now he was a great surgeon and an astute businessman. He could not afford the negative publicity that would reveal his imperfections—of being "found out."

Mollie continued to focus on her brother-in-law as he explained the conditions. First, if the Court believed Mollie was entitled to an action at the upcoming trial, V.I. said she had to request an absolute divorce, not a separation.

Mollie clasped her hands together under the table. She wanted that too.

Second, if the Court granted a divorce at trial, J.R. would agree to award Mollie the care, custody, and education of their two children—a marvelous surprise—but only if she accepted four stipulations.

Mollie shared a wide-eyed glance with Attorney Martin. Neither she nor he believed J.R. would provide Mollie custody without a courtroom battle. Yet she knew any financial settlement she might receive from J.R. would still be fought in front of a trial judge.

Attorney Minahan slid a paper across the table toward Mollie and Martin. First, V.I. said, his brother J.R. would be awarded visitation rights during the school year, and he could take the boys on summer vacations, not to exceed four weeks in any one year. Second, the children would be baptized into the Roman Catholic faith and fully educated in its tenets, practices, discipline, and observances. Third, the children would complete their education in the Green Bay schools.

For Mollie, those stipulations seemed too good to be true.

But then V.I. read the fourth one. He said J.R. would have the sole right to care for their children's medical needs.

At those disturbing words, Mollie's gaze finally met her husband's. He had enticed her with a bushel of apples before dropping in the onion. The fourth stipulation would allow J.R. to conduct syphilis treatments on the boys without her approval.

Attorney Minahan said he and his client would step out of the room so Mollie and Martin could discuss the proposal.

Once the door closed, Mollie told Martin she was afraid to accept the conditions unless J.R. removed the last one about the children's medical care.

Martin believed Mollie might be reading too much into J.R.'s last stipulation. Dr. Robert was her children's primary care physician within the Doctors Minahan partnership. That should not change. Martin said he would talk to Attorney Minahan privately to see what he had to say.

While Martin stepped out, Mollie mulled over her situation. Prior to trial, her husband still had time to amend his counterclaim and accuse her of suffering from melancholia *and* allege she was an adulteress. There were no guarantees Mollie would win the children's custody. Could she risk that possibility by not agreeing to J.R.'s fourth condition?

Martin entered the room. According to Attorney Minahan, Martin said the medical treatment stipulation was a mere concession. If granted,

J.R. would settle the children's custody without controversy. Mollie was to sign the document if she agreed.

Mollie stood and stepped over to the windows. Down on Washington Street, among the pedestrian traffic, she saw a young mother in a wide-brimmed hat holding her children's hands, not letting them go, protecting them from harm—no matter what obstacles came their way.

Mollie returned to the table.

She made a choice.

She took a risk.

Mollie picked up a pen and signed.

Kitten Bertles wedding. Mollie's hand is on her son Robert's shoulder. Little Grace Warren is beside him, and Mollie's son John is to Grace's right. Annie Bertles Evans is to John's right with her hand around his waist. (Roger Minahan Papers)

SURROUNDED BY THE SCENT of magnolia and rose bushes, Mollie sat next to her friends, Mayme and Edgar Warren, at Kitten's June 29, 1910 wedding in the backyard gardens of the Bertles Estate. Mollie's sister, Annie, and her husband Attorney William Lincoln Evans had recently moved into the home and the pair sat to Mollie's right. A decade had passed since Mollie had genuinely enjoyed herself without J.R.'s scrutiny, accusations, and abuse as she was doing that afternoon.

Six weeks earlier, the judge had granted Mollie an absolute divorce. J.R. had celebrated by attending an Elks Club billiard tournament where he had donated a Brunswick-Balke cup for the winner. Mollie had won a far larger prize: the custody of her sons. The judge would soon stipulate

Mollie's alimony and child support since a court order had forced J.R. to open the Doctors Minahan bank account to the judge's scrutiny.

Mollie beamed as her dark-haired sons dressed in white jackets and knee pants carried daisies down a ribboned aisle. John, eight, with a serious face, and Robert, six, with a devilish grin, drew smiles from guests, as did the little flower girl, Grace Warren, Mayme and Edgar's daughter.

An orchestra played the wedding march as Kitten came down the porch steps unattended in her white beaded dress and tulle veil. She had been Mollie's impermeable fence for nearly six months to keep J.R. at bay. Kitten reached the wedding arch and joined her groom, Willard Fish Harris of Racine, Wisconsin. Reverend Edwin A. Ralph from Union Congregational Church performed the service. A breeze stirred trees along the Fox River shoreline. For Mollie, the rustling leaves whispered relief.

During the wedding supper, she gazed at her supportive sisters who had buoyed Mollie up throughout her tumultuous marriage. In addition to celebrating Kitten's new marriage, the sisters quietly celebrated Mollie's release from the hell of hers.

MOLLIE AND THE BOYS watched the Gollmar Brothers Circus parade one month later on Saturday, July 29, 1910. The gamey scent of elephants, camels, dromedaries, and caged lions swirled in the dusty Washington Street air, and a calliope played popular tunes. The next day mother and sons entered St. John's Church for a solemn occasion. When J.R. had proposed the children be baptized as Catholics and raised in that faith, Mollie had freely assented. "Although I attended Union Congregational Church, I had never planned to have them baptized or raised in that faith." As in many situations, Mollie had shied away from anything that would bring on her husband's wrath.

Mollie believed J.R.'s stipulation about their sons' religious requirements had only been demanded for the court's benefit. "He never requested or suggested that the children be baptized, or that they be instructed in the precepts of any religion, whatsoever ... [He is] wholly without religious conviction."

Mollie had initially asked Attorney Martin and his wife, active Catholics, to be the boys' baptism sponsors. But J.R. talked to Father

St. John Catholic
Church (A Souvenir of
Green Bay 1903)

Ricklin and told him he objected since "Mr. Martin was not morally qualified to occupy the position." Mollie and Martin decided "the matter was not worth making trouble over." Instead, the Martins' children agreed to be the Minahan boys' sponsors: Marie, twenty-one, and John, twenty, who would eventually become Wisconsin's attorney general.

Mollie sat beside the elder Martins inside the twin-steepled St. John the Evangelist Church. The two Martin siblings stood on either side of John and Robert while Father Ricklin performed their baptism.

A week later, Mollie was thrilled when Judge Tarrant ruled that J.R. was to pay her a total of $25,000 for her divorce settlement, unpaid temporary alimony, trial preparation costs, and Attorney Martin's fees (about $785,000 in current valuation). Until the boys turned eighteen, their father was also ordered to provide Mollie monthly child support. J.R. would retain the Quincy Street home, and Mollie would receive all the household furniture and furnishings besides J.R.'s library contents, some bedroom furniture, and his mother's engraved silver tea and coffee service. But when J.R. was to provide Mollie her final settlement on October 25, 1910, one year after he had initiated their divorce action, J.R. refused to hand over his wealth. Since the Minahan Building Company franchise was still in litigation, he claimed he could not pay Mollie. In addition, J.R. had taken up his old, spurious claim that Mollie was unfit to have their children's custody.

That October night, rather than celebrating her independence from J.R., Mollie agonized over the unexpected turn of events. She and her attorney should have considered that J.R. would not submit to the Court's ruling so easily. Mollie had recently discovered that J.R. was furious that neither she nor Mr. Martin had notified J.R. about John and Robert's baptism. J.R. alleged that Mollie had known that Martin's eldest son was not morally qualified to stand as sponsor based on his "association with women of ill-repute." J.R. claimed John Martin's appointment as his sons' godfather "was a gross mistake and was made ... solely in furtherance of Mollie's wicked design to use the children and her custody of them as a means of harassing and tormenting him."

The Minahans' divorce decision was headed to the Wisconsin Supreme Court.

Compound "606"

A NEWSBOY TOSSED the February 6, 1911, *Green Bay Gazette* onto the front porch of the Minahans' Quincy Street home, and Mollie stepped out to retrieve it. The court order to restrain J.R. from living there was still in place while she and her sons awaited the Wisconsin Supreme Court's decision. Although nagged by that worry, Mollie focused on the present to maintain a healthy and hopeful attitude. But when she read one of the *Gazette's* articles, her positive demeanor evaporated. J.R. and his brother Dr. Robert would be conducting a clinic at St. Vincent Hospital the next day, and the program would include an address by J.R. titled: "Observations in the Use of '606.'"

Mollie did not know whether his earlier admission—that he had treated John and Robert for syphilis—was the truth. But ever since, she had kept herself apprised of any syphilis treatments their father could have conducted on the boys, including the new "606" compound.

Dr. Paul Ehrlich and Professor Sahachiro Hata (Library of Congress Prints & Photographs)

Working together, Berlin's Dr. Paul Ehrlich and Japan's Professor Sahachiro Hata had recently discovered that the sixth chemical in the sixth series of the dangerously toxic drug atoxyl often destroyed the syphilis bacteria. Ehrlich had coined the phrase, "magic bullet," to describe the "606" wonder drug which could actually cure syphilis. Previous mercury treatments for the disease were deemed ineffective and dangerous. But the new "606" compound could also produce side effects like rashes, liver damage, and "other risks to life and limb." In fact, many believed the new compound's side effects were worse than the syphilis disease itself.

In the ensuing years since J.R. had first accused Mollie of having syphilis, she had speculated whether he had contracted the disease prior to their marriage. If he had, she assumed for the past decade, he had been in a latent stage and had never been contagious, lucky for her. He would also have been treating himself with mercury to protect himself from syphilis's deadly third stage. While mercury would have helped to keep J.R.'s disease at bay, she knew that treatment did not provide a cure like the new "606" compound promised.

Mollie took a deep breath and picked up her knitting, an activity that helped relieve her stress and the stiffness in her fingers. Could the paper J.R. was presenting perhaps include his observations on the use of "606" conducted on himself and also on his sons?

She had to erase those thoughts. For the moment, she had exclusive custody of her boys and could protect them from J.R.'s syphilis treatments.

For the moment...

THE MINAHAN BOYS ran the three blocks home from Howe School on the afternoon of March 13, 1911, and told Mollie that St. John's Church was on fire. It was a block from their two-story brick elementary school and teachers had sent all students home, fearing the sparks could ignite the school's roof. The blaze had started in the church attic and had burned for several minutes before anyone noticed smoke and flames coming from the steeples. The fire had taken hold of the structure's wood frame, and the interior was a roaring furnace by the time fire engines arrived.

While the blaze raged and the scent of smoke permeated Mollie's neighborhood, she received a phone call from Attorney P.H. Martin. He and Attorney V.I. Minahan had made their oral arguments before the Wisconsin Supreme Court Justices in the Minahans' divorce case.

Martin said he was happy to inform Mollie that the Supreme Court had affirmed Brown County Circuit Court's earlier decision. She had finally, officially won.

Mollie was ecstatic. She had defeated J.R., who never lost.

In addition to retaining custody of her sons, Martin said Mollie would immediately begin to receive J.R.'s ongoing child support. When the judgment's October anniversary date arrived, J.R. would be required to pay Mollie her court-ordered alimony. But Martin warned her that J.R. could still appeal the Supreme Court's decision until that date. He also reminded her that the justices had affirmed that J.R. *would* control the Minahan boys' medical care.

Attorney Martin's last two warnings dimmed Mollie's elation as she hung up the phone. He had to be correct about J.R.'s medical care stipulation, that she had read too much into it. Dr. Robert, of course, would continue to be the boys' primary care physician within the Doctors Minahan partnership. Yet Mollie did not know whether to trust her doubts or dismiss them. But what could she do either way?

Over the next two months, as St. John's parishioners raised money to rebuild their church, Mollie built her new life. She could have remained in the Minahans' home until the October divorce judgment anniversary, but when Mollie received her papa's inheritance at long last, she and the boys moved out. While Mr. P.H. Martin completed the Lawe Street home Mollie would lease from him, she rented a house at 803 S. Quincy Street, two blocks from J.R.'s.

THE SCENT OF LILACS drifted in through Mollie's open windows three weeks later. When her cool hand felt seven-year-old Robert's hot forehead, she knew he had a fever. She called J.R.'s brother, Dr. Robert. He promised to stop over after his medical office hours.

A different Minahan arrived.

J.R. stomped into Mollie's front room and said she might be getting his money, but he still controlled the boys' medical care. She could not go around his back and contact his brother again.

Mollie stood stock still. Attorney Martin had been wrong. She had been right to be suspicious of J.R. Until her young sons became legal adults, Mollie would have to protect them from their father's syphilis treatments. But how?

There is no record of what sort of medical care J.R. provided to Robert during the next three months, but his temperature never abated. J.R.'s obsession with syphilis was likely at the top of his mind since a fever was often a symptom in the disease's second and tertiary stages.

When Mollie repeatedly questioned J.R., asking whether he was using a syphilis drug on Robert, J.R. claimed he was not.

The day after the Minahan boys celebrated the 4th of July with their father, J.R. admitted Robert into St. Vincent Hospital for further treatment. Two weeks passed, and Robert's temperature had not yielded. Mollie did not know what to think or do. J.R. was the only one diagnosing and treating their son's condition. She believed J.R. could potentially be using drugs that continued to elevate Robert's temperature.

Mollie had visited her son daily, and she finally called J.R. to see when he planned to discharge their seven-year-old. "J.R. reported to me that [Robert] was getting worse and proposed taking the child to his home for syphilis treatment."

Mollie had dropped into her worst nightmare.

She would not allow J.R. to treat their son for a condition he did not have.

Before J.R. could follow through, Mollie arrived at the hospital, a bundle of Robert's clothes in her arms. She climbed the stairs to his second-floor room. As he dressed, Mollie told one of the Sisters she was discharging her son into her care. "I did not take the child surreptitiously or secretly but openly ... because I deemed it was my right." Mollie immediately took Robert to see Dr. Kelly, a Green Bay children's specialist. He believed Robert's problem was related to certain foods he ingested, and Dr. Kelly prescribed a modified diet.

Mollie knew that J.R. would soon discover that Robert was no longer a hospital patient. She had no time to lose. Once she and Robert arrived home, Mollie made some long-distance phone calls and secured a Door County cottage at the Idlewild Inn until the end of August. She and the boys quickly packed and boarded a train for Sturgeon Bay, Wisconsin. In the late July heat, the passenger car felt like an oven, but Mollie did not care. She and her sons had safely escaped from Green Bay.

A hotel launch motored Mollie and the boys the five miles across the canal to the Inn known for its excellent boating and swimming facilities. A nearby farm provided fresh dairy and produce, and each day the same waitress served the Minahans at their assigned dining room table. Mollie placed Robert on Dr. Kelly's diet, and her son's temperature largely subsided, though it did not entirely disappear. That did not alleviate Mollie's ultimate fear. Each day she expected to receive J.R.'s contempt of court document for denying him the sole right to medically treat their youngest son.

But no such document arrived. In fact, when Mollie and the boys returned to Green Bay in September, instead of suffering J.R.'s wrath, it seemed as if he had forgotten about his youngest son's temperature and Mollie's transgressions altogether. J.R. treated Robert's fever as if it was inconsequential. Mollie, however, was still worried about Robert's health.

In early October, she took him to Chicago to see Dr. Sippy, a stomach and intestine specialist, to get another opinion. He thoroughly examined Robert and observed him for a week. Dr. Sippy reached the same conclusion as Dr. Kelly. He believed Robert was suffering from intestinal indigestion. Dr. Sippy prescribed plenty of fresh air, a slightly different diet, and reasonable exercise. If that did not work, he said Robert could potentially have tonsillitis.

When Mollie had initially arrived at Dr. Sippy's office, she had also asked the physician to examine Robert for syphilis, including a blood test. "[Dr. Sippy] advised me that Robert was not afflicted with syphilis—and [he] advised me most emphatically against permitting Robert to be treated or inoculated with the remedy known as '606.'"

Armed with that knowledge, Mollie returned to Green Bay. Over the next few weeks, while Robert followed Dr. Sippy's diet directions, Mollie's divorce anniversary date finally arrived. To her relief, J.R. had made no further appeals to the Wisconsin Supreme Court. On October 29, 1911, Judge Samuel D. Hastings ratified and confirmed the Minahans' bonds of matrimony were "wholly and forever dissolved." Five days later, the Court ordered J.R. to settle his financial obligations with Mollie, including interest, and he actually paid.

Mollie was a rich woman.

More importantly, Robert's temperature had returned to normal.

Ashes and Abduction

Mollie's 409 Lawe Street home
(Author's photo)

MOVERS HEFTED MOLLIE'S Steinway piano up the front porch steps of her new 409 Lawe Street rental home in mid-December of 1911. She stood beside Attorney P.H. Martin, who had constructed the stucco Craftsman-style modern home per her specifications. Located next door to his and on the same square block as Union Congregational Church, Mollie's home was just steps from St. James Park and the Fox River, perfect playgrounds for her sons. Children were building a snow fort in the park. Their laughter bubbled up into the frigid air, scented by smoke drifting from neighborhood chimneys.

Martin told Mollie she should feel a sense of pride and satisfaction. In the past two years, she had secured a promising future for herself and her children. Mollie had also protected Robert from further syphilis treatments.

A committee of women decorated Turner Hall for the Charity Ball. The Vandenberg Harp Orchestra program would begin at 8:30 p.m. and the dancing at 9:00. Mollie was dressed in her finery when Robert said he did not feel well. She checked her seven-year-old's temperature and noted it had spiked. A sinking feeling settled inside Mollie's chest. Based on her divorce stipulation, she had to call J.R. While awaiting his arrival, Mollie gave her son Castoria, a remedy for stomach pain, bowel problems, and quieting the nerves.

J.R. entered Mollie's home at about 9:00 p.m. She looked on as he examined Robert in his second-floor bedroom. J.R. stepped back and said their son had "serious spinal trouble."

That diagnosis should have horrified Mollie, but she did not believe it. "I have no confidence in J.R.'s ability as a physician to care for or treat diseases of children," Mollie later testified. Before their divorce, whenever J.R. had prescribed treatment for either son, Mollie had consulted Dr. Robert afterward, and he had nearly always changed the treatment.

J.R. called in a prescription for Robert and left. For all Mollie knew, the medicine could be for syphilis.

When the delivery boy dropped off the prescription, Robert was sleeping soundly. Mollie gazed at her child and made a decision. Before giving Robert J.R.'s medicine, she would wait until morning to see whether her son's condition had worsened.

Still dressed in her ballgown, she sat by his bedside and dozed off. In the morning, Robert's temperature had returned to normal. He was up and about, displaying no spinal trouble, while Mollie's body ached from her all-night vigil.

THREE WEEKS LATER, Mollie kissed her boys good night at about 9 p.m. on the evening of January 15, 1912. Their cheeks were still glowing from hours of skating on the frozen Fox River. At the end of Porlier Street, residents had shoveled the ice to produce a neighborhood rink. Mollie had joined in on the fun. She loved to figure skate while watching her boys race around on the ice. John, ever the big brother, kept tabs on daredevil Robert, helping him up each time he took a spill.

Mollie stepped into her bedroom and smiled. Nothing could be better than spending a frosty evening with her boys under a moon-lit sky and returning home, all tuckered out, to mugs of hot cocoa with marshmallows floating on top.

Five hours later, and about four blocks to the east, Station No. 2's firetrucks skidded to a halt in front of J.R.'s Quincy Street home. On the snow-covered sidewalk, he and his servants waited in their nightclothes. J.R. told the fire chief a coughing fit had awakened him, and he had discovered smoke seeping under his bedroom door. While the housekeeper had sent in the alarm, J.R. had located the fire's source in the basement.

Firefighters smothered those flames while men operating the water pumps noticed a fire on the roof. The blaze had crept up through one of the home's partitions and ignited the garret's fifty-year-old pine timbers and beams.

A westerly wind carried large sparks toward other houses. Neighbors fled their homes and lined the streets as firefighters poured on water from three different sources. There was much consternation when the library where J.R. kept his guns and ammunition started to burn. Shells exploded in all directions, miraculously not hitting anyone. If the roofs had not been snow-covered, the entire Astor Heights neighborhood might have burned down that night.

J.R.'s home and contents, including valuable paintings, furniture, trophies, and his extensive medical library, were destroyed due to faulty wiring. "I'm only insured up to eleven thousand dollars," J.R. told reporters. "And I believe my loss might go as high as twenty-five thousand dollars." The fires at Dr. Minahan's home and St. John's Church, both city landmarks, were the worst Green Bay had seen in a decade. If Mollie had requested the Quincy Street home in the Minahans' divorce action, a significant portion of her settlement would have gone up in flames.

J.R. would not let his home's destruction set him back. In fact, he took this moment to leave Astor Heights altogether. His brother, Dr. Robert, purchased the four lots where J.R.'s home had stood to build a stucco Italianate house on that site for his son Eben. A construction crew also began work on J.R.'s new Bay Shore Road home situated on forty acres along the east shoreline of the waters of Green Bay. The University of Wisconsin-Green Bay would later purchase that property, and the road would become Nicolet Drive.

A MONTH AFTER the fire, Howe School's visiting nurse sent Mollie a note stating, "In my opinion, Robert Minahan's tonsils should be removed." Mollie relayed that information to J.R., but he disregarded it—just as he had with Dr. Sippy's diagnosis concerning Robert. About a month later, Robert's temperature elevated again. Mollie knew J.R.'s single-minded belief would be that syphilis was its cause. She took both boys to Chicago to consult with Dr. Billings and another notable physician to gain new ammunition. The two doctors concluded that neither child had syphilis.

On the return train journey, Robert, eight, and John, ten, both handsomely dressed in belted wool suits and matching caps, sat across from Mollie. When John asked his mother why she had taken them to see the Chicago doctors, Mollie told him the truth: His papa wished to treat John and Robert "for a disease, she believed they did not have, and she feared [the] treatment was dangerous."

Upon Mollie's return, J.R. arrived at her Lawe Street home to pick up the boys for their Saturday visit. He first took Robert's temperature, still outside the normal range. Mollie saw the fear in her son's eyes when J.R. instructed the boys to go upstairs so he could talk to their mother. After they departed, J.R. told Mollie that Robert's fever was syphilis related.

"J.R. indicated a purpose to take the child to the hospital to have administered ... '606.' I protested that [Robert] had no need of said remedy."

Mollie told J.R. she had talked to the Chicago physicians. They had said the "606" treatment was "radical, dangerous, and experimental ... especially for children who [were] not even afflicted with that disease." Since J.R. would not listen to reason, Mollie directed her counsel, Mr. P.H. Martin, to officially report Dr. Sippy's and the two other Chicago physicians' opinions to J.R.

Even though Martin confirmed he had met with J.R. and done as Mollie had asked, Martin said J.R. felt his expert knowledge concerning his sons' medical treatment far surpassed that of the Chicago physicians.

Mollie did not know what else to do. But she could not give up.

AS ROBERT AND JOHN walked the three blocks to Howe School two days later, J.R.'s automobile ground to a stop beside the boys. Their father climbed out and called his youngest son over. J.R. told Robert that he had to go to St. Vincent Hospital with Pap. He seized Robert's arm while the young boy cried and kicked, attempting to pull free. J.R. forcefully threw Robert into the vehicle, and they drove away.

J.R. later testified, "Mollie told the children that their father would kill them by giving them powerful medicine for a disease they did not have. She had so frightened them that Robert violently and loudly resisted when I took him to the hospital."

John ran home and told Mollie, who raced the six blocks to St. Vincent. A receptionist told Mollie that a hospital aide had transported Robert from Dr. Minahan's surgical suite into a second-floor private room.

Mollie's body faltered. She was too late. She climbed the central stairway, and a nurse confirmed Mollie's worst fears: J.R. had given Robert the "606" treatment and a potent sedative.

Mollie entered her eight-year-old's room. His eyes were closed, his breathing heavy. Mollie had read how doctors administered the "606" compound. Robert would have had to lie face down, likely restrained by aids, as his father injected the acidic solution into both of his son's buttocks

St. Vincent Hospital in 1910 (Postcard)

"deeply, slowly, and gently." Adult patients described the injections as horribly painful, the torment sometimes lasting six or more days. Physicians often used narcotics to control the pain.

Mollie tried not to imagine the torment her boy had suffered. She smoothed the cowlick on his damp head, knowing she could not change what had already happened, though desperately wishing she could. She had to make the best of the terrible situation for her child's sake.

J.R. had not paid for a private nurse, so Mollie went to the hospital each day. After J.R. administered morphine to subdue the pain in Robert's injection sites, Mollie followed her husband's directions: feeding her son soft foods, bathing him, and keeping him on his side. She tried everything she could to appease J.R., to avoid arousing his anger, to alleviate further anguish for her boy.

Inside Robert's young mind and tormented body, he would have watched Mollie in his lucid moments, trying to figure out what was going on. What would she have said if his dark eyes had gazed up into hers and he had asked her whether Pap had tried to kill him?

Robert's pain finally subsided after two weeks, and J.R. claimed there would be no residual effects. At their son's hospital discharge, J.R. told Mollie that Robert's second "606" treatment was imperative. She had to return him to the hospital in one month.

Out of her son's hearing, Mollie vehemently told J.R. that would never happen.

Last-Minute Escape

MOLLIE STOOD on the front porch of her Lawe Street home and watched her boys head off toward school. A Ford Model T roadster drove past as she twisted a handkerchief in her painfully stiff hands. Thankfully, J.R.'s vehicle was nowhere in sight. Constant worry had frayed her nerves, and her rheumatism had flared. Not only was her youngest son's second "606" syphilis treatment, demanded by J.R., drawing near, but Daisy, her former sister-in-law and friend, had suffered an appendicitis attack in Paris.

Dr. William E. Minahan and wife Lillian (Roger Minahan Papers)

V.I. Minahan had received that news in a telegram from his forty-five-year-old brother Dr. William E. Minahan. He, his wife Lillian, and Daisy were on a three-month European tour. The rotund, nearly six-foot-four Dr. Will, a Chicago Rush Medical graduate, had operated on Daisy. Since she was in no condition for extended travel, Dr. Will's telegram stated the three had decided to forgo their planned tour and return home. But the Minahans' steamer had been delayed at the Queenstown, Ireland departure harbor due to a British coal strike. Dr. Will's telegram said he had rebooked first-class accommodations on the Titanic's maiden voyage.

Mollie's sharp gaze followed her boys until they turned north onto Madison Street and disappeared from view. She finally stepped back inside her home, willing the phone to ring. Mollie had decided she could not sit back and hope that J.R. would not abduct Robert to administer his second "606" treatment. She had sent a telegram to her sister, Kitten, who now lived in New Mexico, to ask whether Mollie and the boys could come for a visit. She had also placed three long-distance phone calls to Kitten, at different times of the day, but no one had answered.

Even though the boys would miss the last few weeks of school, their escape from Green Bay was imperative.

ABOARD THE TITANIC, after three days at sea, the Minahans attended a lavish dinner in the First-Class Dining Salon. Their party included the ship's captain E.J. Smith, Colonel and Mrs. John Jacob Astor, and President William Howard Taft's aide, Major Archibald Butt. The Minahans and their party entered the Café Parisian after dinner for late-night refreshments, conversation, and cards. Dr. Will puffed on his cigar while perhaps telling a story he had often repeated. Some years back when he was planning his first trip to Europe, a mystic revealed he would "lose his life on his second trip abroad." That declaration had caused his friends "considerable merriment." They told him he had no reason to fear the mystic's prediction as of yet. But on Dr. Will's current excursion, although he had not put any credence on the prophecy, he increased his life insurance to $60,000, just in case.

That night of April 14, 1912, his story would have caused his companions merriment as well since newspapers reported, "It was the boast of the White Star... the [Titanic] was unsinkable."

ON THE AFTERNOON of Monday, April 15, Mollie was thoroughly rattled. She still awaited a return call from Kitten while another concern troubled Mollie's mind. Community news had circulated about a Titanic disaster. The details, however, were sketchy since the steamship was out of cable range. When Mollie heard the newspaper land on the front porch, she raced out and read the headline: "Titanic Hits Iceberg in Ocean; But all Passengers are Saved."

Mollie released her held breath as the boys arrived home from school and gathered around her. A companion article named their Uncle Will, Aunt Daisy, and Aunt Lillian. According to an Associated Press dispatch, the local Wisconsinites were in "no danger." All passengers had been "safely transferred to steamers of the Allan line." That news reassured Mollie until she read conflicting articles. A Minia cable ship dispatch reported the Titanic was sinking, and steamers were towing her toward Cape Race. The White Star Line's Manager denied the Titanic had sunk. As far as he knew, the vessel was afloat, making for Halifax under her own steam, aided by an Allan liner.

Attorney V.I. Minahan arrived at Mollie's home. He was clearly distraught. V.I. informed Mollie he had just dropped J.R. off at the train station. Her children's father was traveling to New York to gather accurate information about the Titanic disaster and meet the steamer or its rescue ship when one of the vessels docked in Manhattan.

Of course, Mollie was concerned for the three Minahans' fates, especially Daisy's. Yet Mollie was relieved that J.R. would be out of the city. Once she heard back from Kitten, J.R.'s absence would simplify the boys and Mollie's departure.

ON APRIL 16, Mollie read that the Carpathia rescue steamer had come into telegraph range and sent a dispatch stating: "The Titanic has struck an enormous berg and sunk." She and the rest of the world were stunned to learn only 700 passengers and crew out of the estimated 2,224 onboard had been rescued.

V.I. Minahan alerted Mollie that he had received a telegram from the Carpathia via Halifax, stating, "Come. Lillian and Daisy at my home. 1975 Broad Street, Newark, N.J. Signed C.E. Henry Stengil." V.I. said the message was distressing. When the Carpathia docked in New York carrying the Titanic survivors, the passenger, Henry Stengil, appeared to be taking Lillian and Daisy to his New Jersey home. The message would have included Dr. Will's name if he had survived.

Just hours later, a devastated V.I. called Mollie again. He had received a telegram from J.R. stating, "All hope is gone." J.R. had communicated with the White Star Line and obtained an official survivor list. Dr. Will's name was not on it.

Mollie told V.I. how sorry she was for his loss. Yet, each time the phone had rung, Mollie had hoped the person calling would have been Kitten.

THE CARPATHIA berthed at Pier 54 four days after the Titanic struck the iceberg, and J.R. met Daisy and Lillian as they disembarked. "I rushed them to the Hotel Astor," J.R. told the press.

The two women had sustained many bruises and J.R. treated them for shock. He also ordered new wardrobes for them and provided a White Star Line official a description of Dr. Will, in hopes of recovering his brother's remains.

White Star Office after Titanic Disaster where J.R. left description of his brother Dr. Will (Library of Congress Prints & Photographs)

J.R. escorted Daisy and Lillian by train back to the Chicago LaSalle Street Station. He called V.I. to tell him they would reach Green Bay by about 7:00 p.m., and J.R.'s brother relayed that message to all the Minahan relatives, including Mollie.

Although she wanted to express her sincere condolences and support to Daisy and Lillian, Mollie's priority was her youngest son. The date for Robert's second "606" treatment had arrived. Mollie still had not heard from Kitten, but she and the boys had packed for their departure. If her sister did not call in the next few hours, Mollie would need another plan. She and the boys had to leave before J.R. returned.

There was no other option.

ON THE FINAL train leg between Milwaukee and Green Bay, Daisy and Lillian agreed to share their harrowing stories with the press. "It will be absolutely impossible to describe the scene when the vessel sank," Daisy said, seated beside Lillian and across from reporters at a dining car table. Just hours before the disaster, Daisy said the Minahans had left the Café Parisian and located chairs on the First-Class Promenade deck. In the crisp air and starlit night, old sailors told them they had never seen the sea so calm and glassy. At around 9:30, the temperature suddenly dropped, and they returned to their cabin.

"I had been sleeping soundly for about two hours," Lillian said, "when [I was] awakened by frantic cries outside our door. My husband peered into the corridor and saw Mrs. John Jacob Astor running frantically and shrieking, 'The boat's sinking!' ... And we felt the huge ship reclining upon its portside. My husband threw several blankets about me, hurried into some clothes himself, and ran to the adjoining stateroom where Daisy was sleeping. After throwing a blanket about her, he took us to the main deck where we found everything in confusion. Lifeboats were being lifted down into the sea, and two were already being put off with frightened and hysterical women."

MOLLIE PACED in her Green Bay home, her eyes watching the clock as the telephone rang. Kitten's voice came over the line from New Mexico. She and her husband had just arrived home from a two-week trip, and she had read Mollie's telegram. Of course, Mollie and the boys were welcome to stay at Kitten's home for as long as necessary.

Relief flooded Mollie.

She had no time to waste.

BEFORE EACH of Lillian's words, there was a "barrier of choked sobs." Daisy came to her aid. "I never saw such calm composure and cool bravery in my life as the men of the first and second cabin displayed. Colonel Astor seemed to be the controlling figure. He and Mr. Butt, Mr. Guggenheim, Mr. Widener, and Mr. Thayer clustered in a group as if they were holding a quick consultation as to what steps to take." Daisy said Mr. J. Bruce Ismay, one of the Titanic's owners, also joined the group before Colonel Astor came forward with the cry, "'Not one man must leave the boat until all the children and women are cared for.'"

"There was a heart-rending wail from the steerage as the words that the ship was sinking went up," Lillian added. "Women, clinging to their babies and children, were frenzied ... My husband was aiding with the lifeboats, and he told us to be brave, and all would be well."

A wide-eyed porter refreshed the two women's water glasses as Daisy continued. "We heard a number of shots as the boats were being lowered ... It was the officers who were keeping the steerage passengers from stampeding the small boats."

"The last boat was being lowered," Lillian said, "and it seemed as if there were over a hundred women waiting to get in. Fifty persons had already filled it when my husband nearly carried me and Daisy to the side of the half-sunken vessel and lifted us in ... Colonel Astor assisted him, and Mrs. Astor was put into the same boat with Daisy and me."

Tears filled Lillian's eyes as she recalled her husband's last words, "'Be brave,' [and] he kissed me for the last time."

AΠ OPEΠ-AIR taxi pulled up outside Mollie's Lawe Street home. The vehicle was roomy enough to stack the family's trunks inside. A neighborhood teen helped the driver load them into the rear and strap them down. Mollie and her two sons climbed in. She had secured three seats on a train heading south within the next sixty minutes.

Chicago & Northwestern train depot
(Postcard)

The Chicago, Milwaukee & St. Paul train carrying Daisy, Lillian, and J.R. steamed into its Washington Street depot as Mollie and her boys' taxi drove past. They arrived at the Chicago & Northwestern depot on the Fox River's west side with just minutes to spare.

As their train headed south, Mollie finally took a calming breath. Her gaze landed on her eight- and ten-year-old sons—her boys—who gave meaning to her life. John's nose was already in a book, Robert's pressed against the window, his cowlick sticking up.

For the second time, she had disobeyed J.R.'s sole right to treat her youngest son.

Seizing Medical Rights

MOLLIE SIPPED SWEET TEA on the front porch of her sister's Silver City, New Mexico, home, situated at the foot of the Mogollon Mountains' Pinos Altos Range. Kitten's husband worked as an engineer for the nearby Chino Copper Company, which operated a large open-pit mine. The pinging noise of BB guns resonated from the backyard. Under a hired man's supervision, Mollie's sons were shooting at cans, pretending to be outlaws in the city's infamous Billy the Kid's gang.

More than two months had passed since Robert's discharge from St. Vincent Hospital. For the moment, Mollie had protected her son from J.R.'s second "606" treatment. Mollie's health had also improved in the dry New Mexico heat.

Kitten returned from the postal box with a letter for Mollie.

As soon as she and her boys had arrived in New Mexico, Mollie had written Daisy to offer condolences for the tragic loss of her brother and sympathy for Daisy's and Lillian's horrendous ordeals. Mollie opened her former sister-in-law's response. Daisy reported that the cable ship Mackay-Bennett had recovered Dr. Will's body clad in a black suit and overcoat. His pockets contained a gold watch, clinical thermometer, English and American cash, and a letter of credit for $2500. His remains were among the 190 transported to the Halifax Mayflower Curling Club ice rink. Daisy's brother, V.I., had traveled there and brought Dr. Will's body back to Green Bay. J.R. and Dr. Robert had performed the autopsy and determined their brother had frozen to death in the 28-degree water.

Those freezing elements had also impacted Daisy's health. She had written her letter from the Wood County Sanitarium. Three years earlier,

Daisy had contracted tuberculosis. That infectious disease killed one out of seven people in those days. The hours Daisy had spent in the lifeboat had exacerbated her condition, prompting her need for extended medical care.

Mollie read Daisy's closing words, which cautioned Mollie about J.R.'s fury. When he had discovered Mollie had taken the boys out of Wisconsin, J.R. had told Daisy he believed Mollie's departure was solely to defeat his "right to the medical supervision of the children."

As before, when Mollie and the boys had escaped to Door County's Idlewild Inn, Mollie feared J.R. would procure an order charging her with contempt of court. Each day Mollie's heart sped up as Kitten checked the mail. But when nothing arrived by early September, when Mollie and the boys departed for Green Bay, she still could not relax. Although their visit had provided her sons a summer of safety, Mollie had returned to the same stark reality: She had custody of the children, yet J.R. controlled their medical treatment until they reached adulthood. John was ten and Robert, eight. In her younger son's case, Mollie realized she would have to keep tabs on his father's medical actions for ten more years.

That caused Mollie acute stress.

She thought J.R. would immediately kidnap Robert from the street for another "606" treatment. But J.R.'s new financial endeavor seemed to have supplanted his concern for Robert's condition. J.R. had purchased the Green Bay Theater, adjacent to the Minahan Building, and renamed it the Jay-are Theater. Work had begun to redecorate, remodel, and renovate its interior. Her former husband's goal was to make the theater the city's premier house and the "best equipped in the state," surpassing those in Milwaukee.

Even though J.R. seemed to have forgotten about Robert's second "606" treatment, that did not alleviate Mollie's fear. Each day, she awaited her children's return from school. Each day, she expected the worst. Soon after her Green Bay return, Mollie was diagnosed with melancholia. "[That] condition of nervousness is the same that I suffered prior to my divorce ... and was occasioned by J.R.'s cruel and inhuman treatment ... In the fall of 1912, I was confined to my home for rest under the care of a nurse."

A shawl covered Mollie's shoulders as she rocked on her front porch in mid-September. In past years, she had relished the temperate fall days, clear blue skies, and the vibrant colors of goldenrod, black-eyed Susans, and purple asters blooming along the Fox River. She had especially enjoyed the cool and crisp evenings conducive for sleep. But after Mollie's return from New Mexico, nothing seemed to lift her spirits and sleep eluded her.

The repetitive chopping noise of a push-reel mower in the Martins' yard competed with the sound of J.R.'s automobile as he pulled up. John and Robert had spent the weekend at their father's new Bay Shore home.

J.R.'s vehicle drove away as the boys ran up the porch steps, flushed with excitement. Robert said they had gone fishing and swimming and built a fort in the woods adjacent to Pap's new house. John said Pap's shoreline house was just as modern as their Green Bay home, with hot and cold water, a bath, electric lights, and furnace heat. That Pap had even hired servants to cultivate a garden, raise chickens, and milk two cows. Robert added that the automobile drive from Pap's home only took fifteen minutes.

The boys' enthusiasm sunk Mollie into a deeper depression. That seemed to give J.R. pleasure when he picked them up in early October. Mollie heard him tell the boys that their mother had suffered a "nervous breakdown." That was why she was "particularly cross and irritable and unable to sleep at night."

In private, J.R. told Mollie her untreated syphilis was responsible for her melancholia. In syphilis's tertiary stage, it could produce brain changes.

But by mid-October, Mollie's depression improved. Her sister, Annie, had encouraged Mollie to focus on the positive aspects of her life. Mollie's sons were healthy. They loved and respected her. And their father had not followed through with Robert's second "606" treatment, likely due to J.R.'s continued preoccupation with his business endeavors. The Jay-are Theater renovation was behind schedule, and the Minahan Building Company's ongoing litigation with Wisconsin Public Service continued to create negative press for J.R. and his brothers.

In Brown County Circuit Court that week, Green Bay's former mayor Dr. Robert E. Minahan swore he had never been a Minahan Building Company stockholder. He testified he had given his son Eben cash, a law library, and furniture on his twenty-first birthday. Attorney V.I. Minahan provided proof that Eben, rather than his father, had invested that gift money into the Minahan Building Company. The stockholders were Eben and his two uncles, Attorney V.I. Minahan and Dr. J.R. Minahan. *The Green Bay Gazette*, V.I. argued, had errored in their reporting.

Many in the Green Bay community still felt the Minahans had conducted a shady deal, using Dr. Robert's mayoral influence to secure the business district's power and light franchise for his brothers' and son's benefit.

Nevertheless, the litigation parties finally settled the case in the Minahans' favor. A half-page notice ran in the *Gazette* stating, "Wisconsin Public Service has absorbed the Minahan Building Company's lighting and power business."

J.R. had made a lucrative deal: Wisconsin Public Service had awarded the Minahans substantial stock to halt the franchise business. Moreover, J.R. did not have to share his proceeds with Mollie.

OVER THE FIRST QUARTER of 1913, the Minahan boys had been healthy, and, thankfully, no issues concerning their father had arisen for Mollie. But in the spring that changed.

Mollie helped the boys pack for a weekend visit with their father when she noticed a rash on Robert's face. Reluctantly, she wrote J.R. a note, asking him to examine Robert. On the boys' return, J.R. stepped into Mollie's house and said he had diagnosed Robert with a bad case of eczema.

After J.R.'s departure, Mollie sensed the boys seemed "discontented." John said Pap had commented "upon his wealth and upon [Mollie's] lack ... And upon the fact that she was living in a rented house. And upon the dress of the children." Mollie called Attorney Martin and asked whether she should refuse to let the boys visit J.R. at any time other than that provided in the judgment. "Mr. Martin advised that I had better overlook the matter ... With time, J.R.'s feelings would become less bitter, and the comments would likely cease."

Two days passed. When Robert returned from school, a different rash covered his face and body. Mollie asked J.R. to stop over. After he examined Robert, J.R. told Mollie their son's condition had changed. He had "poisoned blood," and Robert required hospital treatment.

J.R.'s diagnosis was "ambiguous and indefinite," Mollie later testified, and she questioned whether he was planning to treat Robert for syphilis.

J.R. assured Mollie he was not. Yet she knew his obsession with that disease was never far from his mind. His false belief that she had contracted syphilis had persisted for more than a dozen years, and nothing could convince him otherwise. That belief had ruined her marriage, but most disturbingly, it was detrimentally affecting her sons.

J.R. admitted Robert into St. Vincent Hospital. Mollie believed her boy would only be there for a few days, but when his rash did not disappear, those days turned into a week, then five weeks. Like the year before, J.R. was the only one diagnosing Robert's condition and deciding which drugs to use.

In July of 1913, Mollie finally cornered J.R. near Robert's hospital room. "I asked him what his diagnosis was ... What treatment he had given, was giving, and intended giving. J.R. replied it was 'the same old story'... He had given Robert Cypridol (a syphilis drug) and an iron tonic ... After Robert rested ... J.R. said he would give him further treatments."

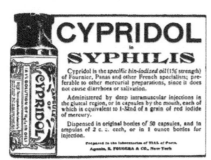

Cypridol directions (Western Canada Medical Journal)

Mollie was tearful and full of bitterness. She asked why he had not given Robert the "606" treatment he had begun the year before. "J.R. said he did not dare to because Robert's heart was in such bad shape. I asked if his heart had not been in bad shape the year before when the '606' was administered. 'It had not been,' J.R. said, [and] I asked if it was not probable that the '606' treatment had injured Robert's heart ... J.R. said, 'No, not at all.'"

Mollie told him he was lying, and she was taking Robert home. J.R. strode to the nursing station and told a Sister he wanted round-the-clock private care for his son. The staff had to prevent his wife from discharging Robert as she had done in the past.

Mollie left the hospital and called Attorney Martin at his Minahan Building office. She told him about her youngest son's ongoing hospital stay, J.R.'s syphilis treatments, and his claims about Robert's heart. She begged Martin to find a legal action she could pursue. Mollie needed Martin to feel at least a tinge of what she was feeling, and when he said he would drop everything and meet her at his house within the hour, she knew her desperate words had touched him.

As Mollie hung up the phone, there was a knock at the front door. She opened it, and a young man handed her a document. He said she had been served. Mollie gazed down at J.R.'s court petition for their children's sole custody, and her heart nearly stopped.

The Suitable Parent

IN THE MUGGY July heat, Mollie marched out onto her home's front porch, fanning her face with J.R.'s custody petition. She had read the document a half dozen times, and she could nearly repeat each lie by heart. J.R.'s closing words had especially riled her up. He claimed, if the boys were left in Mollie's custody they would be "ruined morally as well as physically" and would be "wholly unfit to properly carry the responsibilities of their manhood."

Mollie's gaze landed on her eleven-year-old son, sitting on the porch steps beside a neighborhood friend.

Nothing could be further from the truth.

She watched as John organized his fishing gear, his excited voice discussing the upcoming Perry Victory Centennial with his friend. That event would celebrate the anniversary of Commodore Perry's naval victory over the British in the War of 1812. In addition to a Washington Street parade, visitors would be invited to board Perry's reconstructed Niagara flagship, scheduled to arrive in Green Bay on August 10. John couldn't wait for that week-long event. Yet Mollie knew he worried, as did she, that his younger brother would miss out. Robert could still be locked inside St. Vincent Hospital where his papa held the key.

That angered Mollie and broke her heart.

She told John she would be at the Martins' home as the boys set off for the Fox River—but not before she cautioned John to be careful on the docks. One complaint within J.R.'s petition was that Mollie lacked concern for her boys' safety. J.R. alleged that John and Robert could be gravely injured or killed since Mollie allowed them to go down to the railroad tracks and out on the Fox River docks.

J.R. had contrasted that with his new waterfront home, which he said afforded their sons "a safe, shallow playground." J.R. also said, because of his training, the boys naturally turned to the woods, the water, and outdoor sports. Those activities, J.R. alleged, gave them no time or inclination to indulge in habits dangerous to their health and moral welfare—elements he implied were rampant near Mollie's more urban home.

She believed J.R.'s allegations were blatantly false. Mollie had never allowed either boy to play near the tracks, and Robert was not permitted to step onto the docks unattended. However, in the last few weeks, she had allowed John to fish there. The water was shallow, and John was an excellent swimmer. He had always been careful and deserved her trust.

Mollie strode up Lawe Street and turned north onto Madison Street. Strains of music carried on the breeze across from St. James Park. The City Band was tuning up for that evening's concert—another enjoyable event that Robert would miss—all because of his father.

Mollie sped up the Martins' 736 S. Madison Street walkway. She typically admired her attorney's magnificent Queen Anne Revival home, its turret, gables, bay windows, and intricately designed brick chimneys. But Mollie's full attention was on J.R.'s custody petition, still gripped in her hand.

Mr. and Mrs. P.H. Martin's 736 S. Madison Street Home (A Souvenir of Green Bay 1903)

She climbed the porch stairs and rang the bell. A maid answered and said that Attorney Martin had just arrived home. She escorted Mollie into his library where he sat behind his desk.

Mollie handed Martin J.R.'s petition and told him he had been wrong. That J.R.'s bitterness toward her would never cease until he got full custody of the boys.

Mollie could tell her attorney was taken aback by her accusing tone as his eyes quickly scanned the custody petition. She knew she was being unfair. He had been caught off guard just as she had been when served J.R.'s petition an hour before.

Mollie took a deep breath and apologized for taking out her frustration on him. She said she knew that Martin and his wife cared for Robert. How after church services, they had often invited her son to stop over at their home to read the "funny papers" from their New York Sunday newspaper. How Robert had laid on the Martins' front room floor, just down the hall, engrossed in the antics of "Happy Hooligan," "Little Nemo in Slumberland," and "Krazy Kat."

Mollie longed for Robert to have that carefree joy again.

Martin said he did too, and he would do all he could to accomplish that for Mollie.

She nodded and finally sat down. Mollie told Martin she believed J.R.'s primary motivation for the custody action was to enable him to continue to treat Robert for syphilis. In the petition, J.R. had falsely claimed that the boys had always been "sickly" and required "persistent treatment to thoroughly eradicate" the syphilis disease inherited from her. But J.R. said that Mollie had always objected, claiming the treatment was "wholly unnecessary and positively injurious to the children."

Indeed, she had objected, Mollie told Martin. But it was not due to incompetence, as J.R. implied, but because the boys did not have syphilis—according to other doctors. Martin knew that too. The boys' syphilis diagnosis did not exist outside of J.R.'s mind.

Mollie hesitated before asking Martin to look at the petition's last paragraph concerning the two of them. How J.R. alleged that Mollie had induced Mr. Martin to take "considerably more than a professional interest" in Mollie's divorce case. That J.R. claimed "a singularly cordial and intimate relation" had sprung up between Martin and Mollie when he had called on her at her home, presumably for consultation. And, after the divorce judgment, J.R. alleged Mollie and Martin's intimate relationship had continued. J.R. said it was especially evident when Mr. Martin had constructed a rental house for Mollie next door to his.

Throughout her marriage, Mollie had dealt with J.R.'s adultery claims, but his current insinuations, directed not only at her but Attorney P.H. Martin, were the last straw. Mollie said it was hard to believe that she had ever loved J.R. It was just as hard to believe that her former husband and Martin had ever been friends.

COLUMBIA COUNTY'S Judge M.L. Leuke presided at the Minahans' three-day custody battle in late July of 1913. At the trial's conclusion, he ruled: "The Court finds no reason, whatsoever, why the Minahan children's custody should be taken from Mollie B. Minahan."

Mollie could not hide her relief and victory smile, while J.R. displayed no emotion.

What was more, his action had backfired. In addition to denying J.R.'s custody application, the judge had adjusted the children's medical care stipulation. Attorney Martin had argued that the Court should no longer award J.R. the sole authority for his children's medical treatment.

The judge agreed.

In the future, when either child needed medical care, the judge had ordered that J.R. or another physician, deemed appropriate by both parents, could administer that treatment. All doctors had to conduct the boys' care at Mollie's home, except when its nature or the child's condition necessitated hospital treatment. In that case, the physician could not detain the child away from home any longer than necessary.

Mollie knew the very best way to celebrate the judge's decision. For nearly three months, J.R. had imprisoned Robert inside St. Vincent Hospital. Mollie went straight to his second-floor room and discharged him into her care. As she and Robert walked down the hospital stairs hand-in-hand, a surge of exhilaration filled Mollie. In less than two weeks, her nine-year-old would get to climb aboard Commodore Perry's ship with his brother.

Mollie smiled at that marvelous and rewarding thought.

The Walk

FOUR YEARS HAD PASSED since Mollie had retained custody of her boys and no court battles had ensued. But Mollie would not let her guard down. She carefully negotiated every medical decision with J.R., the memories not fading for her nor Robert. That was evident on February 26, 1917. As a Sister wheeled Mollie's now thirteen-year-old into St. Vincent Hospital's operating room, Mollie watched him tremble with fear. It was the same surgery suite where his father had administered Robert's "606" treatment five years before.

That afternoon, a neighborhood boy's "BB" gun's lead shot had embedded below Robert's eye, so close Mollie worried her son might lose his sight. She had immediately notified J.R., and he had met them at St. Vincent.

Mollie waited within the hospital's chapel, willing the quiet space to calm her fears. J.R. finally stepped inside, dressed in white scrubs stained with blood. He said he had successfully removed the lead shot near Robert's eye, and his sight would not be affected.

For once, Mollie offered J.R. her profound thanks. His skilled hands had helped Robert rather than harming him.

LATE ON THE EVENING of April 2, 1917, Mollie heard the sound of "Extra! Extra!" outside her Lawe Street home. With three cents in her hand, she stepped onto the lighted front porch, and a newsboy ran up the steps to hand her a late-breaking *Green Bay Press-Gazette.* Back inside, Mollie read the news she and most of the country had dreaded, yet expected. Europe had been waging its Great War for two years while

America had remained neutral. But after German submarine warfare had escalated in the Atlantic, following the Lusitania's sinking, and Germany's attempt to meddle in U.S.-Mexican relations, America could not stand by any longer. That evening, President Woodrow Wilson had delivered an address, asking congress to declare war against Germany, "to make the world safe for democracy."

When the Brown County Red Cross former chairman moved to Chicago, the organization's 800 female members elected Mollie chairman. She would now lead the county's Red Cross efforts for the young men going overseas. Congress reinstated the Selective Service Bill, and President Wilson issued a proclamation requiring men from age twenty-one to thirty-five to register for the draft by June 5, 1917.

On that day, Green Bay held an impressive parade for the young men called to serve their country. Local boys in batteries B and E, who had already registered, led the way. Civil War and Spanish-American War veterans marched along with the Boy Scouts and 500 railroad men. Dressed in her Red Cross uniform, Mollie carried an American flag and led the Brown County chapter right past the Minahan Building. Sixty of the 2,363 Brown County men who enrolled for service that day would be among the Great War's fatalities.

Mollie leading the Red Cross brigade past the Minahan Building (Courtesy of the Neville Public Museum of Brown County)

The government commissioned J.R. as a medical corps captain, scheduled to leave in mid-1918 for hospital base work in France. Battlefield surgeries and syphilis were bound to fill his schedule. Over one million French troops had already contracted the venereal disease. In some instances, soldiers had deliberately infected themselves with matchsticks passed from one to another to avoid serving on the front lines.

Mollie stepped into her Brown County Red Cross office within Green Bay's

John & Robert's friend Grace Warren with other Junior Red Cross girls (Courtesy of Beverly Hart Branson)

Federal Building on December 6, 1917. *Press-Gazette* reporter Max Rosen waited inside to interview her. Since Mollie had assumed her leadership position, she had boosted the county's Red Cross volunteers by more than ten-fold. Mollie had gained the Green Bay merchants' cooperation to devote much of their advertising space to the National Red Cross War Fund Drive, and she had raised money through endeavors like Red Cross Tag Day and Theater Day. However, her primary role was to manage Brown County's largest manufacturing operation, and she performed that job for free.

At age 42, Mollie was headlining more news than J.R.

As she gave Max a tour of the Red Cross facility, Mollie explained, "We're divided into six departments with a complete staff of female managers, overseeing eight-thousand women, turning out six-hundred garments and thousands of bandages each week. Efficiency is our motto, cleanliness our byword, and thrift our distinctive feature."

Max later reported, "I have never felt so completely useless while I followed Mrs. Bertles Minahan ... and learned how the raw material was procured, cut, sewed, and shipped out." Anyone who read Max's two-full-page-article could not help but recognize Mollie's business savvy and her war effort contribution.

MOLLIE AND ROBERT sat inside the Appleton High School auditorium on February 8, 1918, to watch the Appleton, Marinette, and Green Bay triangular debate. The East High School's three-boy team included John Minahan. Mollie knew that all who met her eldest son considered him a student

East High Forensic Team: John Minahan on the right. (East High 1918 Yearbook)

of "exceptional mental abilities, popular with young and old." As a junior, he was an excellent forensic debater and orator as she had been.

At that night's debate, the question was: "Resolved that the national government should own and operate the railways." The issue was vital to the public since the U.S. government, while at war, currently supervised all railroads. Although John's team did not take home that evening's trophy, Mollie and Robert agreed that John had done an excellent job. His goal was to win the state oratorical contest before graduating, and

Mollie believed he would do it.

John had already achieved another goal. Four months earlier, after J.R. had taken his sons deer hunting in Forest County, John had brought home a 250-pound buck while his brother and father had returned empty-handed. When J.R. had dropped the boys off, J.R. had boasted to Mollie about John's hunting prowess, and she had noticed the hurt in her youngest son's eyes. It saddened her to know that throughout Robert's life he had felt his big brother was Pap's favorite son.

GREEN BAY'S scarlet fever season arrived in Brown County. Every positive case was to be immediately reported and quarantined. When Mollie returned from a Glenmore Red Cross address, she received a call from the East High School nurse. A student in John's class had a confirmed scarlet fever case. John had to be quarantined for seven days to determine whether he had contracted the disease.

Mollie made the hard decision and sent Robert to J.R.'s home without his big brother's watchful eyes. But she couldn't put Robert at risk of contracting scarlet fever. That bacterial disease resulted in the death of nearly 15 percent of those affected and had likely instigated Mollie's lifetime of rheumatism.

A few days later, John did develop the telltale scarlet fever symptoms: a sore throat, fever, and rash of small spots, evenly diffused and bright red on his neck and upper chest. Medical advances had taken place since Mollie had contracted the disease at age nineteen. Scientists had developed a scarlet fever serum extracted from horses' blood, reducing the disease's mortality rate by 40 percent. Although scarlet fever was more prevalent among children, Mollie had to be quarantined for seven days to see whether she developed any symptoms.

Nearly every day, Mollie took long walks on the River Road (the current Riverside Drive). She had never lost her taste for physical exercise, which had become crucial due to her work strain. On top of that was Mollie's current worry about John. In addition to his scarlet fever health risk, she feared he might contract rheumatism as she had.

Normally Mollie walked with her sister, Annie, or another female friend, but on February 26, 1918, she told John's private nurse of her intent to walk alone. Snow had fallen in the early morning hours and the temperature was about eight degrees. Instead of striding down the road, Mollie chose the railroad tracks, two blocks west of her home, likely to avoid well-traveled areas if she had indeed contracted scarlet fever.

Hochgreve Brewery (A Souvenir of Green Bay 1903)

The Chicago, Milwaukee & St. Paul Engine No. 91, a way-freight pulling two cars and a caboose, had originated in Milwaukee. It had arrived in De Pere, five miles south of Green Bay, nearly an hour late and should have chugged past Mollie's home before her walk's 3 p.m. departure. At about 3:50 p.m., the train headed toward its Green Bay depot.

Mollie had walked two miles south on the railroad tracks, up to Hochgreve Brewery (the current 2200 Riverside Drive office building), then turned back and was about a half-mile from her home.

Engineer Carl Fogle's train rounded the bend. He saw Mollie striding along the railroad bed, her back to him, about forty yards north of the Chicago and Northwestern bridge that crossed the Fox River. Frantically blowing the whistle, Fogle applied the engine's brakes while warning blasts exploded from the bridge tender.

Mollie did not have enough time to react.

The engine struck her at 3:55 p.m.

The locomotive screeched to a stop and Conductor Robins jumped off.

The train had mangled Mollie's body. Blood was everywhere. A deep gash cut across her forehead. The steel wheels had severed one of her legs at the knee, the other at the ankle. The conductor checked Mollie's breathing and pulse as Engineer Fogle joined him. Robins looked up and grimly shook his head.

The conductor notified Sheriff Nic Ryan. Since Mollie had no identification on her, the sheriff called the Snavely Livery Company to transport Mollie's body by ambulance to R.J. Coad's Undertaking Parlors on West Walnut Street.

When Mollie had not returned to her Lawe Street home for the dinner hour, John's worried nurse had contacted Mollie's sister, Annie. Her husband, Attorney William Lincoln Evans, had heard the catastrophic news about a train killing a woman along the railroad tracks. He immediately went to the undertaking rooms. At 7:30 p.m., Evans performed the grievous task of identifying his sister-in-law's body.

Dr. T.J. Olliver performed the autopsy. His report stated: The gash on Mollie's head had produced instantaneous death. The Brown County coroner ruled Mollie's passing "accidental," but some in the community speculated. Mollie had to have heard the whistles in the seconds before her death. Had she turned around? Had Mollie seen the massive engine bearing down on her? Had she frozen in fear? Or had she attempted to reach safety and slipped on the icy roadbed?

And what narrative had J.R. constructed? Instead of an accident, would he have suggested that due to melancholia, caused by Mollie's work strain and John's scarlet fever infection, she had walked on the tracks with a death wish. The Brown County Local History & Genealogy librarian, Mary Jane Herber, still questions whether Mollie might have committed suicide, potentially a century-old gaslighting theory nurtured by J.R.

ANNIE AND HER HUSBAND planned to hold a private funeral for Mollie at their home. But those who had worked with Mollie convinced the family the entire community was mourning her loss. They wanted to publicly express what she had meant to Brown County. The Kiwanis Club, where Annie's husband was a member, adopted the following resolution: "That in the sudden accidental death of Mrs. Mollie Bertles Minahan, the family has been deprived of a loving mother and sister, and though we must submit to the will of her Creator, who gave and has taken her, we can not refrain from expressing our regret and heartfelt sympathy to the bereaved, especially her children, whose interests she so earnestly guarded."

Out of respect for Mollie, the banks and retail district establishments suspended business during her funeral service, as did Brown County's Red Cross chapter and East High School, where John, sixteen, and Robert, fourteen, were students.

Union Congregational Church overflowed with Mollie's family, friends, and supporters. Elders quickly arranged parlor seats attached to the main auditorium to accommodate the large crowd. The Reverend

Union Congregational Church 1907 (Postcard)

Edwin A. Ralph stood behind the podium. He spoke from his heart as he said, "Our friend lived in this age, caught the spirit of these great times ... met today's challenge for loyal, tireless, skillful service with a life in complete readiness, not only to help but also to lead ... It is no small thing to live in a community like this for forty years and win a commanding place in its life."

J.R.'s goal had been to destroy Mollie with his lies about syphilis. He had not succeeded.

She had accomplished her goals: "to rise again ... to broader fields of work, a potency in school and city."

Most importantly, she had fiercely protected her sons.

But what of Mollie's boys now, who had landed back into their father's care.

THE
Sons

"To let a sad thought, or a bad one, get into your
mind is as dangerous as letting a scarlet fever germ
get into your body. If you let it stay there ...
you may never get over it as long as you live."

—FRANCES HODGSON BURNETT, *The Secret Garden* (1911)

John Bertles Minahan

Green Bay East High School – Junior Class Boys – John B. Minahan, front row, third from right

EVER SINCE JOHN'S BIRTH, Mollie had strived to protect him and his younger brother. Nobody could take her place. Piano music no longer played, no perfume filled the air, no knitting basket rested by a chair. Through his father's Bay Shore home windows, John, a high school junior, would have looked out onto the waters of Green Bay, connected to the Fox River. Memories of rowing beside his mother in her small launch would have constricted his chest. He would have missed her hand's light stroke on his cheek and her kiss on his forehead as she strained on the tips of her toes to reach that spot.

John B. Minahan – Junior Class President (East High 1918 Yearbook)

Mollie's sister, Annie, whom Mollie had called on in the past to watch out for her boys, would have tried to remain engaged in their lives. Yet, with the animosity and accusations J.R. had levied on Annie, it would have been difficult for her to do so until J.R. left for military duty in the summer of 1918. Since the Minahan boys had already lost one parent, the military dispatched J.R. to a U.S. medical corps hospital instead of overseas to protect his life.

But before J.R. departed, knowing Mollie was out of the way, had he finally provided his fourteen- and sixteen-year-old sons the "persistent" syphilis treatment he claimed was imperative so his boys could "carry the responsibilities of their manhood?" Neosalvarsan had replaced "606" as the primary cure for syphilis. Although the new drug was easier to administer, its side effects were nearly the same, such as rashes, liver damage, and "other risks to life and limb." Before leaving for military duty, had J.R. perhaps administered this drug to both boys to "thoroughly eradicate" any syphilis inherited by their mother?

John and Robert likely stayed with Dr. Robert's son Eben Minahan during their father's absence. The probate court, settling Mollie's inheritance, had appointed Eben Guardian ad Litem for the Minahan boys' rights and protection. But when the Bluejacket Band of the Great Lakes Naval Training Station arrived in Brown County in late September, the Minahan boys required extra protection, as did all citizens. Seven of the band's thirty members had caught the Spanish Influenza in stops along the way and had been hospitalized. By the time the remaining members reached Green Bay, four additional Bluejackets were admitted into St. Vincent.

Nevertheless, the nineteen members that were left still played concerts and marched in parades throughout the county, while restaurants like De Pere's Union Hotel fed the band for free. All the while, the Bluejackets, unknowingly, kept spreading the Spanish Flu.

Soon, the county's cases reached 100.

Since most of the doctors and nurses were in military service, only nineteen physicians remained in Brown County to serve a community of 30,000. Two of those doctors were soon dead, as was Father O'Brien, who had aided Mary Cenefelt in her battle against Dr. Minahan. The city's theaters and schools all closed. Not even the gauze masks the Beaumont House barbers were required to wear provided protection. Cases reached 500.

Then, by November 1, there was a noticeable decline in reported cases. The county lifted the theater ban, and John and Robert returned to East High School.

Three days later, the Austro-Hungarian empire agreed to an armistice. Kaiser Wilhelm abdicated on November 9, 1918, and Germany signed a truce two days later, effectively ending the war. The U.S. had suffered more than 100,000 deaths, including 45,000 who had died from the Spanish Influenza before arriving in France.

Armistice Parade – Includes Roger Minahan (Dr. Robert's grandson) and Grace Warren (daughter of Mollie's friend Mayme) (Courtesy of Beverly Hart Branson)

News of Germany's unconditional surrender exploded in Green Bay, and the jubilant citizens celebrated on the streets and held a parade.

A new influenza surge followed, and the caseload reached 800.

As 1918 drew to a close, the infections dwindled to nearly nothing, and the schools reopened on December 30. John, his brother, and their Green Bay relatives had all survived.

IN THE SPRING of 1919, J.R. returned to the city in time to see John win the Wisconsin statewide declamatory contest, speaking confidently about "The End of Autocracy." J.R. would once again have bragging rights about his "favorite son." A few weeks later, John stood tall and confident among Green Bay East High School's sixty-nine seniors while giving one of the Class of 1919's graduation speeches. Those present would have commented that John was indeed his mother's son.

Lawrenceville Academy Yearbook Photo of John Minahan 1920

That same month, Congress passed the 19th Amendment giving women the right to vote. Mollie would have relished that event—but not the one that occurred in September of 1919.

According to the custody agreement, Robert was to complete high school in Green Bay with his lifelong friends. But with Mollie gone, J.R. decided unilaterally that New Jersey's Lawrenceville Academy, one of the nation's premier prep schools rooted in British boarding school traditions, would be the best education for both John and Robert. That decision by J.R. could have been part of Robert's undoing.

As a high school sophomore, Robert resided in the Circle or Crescent House, while his older brother lived in one of the Fifth Form Houses to begin his pre-med studies. The school virtually segregated the two boys from each other. In John's third year away from home, he began his university studies at Princeton, while Robert, who had completed his secondary school education, launched into his Lawrenceville pre-med coursework.

Soon after the boys' Green Bay departure, their fifty-nine-year-old father purchased an Astor Heights' New England Cape Cod at 1030 S. Monroe Avenue and quietly married his third bride, Hattie Johnson, his forty-four-year-old head surgical nurse.

Hattie Johnson Minahan, J.R.'s Third Wife.
(Roger Minahan Papers)

Born to Norwegian emigrants, Hattie had earned nursing certificates at Lake Geneva Sanitarium and at St. Mary's Hospital Training School in Green Bay. She worked as a private nurse in the city until J.R. hired her. Hattie would say, "[Dr. John and I] worked together like four hands connected to one brain."

Six months after the new Doctor and Mrs. Minahan's wedding, John returned home from Princeton due to illness and stayed there for nine months. No records provide insight into John's ill health. Even if his father had not administered the syphilis drug Neosalvarsan to his sons following Mollie's death, J.R. had still claimed he had treated both boys prior to her death with other syphilis drugs like Cypridol and "606." In March of 1922, John could have been suffering from those drugs' side effects.

Another possibility is that he had contracted tuberculosis also called TB. A clue to that is based on a letter he wrote to Hattie soon after he resumed his pre-med studies at the University of Chicago in January of 1923. John wrote that a "hard cold and cough" had confined him to bed.

TB's symptoms included fever, chills, night sweats, and a persistent cough, where the patient expectorated thick white phlegm and blood. John's Aunt Daisy had recently died from tuberculosis, also called consumption, or the "Great White Plague," due to the extreme paleness of those affected. Most doctors advised their TB patients to rest, eat well, and exercise outdoors, but there was no cure. The disease's recurrence haunted those who had survived their first bout. They feared subsequent ones, which could destroy any hope for a normal life.

John was a savvy medical student, dating eighteen-year-old Susanne Smith, the Green Bay Foundry and Machine Works president's daughter. John would have known that individuals with TB, in an active stage, should not be intimate with a partner nor marry. After his health had deteriorated again, what thoughts were going through John's mind?

To provide a climate more conducive for his son to regain his health, J.R. arranged to take John and his university friend, Al Hoff, a Maroon football star, on a week-long New Mexico hunting expedition.

The day before J.R.'s scheduled departure for the University of Chicago, he conducted an operation at St. Vincent Hospital on seventeen-year-old Rose Wendricke. Thirteen years earlier, she had swallowed an inch-long brass nail, which had lodged in her left lung, placing her life in peril due to pulmonary infection and tuberculosis. After the risky but successful surgery, a reporter interviewed Dr. Minahan. "It was necessary to open her chest and temporarily sever five ribs," J.R. explained. "At one period of the operation, the girl's heart stopped beating. I discovered ... by moving the heart slowly and then releasing it to a normal position, I could regulate its action. I finally had it in [a] position where I could make the incision to remove [the nail] from the lung."

J.R. boarded the train the next day. Seated inside a passenger coach, he would have nodded to those fellow travelers eyeing him over their *Green Bay Press-Gazette* newspapers as they read about his prior day's surgery, alleging him to be the first to move and restart a human heart. The Associated Press had picked up that news and published it in numerous U.S. and Canadian newspapers. Minahan's medical ego would not have allowed him to correct that article's slight mistake. J.R. might have been the first surgeon to "move" a human heart to access the lungs. But in 1901, Norway's Dr. Kristian Igelsrud was the first physician to successfully perform a human resuscitation by utilizing an open-chest cardiac massage.

J.R. arrived at his son's University of Chicago Alpha Tau Omega chapter house on February 2, 1923. Detective Sergeant Hanson greeted J.R. rather than John.

At 7:00 a.m. that morning, the detective told J.R., his son's fraternity brother had found John reclining in his bedroom chair, a shotgun between his legs, a full charge to his face, and the top of his head blown away. The autopsy pathologist later deduced that John had placed the gun muzzle in his mouth before pulling the trigger.

The detective told J.R. they were still determining whether his son's death was an accident or suicide. The last person to see John alive was his fraternity brother, Al Hoff. The night before, Hoff told the detective that John had been in the best of spirits, still preparing for the trip, although his automatic rifle's ejector was not working to his satisfaction. At 3:00 a.m., Hoff said, he had told John to let it go before Hoff went off to bed. He and most of his fraternity brothers thought John had accidentally shot himself. One of John's friends told Detective Hanson that John had never appeared despondent or talked of death, but he had recently appeared "restless" and had suffered from "indifferent health for months."

The Los Angeles Times printed an exclusive Chicago dispatch that day, mentioning John's health. It said, "A surgeon who had just saved a girl from threatened tuberculosis and probable death ... turned from his honors to discover that the disease ... he had defeated had taken its revenge. His son, a victim of the white plague, had just been found dead in a University of Chicago fraternity house, a shotgun resting with its stock between his knees. The police call it a suicide."

Detective Hanson knew that young men most likely committed suicide due to physical or mental illness. But Hanson also speculated whether John had taken his life after being jilted by his sweetheart, Miss Susanne Smith, living at Chicago's Shorecrest Hotel. The detective had discovered a note she had written to John inside his pocket.

Susanne told the Chicago detective, "There was nothing in the note to cause him to think I was breaking with him ...We were not formally engaged, but we had what might be called an understanding. I know he was going on a hunting expedition for his health, and I wrote him a sympathetic note. I merely wished him good luck and told him I was sorry he was going to leave, even for so short a time."

Outside the Alpha Tau Omega chapter house, the wind swelled, and tree branches snapped against the fraternity's front room windows. Inside, Detective Hanson interviewed J.R. He said his son had a habit of blowing into a gun barrel while cleaning it, and J.R. had cautioned John not to do so. "There was no reason for my son to take his life." J.R.'s impassive gaze met the detective's. "[John] was in excellent health, with the exception of a slight cold ... He was not troubled with melancholia. He had no worries, and his disposition was the best."

Throughout J.R.'s life, he had controlled the narrative with his proven genius in medicine and finances. His many followers had aligned themselves with a winner and would not believe any troubling information about his boys. His admirers would not readily give up their trust in Dr. J.R. Minahan, the model father, whose brilliant sons were following in his footsteps. There was no reason not to believe the words that came out of J.R.'s mouth.

The news of John's death and the question of its cause made national headlines. The Sioux City Journal said, "After Dr. J.R. Minahan's former wife's death, he devoted himself to his boys ... The busy surgeon was never too engrossed to wait on John and Robert. If necessary, he would cross a continent to gratify the whim of the favorite son, John."

J.R. and his nephew, Eben Minahan, attended the coroner's inquest. Based on the testimony of J.R., John's student friends, and Detective Hanson, who now said John's death could have been unintentional, the jury ruled John's death accidental.

J.R. buried his son in Green Bay's Woodlawn Cemetery on February 5, 1923, exactly three weeks before the fifth anniversary of his mother's death. John was interned in a lot just west of those reserved for Dr. Minahan and his third wife, Hattie. About twenty yards to the north was his mother's grave. Space remained on both sides of Mollie's simple marker, as if waiting for her sons and their future families to join her.

J.R. had not relinquished his son's custody, even in death.

Robert Bertles Minahan

1918 Freshmen East High photo. Robert Minahan is first on far left.

IN THE GREEN BAY East High School 1918 *Aeorplane* yearbook, Robert, or Bobbie, as friends called him, seemed to be a jokester in his freshman photo. Perhaps that was a coping method to hide his emotional pain caused not only by his father's years of abuse but from his mother's recent death. To lose her at age fourteen in such a horrendous fashion would have shattered Robert even more, especially losing a mother who had loved him unconditionally, who had steadfastly nursed him at his hospital bedside, who had orchestrated his escapes from his father's syphilis treatments, and who had been brave enough to divorce his abusive father and fight for her sons.

One consolation for Robert would have been that his mother's untimely passing had saved her the anguish of dealing with John's death, as Robert currently was.

After his brother's February 5, 1923, funeral, Robert remained in Green Bay and did not complete his Lawrenceville pre-med spring term. Even so, the school provided him a full-page spread in their Olla Podrida yearbook where Robert had earned nicknames of "Bip and Min." In one photo, he wore a jaunty derby, a white shirt, and a tie. The caption read: "[Robert] was

Robert B. Minahan's Lawrenceville Academy Yearbook Photo

a gifted orator whose tongue can arouse sentiments of love and hate in the school-boy breast ... We cannot help but prophesy a great future for him."

The summer following John's death, Robert posed for a family photo in front of his father's Monroe Avenue home. Robert characteristically grinned while J.R. stood beside him, stoic and tall. Robert, the son his father initially claimed was not his, was J.R.'s only hope to carry on the Minahan name. He was the sole heir to J.R.'s vast fortune and Mollie's trust fund. Since John had passed away before reaching age twenty-five, he had not received his half of Mollie's inheritance. Robert would now receive the entire amount of $31,000 when he turned twenty-five (about $540,000 in current valuation).

Soon after that photo, the police arrested Robert twice for speeding.

Photo in front of J.R.'s home. Back row: Jessie (sister to Tracy Minahan), John R. Minahan, Robert B. Minahan, Robert E. Minahan, Victor I. Minahan. Middle row: Tracy Minahan, Nellie (Tracy's mother), Mrs. Copp, Bertha Minahan (V.I.'s wife), Hattie Minahan (J.R.'s wife). Front row: Eben's children (Roger and Nancy to the left and Robert E. to the far right.) The two small children are Mary and Victor (V.I. Minahan's children) and stepbrother John Torinus (Roger Minahan Papers)

For the next eighteen months, he remained at home rather than returning to Lawrenceville or attending college. During that time, after losing his mother and brother, had Robert's thoughts churned up the past? Had he questioned why he had been hospitalized so many times as a child? Robert had been eight when his mother had told him his papa wanted to treat him for a disease he did not have. At age nineteen, Robert had completed a semester of pre-med coursework and was a legal adult. He could have gained access to his medical records from

St. Vincent Hospital and uncovered the specific syphilis treatments his father had given him: "606," after J.R. had abducted him from the street, and Cypridol, just before J.R. had filed for his sons' custody. His father could have made a notation about Robert's heart, which J.R. had told Mollie was in "such bad shape"—unless that had been a lie.

Did Robert trust his mother's belief that he had never had syphilis or the opposing view of his father, one of Green Bay's top surgeons, who had potentially administered Neosalvarsan to Robert following his mother's death? And could the revelation that his heart was in bad shape have weighed on Robert's mind? Could he have discerned Mollie's truth among his father's lies?

Robert finally enrolled at Northwestern University in September of 1924 and moved into the Sigma Nu fraternity house on the university's quadrangle.

As Robert began his second semester of studies, *The Manitowoc Herald News* reported that fifty-nine-year-old Mary Cenefelt had died of cancer on February 1, 1925. Dr. Minahan's former maid had been in a Green Bay hospital for over a year. Whether her cancer was due to the decades of drugs she had taken to treat her infected womb is unknown. Either way, Mary lived a hard life under Minahan's black cloud. She had been a courageous fighter for her time, an uneducated servant who had stood up to the man who had used every power he had to silence her.

Mary Cenefelt's grave in St. James Cemetery Cooperstown. (author's photo)

J.R. had attempted to destroy Mary, like he had Mollie. Although he had ruined Mary's health, the Wassermann syphilis test would have proved Mary did not have the "unmentionable disease." Otherwise, four years before her death, Reverend August Dusold from Waupaca, Wisconsin, would not have hired her as his housekeeper, thus reinstating Mary's good name.

Three priests performed Mary's Cooperstown funeral mass and burial in St. James Cemetery. Inscribed below her mother's name on the cross-topped granite monument reads: "MARY 1865–1925." She was actually two years older than she had testified to in all her court proceedings. Mary had admitted to her first trial attorney J. Calvin Stewart that she didn't know anything about "arithmetic." She likely had been unable to subtract her birth year from the current year to provide her accurate age.

The week of Mary's funeral, J.R. received "an alarming letter" from Robert. He wrote that he was "growing despondent." February marked the anniversary of his mother's and brother's deaths. The letter closed with, "Goodbye, dear Dad. Find some way to forgive me. I haven't the courage to go on."

J.R. called Chicago relatives and told them he believed Robert had suffered a mental breakdown from overstudy.

J.R. was controlling the narrative again.

The relatives investigated whether Robert was at his fraternity house, but nobody could locate him. That same night, J.R. arrived in Evanston, Illinois, and talked to Robert's fraternity brothers, university officials, and other student body members. No one could shed light on his son's whereabouts.

ON THAT SAME frigid evening, eighty miles north of Northwestern University, the stars were bright over Milwaukee's Juneau Park. A man walking his dog heard a gunshot and located the park police callbox to report the incident. Patrolman John Dickson responded and hurried up the lakeshore bluff. He emerged from the shadows, a revolver in one hand, and a flashlight in the other. The patrolman primarily dealt with problematic vagrants and "mashers," a term used for sexual harassers. A gunshot was different.

At the foot of Oneida Street, Dickson's flashlight beam lit up a young man slumped over on a park bench in a brown velour hat, a sheepskin-lined mackinaw, and black oxfords. He faced Lake Michigan, a revolver clutched in his right hand, a bullet hole piercing his right temple.

Patrolman Dickson checked for signs of life but found none.

The victim had drawn his last breath sitting atop the "lost neighborhood of block 106" where Milwaukee's affluent founding citizens had once resided.

Authorities transported the unidentified body to the Milwaukee County morgue. Coroner Henry Grundman recorded the young man's height at 5-feet 9-inches tall, hair black, and face smoothly shaven. Underneath the mackinaw, the victim wore an expensive dark gray suit. Inside its pocket was a note signed by a woman named "*Louise.*"

The inscription read: *"Dear Charles, I might just as well tell you now, as later, that everything is over as far as you and I are concerned. I don't love you, and I never did. Buddy Hills and I will be married by the time you get this, so there is nothing you can do."*

The note led police to believe the victim's name was "Charles" and, based on "Louise's" unrequited love, he had committed suicide. But that supposition seemed contradictory to the laundry initials stitched inside the young man's clothes.

J.R. WAS STILL at Northwestern when family members contacted him. They had read the *Milwaukee Journal* article about an unidentified youth who had committed suicide in Juneau Park. The paper had included the specific clothing marks, "J.R.M." and "R.B.M."

Robert B. Minahan
(Roger Minahan Papers)

J.R. called the Milwaukee authorities and told them the unidentified victim could be his son. An old friend of Dr. Minahan's, Attorney William H. Timlin, met him at the Milwaukee County morgue. When the coroner drew back the shroud, J.R. said, "It's Robert."

J.R. could not explain the note in his son's suit coat pocket. He told authorities, "The fact that it is addressed to 'Charles' indicates it was not intended for my son. Robert was not in love, as far as I know, and I have never heard the name Louise nor Buddy Hills mentioned by him."

Authorities suggested scholastic difficulties for the boy's act, but J.R. said Robert's first Northwestern semester record had been excellent. Other than mentioning overstudy again, J.R. told authorities there was no reason for Robert to take his life.

Detectives conducted interviews on the university campus. Nobody seemed to know the Buddy Hills or Louise mentioned in the note. The investigators believed the "love letter" was fictitious, and Robert had hoped Milwaukee authorities would never identify his body and bury him as a John Doe.

Robert's passing did not require a coroner's inquest. His death certificate designated "suicide" as the cause.

For once, J.R. had been unable to control the narrative, the community whispers, the ongoing gossip that he had failed his youngest son.

Both John and Robert died in February at age twenty-one. Neither had received any portion of their mother's trust fund. But Mollie had made certain, in the incomprehensible circumstance that both of her boys perished before reaching age twenty-five, that J.R. would not get her money. The trust document's subsequent benefactors were Mollie's siblings, each to receive an equal share.

J.R. buried his youngest son, Robert Bertles Minahan, next to his brother, John Bertles Minahan, their 10-inch-tall rectangular granite stones, a matching pair. It was what Mollie would have wanted, her boys placed together, Robert under his big brother's eternal care.

The Surrogate Son

J.R.'S SONS HAD BOTH DIED at age twenty-one, and he had no namesakes to carry on his legacy. In his eyes, that would have been unacceptable. His two brothers living in Green Bay, Dr. Robert and Attorney V.I. Minahan, both had male heirs. J.R. had to do something about that situation. In 1925, the city had emerged as the world's largest toilet tissue producer and nearly 26,000 cars moved through Green Bay's port, while J.R. began to nurture a relationship with his nephew, Victor Minahan McCormick.

Dr. John R. Minahan
(Roger Minahan Papers)

Vic's father, John McCormick, the husband of J.R.'s sister, Mary, had been nicked by a police bullet in 1901 while escaping from a Green Bay "house of ill repute." The couple divorced, and John McCormick departed for California, "never to be heard of again." He left J.R.'s sister with two-year-old Phyllis and four-year-old Vic.

Vic McCormick attended Marquette University and donated money for a dorm named for him.

By 1925, the ample-sized and deep-voiced Vic had graduated from St. Norbert College and earned a Marquette University law degree. He joined his Uncle V.I. Minahan's firm, but not for long. His uncle kicked Vic out after catching him snooping inside his Uncle Robert's desk. That incident, however, did not deter J.R. from hiring his nephew to manage J.R.'s considerable wealth.

Vic was an excellent extension to his uncle, the front man to handle his legal work and complex negotiations. The two men often congregated in

J.R.'s sixth-floor Minahan building office, their talk spiced with anecdotes that got "better and better" with each retelling. One of Vic's first moves was to recommend that his uncle buy significant Hoberg Paper Company stock to keep it afloat. That company would become Charmin Paper and eventually be purchased by Procter and Gamble.

A relationship also transpired between J.R. and De Pere's St. Norbert College, founded in 1898 by his friend, Abbot Bernard Pennings. The two men's connection, J.R.'s third wife Hattie said, had become "warm and lasting."

Hattie had given up her nursing work to focus on local social causes and cultural endeavors. She hosted the Methodist Church Home missionary group, participated in the Shakespearian Club, was the Art Club's president, and held that same title in the Women's Medical Auxiliary Society.

Owing to Dr. Minahan's untarnished surgical reputation, his name continued to instill confidence in the Brown County community. During the 1932 Great Depression national banking crisis, J.R. offered to throw his fortune behind the People's Saving and Trust Company, where he sat on the board. On a local radio broadcast, he reassured the public they should not withdraw their money, their deposits were safe. J.R.'s action essentially stopped that bank from defaulting while protecting his own assets.

A decade after Robert's suicide, J.R. donated land and money to build a stadium for St. Norbert College, aptly named the J.R. Minahan Stadium and Athletic Field. Upon his death, he also promised to bequeath the land adjoining the stadium to St. Norbert College.

Dr. J.R. Minahan breaking ground in 1937 for the J.R. Minahan Stadium and Athletic Field (Roger Minahan Papers)

While securing his name's legacy, J.R.'s obsession with syphilis continued.

Two local papers had merged to become *The Green Bay Press-Gazette,* and J.R.'s attorney brother, V.I. Minahan, had become its president. Inside the newspaper's office, the year after Mollie's death, "Curly" Lambeau, the former East High and Notre Dame football star was elected captain of the city's football team, eventually named the Green Bay Packers. Significant ties remained between V.I. Minahan and the team, which likely extended to his brother, J.R., who testified as an expert medical witness in the Willard J. Bent vs. Green Bay Packers civil trial.

The fifty-one-year-old Packers fan had fallen twelve feet onto the pavement from a dislodged City Stadium bleacher. In Willard Bent's lawsuit, he claimed he had broken a vertebra, and his injury was permanent. The plaintiff's attorney only questioned J.R. about the man's x-ray results and possible pre-existing arthritis condition. But before the defendant's attorney cross-examined J.R., he told Packers' President Leland Joannes, "The trouble with this son of a B ... is that he is full of syphilis."

When the Packers' attorney questioned J.R. the next day, he testified he had examined Bent's blood and the results proved he was in an active syphilis stage, thus more susceptible to injury. Nevertheless, the jury decided the Packers were responsible for Bent's physical condition and awarded him substantial damages, sending the Packers into receivership and nearly folding the team.

J.R. had always shunned religion, but when a stroke limited his medical practice at age seventy-five, his friend, Father Dennis Burke, later to become St. Norbert College's president, received J.R. into the Catholic church. Soon after, J.R. was named St. Norbert's building fund campaign general chairman, and he pledged $50,000 (about $1 million in current valuation). Eight months later, J.R. passed away from stroke complications.

There is no proof that Dr. Minahan ever had syphilis. Nobody but J.R. knew the reason behind his lifelong obsession with the "unmentionable disease." But if he had lived two years longer, he would finally have witnessed its safe cure. At Staten Island's U.S. Marine Hospital in 1943, Dr. John Mahoney and two other physicians injected four syphilis patients with penicillin, discovered in 1928, and found a syphilis cure that had little or no side effects.

Hattie Minahan, J.R.'s wife of twenty years, held her husband's funeral service at St. Joseph Church on St. Norbert College's campus, where Abbot Pennings spoke: "Dr. Minahan's charity was one of his finest qualities ... His interest in education was shown by his frequent visits to St. Norbert College and his benefactions ... We have lost a good friend in Dr. Minahan."

In J.R.'s will, he left Hattie their home and a trust fund, providing her only $6000 a year (about $122,000 in current valuation). J.R. also bequeathed a one-time gift of $5000 to his female Minahan Building manager and the same to his thirty-two-year-old female laboratory technician (about $100,000 apiece).

J.R.'s nephew, Vic McCormick, inherited the rest of J.R.'s wealth of about $1.25 million (nearly $25 million in current valuation) and the Minahan Building, soon renamed the Minahan–McCormick Building.

Tony Walter, the grandson of V.I. Minahan, stated in an interview, "This is table talk, but Vic Minahan was J.R.'s nephew *and* his attorney. Since J.R. had some dementia before he died, Vic worked out all the paperwork so he would inherit all the money. Vic McCormick separated himself from the Minahans from that time on."

J.R.'s will had not bequeathed the promised St. Norbert College $50,000 pledge nor the land adjoining the stadium. "Vic McCormick perhaps [felt] guilty ... and came up with the money," V.I. Minahan's son-in-law, Mike Walter, wrote. Vic also donated the promised land to the Norbertine Fathers, where St. Norbert College constructed its new abbey.

Vic McCormick & Dorice Dupuis (Press Gazette Wedding Photo)

A decade after J.R.'s death, Vic gave the college an additional $1 million and pledged $500,000 in Proctor & Gamble stock. In return, the college erected the John Minahan Science Hall in 1967, renamed an existing St. Norbert residence hall the Victor McCormick Hall, and built a new dormitory named for Vic's mother, Mary Minahan McCormick. She had died from a barbiturates overdose in 1945. Since a Bible was in her lap, the church accorded her a Catholic funeral. But when Vic refused to provide St. Norbert the pledged P&G stock, claiming it had split and the portion he had given covered the shares promised, the college took the suit to the Wisconsin Supreme Court and won.

Vic was a bachelor until age seventy-one when he met thirty-year-old Dorice Dupuis, a Quebec dressmaker. In their wedding photo, Vic, with his large physique, little hair, dark-framed glasses, and ample double chin, stood beside his stunning bride. Dorice gained power of attorney when Vic turned senile. Before his death at age eighty-eight, she transferred Vic's *and* J.R.'s fortune into her name.

Author's Final Note

THE CITY OF GREEN BAY demolished the block that housed J.R.'s medical office in 1977 to construct Port Plaza Mall, subsequently replaced by Schreiber Foods. That same year, my husband and I purchased our 644 S. Jackson Street home within the Astor neighborhood. After our Queen Anne Victorian's construction in 1899, the year J.R. and Mollie married, our three-story house had eventually been converted into a group residence. While we worked to bring our home back to its original grandeur, the U.S. Department of Interior added the Astor neighborhood to the National Register of Historic Places. Nearly 170 homeowners helped to research their home's history to provide input for the Astor Historic District book, published in 1981.

During that endeavor, I discovered Attorney Victor I. Minahan, who had represented J.R. in his divorce and custody trials and had become *The Green Bay Press-Gazette's* president and editor, had lived in our home. The house of Mollie's friend, Mayme Comstock Warren, had also shared the same backyard fence as ours. The original St. Vincent Hospital, refurbished into J.R. and Mollie's home, had been situated across the street from the Warrens' before J.R.'s house burned down.

The Astor neighborhood's past fascinated me. I would push my children's strollers up and down the tree-shaded sidewalks and admire the former homes of Judge Hastings, Dr. Robert E. Minahan, Attorney Patrick H. Martin, and Dr. John R. Minahan. The mansion-lined streets seemed a beautiful, storied neighborhood. But when I decided to write a book about the Minahan family, I uncovered Mary's and Mollie's court transcripts. The Astor neighborhood, I realized, contained its own dark secrets. Rather than celebrating the Minahan brothers' many achievements, the book I planned to write took a dramatic turn. To give

Mary and Mollie a voice to tell their courageous accounts was important to me. I realized their stories had been erased from the Minahan family history, especially that of Dr. John R. Minahan.

Demolition crews leveled the Minahan–McCormick Building in 1984 to build a Washington Street multi-level parking garage. In 2009, St. Norbert College played its last game in Minahan Stadium. The new Schneider Stadium, funded by the Schneider National trucking family, was constructed on a different site. The modern Gehl–Mulva Science Center dedicated in 2015 replaced the one named for J.R.

The city of Green Bay and St. Norbert College have destroyed all structures bearing Dr. John R. Minahan's name. However, the family name has been kept alive due to J.R.'s brave brother, Dr. William E. Minahan, who perished on the Titanic. His massive granite tomb, with its prominent MINAHAN name, is visible to all who utilize the Fox River Bike Trail constructed over the railroad bed where Mollie took her last breath.

J.R.'s third wife, Hattie Johnson Minahan, survived her husband by eighteen years. Shortly before her 1959 death, Hattie wrote a letter to Dr. Robert E. Minahan's grandson that said: "*It is too bad that humanity has a spark of envy in it, so that it can enjoy repeating, and enlarging upon it, scandalous stories about really successful people. Just who may not have erred here or there, and what can we do about mistakes except to try to correct them? Perhaps, the soul has that opportunity as well.*"

Within Green Bay's St. Vincent Hospital at 835 S. Van Buren Street, a photo hangs of the original 626 S. Quincy Street hospital. For decades, an oil painting of its "godfather," Dr. John R. Minahan, hung on the hospital's first floor landing. His lies destroyed lives, yet his reputation went largely unchallenged as he rested behind the security of being a man of wealth and privilege. No one doubted Dr. Minahan's skill and motives when he first admitted Mary Cenefelt into St. Vincent Hospital

Dr. John R. Minahan
Oil Portrait
(Roger Minahan Papers

after her brutal rapes and abortion. Few people recognized the abusive hell he put Mollie and her boys through when they lived inside that same French-mansard-roofed mansion.

Mary and Mollie both suffered within that structure, yet each found the courage to fight back against Dr. John R. Minahan—a man of power and prestige—just as brave women in the twenty-first century continue to do.

Reading Group Guide

1. Discuss the power plays Dr. Minahan used against Mary and Mollie to keep them silent for so long before each fought back. In this day and age, do you believe women dealing with similar sexual and mental abuse would handle their situations differently?

2. Did you empathize more with Mary's situation or Mollie's? Discuss the reasons behind your feelings.

3. Discuss how that era's medical misinformation and lack of medical discoveries affected the lives of Mary and Mollie, i.e.: syphilis, hysteria, insanity, rheumatism, etc.

4. Dr. Minahan was a narcissistic closet abuser who reveled in the community's accolades for his surgical skills and business savvy. What men in our era remind you of doctor Minahan and why?

5. How do you feel the ultimate court decisions for Mary and Mollie were influenced by their differing social statuses?

6. Would you have signed the divorce stipulation, like Mollie, which gave J.R. the sole authority to treat their children's medical needs?

7. Do you believe Mollie's death was an accident or suicide and discuss your reasoning?

8. Do you believe the death of Mollie's eldest son John was an accident or suicide? Discuss your reasoning.

9. Discuss all the obstacles Mary and Mollie faced as females to seek justice, and discuss whether those same obstacles exist in today's society.

10. The prologue states: "Disturbingly, these women's intimate narratives embody the battles dominating headlines today: men's entitlement versus women's liberty, wealth versus poverty, and false information versus scientific fact." Discuss the parallels between this story and today's news headlines.

Bibliography and Citations

PRIMARY RESOURCES

Every chapter in THE MAID section includes Mary Cenefelt's sworn deposition testimony from the UWGB Archives: Minahan vs. Cenefelt—Brown Series 65 Box 341, Folder 2 (Court box 230). In addition, the quotes for Mrs. Emma Nolan's witness deposition are included in this box. (Note: There were no court records saved that included Mary's cross-examination testimony by Attorney P.H. Martin. To portray this in the Bold and Badgered chapter, the author used Mary's May 14-15, 1897 sworn deposition testimony conducted by Mr. Martin. The author made this decision since questions asked by the opposing attorney during a plaintiff's deposition are often similar or even the same as those used at trial.)

Every chapter in THE SOCIALITE section includes Mollie Bertles Minahan's sworn testimony from the UWGB Archives: Minahan vs. Minahan divorce—Brown Series 65 Box 471 (Court box 321). In addition, the defendant and witness testimony of Dr. J.R. Minahan, Kitten (Katherine) Bertles, Julia Marique, and Dr. C.W. Oviatt are included in this box.

BIBLIOGRAPHY

Addams, Jane. *The Spirit of Youth and the City Streets.* New York: Macmillan, 1909; BoondocksNet Edition, 2001.

Bowen, Elliott. *In Search of Sexual Health: Diagnosing and Treating Syphilis in Hot Springs, Arkansas, 1890-1940.* John Hopkins University Press. 2020.

Beecher, Catherine E. and Stowe, Harriet Beecher. (1896). *American Woman's Home: Or, Principles of Domestic Science.*

Bialynicki-Birula R. "The 100th anniversary of Wassermann-Neisser-Bruck reaction." National Library of Medicine.

Branson, Beverly Hart, (Sturgeon Bay) married to descendant of Mayme Comstock Warren, provided photos, notes, and newspaper articles.

Capps, Joseph A. MD. "Dr. Frank Billings." Northwest University Medical School. Ncbi.nlm.nih.gov

Chapelle, PH. "The Therapeutical Use of Cypridol (A Specific Bin-iodized oil) in Syphilis." (1901). National Library of Medicine Digital Collection.

Cohen, Sheila Terman. (2016). Jews in Wisconsin. De Pere Historical Society.

Cushman, Clare. (2001). "Jury Duty." Supreme Court Decisions and Women's Rights: Milestones to Equality. Washington, D.C.: Congressional Quarterly Press and the Supreme Court Historical Society.

Cruea, Susan M. (2005). "Changing Ideals of Womanhood During the Nineteenth-Century Woman Movement." General Studies Writing Faculty Publications.

Dawson, Milly. Medically Reviewed by Sanjai Sinha, MD. "The Dangers of Syphilis during Pregnancy." Everydayhealth.com/syphilis

D'Cruze, Shani. (1992). Approaching the history of rape and sexual violence: notes towards research, Women's History Review, 1:3, 377-397, DOI: 10.1080/09612029300200016.

Dickenshied, Jacqueline. "Kellnersville European Roots Begin in Bohemia." (1981, Apr 19). Manitowoc Herald-Times.

Donovan, Brian. (2016). Respectability on Trial: Sex Crimes in New York City, 1900-1918. Albany. State University of New York Press.

Eschner, Kat. "The First Syphilis Cure Was the First 'Magic Bullet." (2017, Aug 31). Smithsonian Magazine.

Fournier, Alfred. (1882). Syphilis and Marriage. New York: D. Appleton and Company.

Goldsmith, Wm. B., M.D. (1885). "Syphilis and Insanity." New England Journal of Medicine.

Gray, M. Scott and Philip, T. The Royal Infirmary, Edinburgh. (1963). Syphilitic Arthritis Diagnostic Problems with Special Reference to Congenital Syphilis. Ard.bmj.com.

Green Bay Daily Advocate—Brown County Library

Green Bay Gazette—accessed on Newspapers.com

Green Bay Press-Gazette—accessed on Newspapers.com

Green Bay Weekly Gazette—accessed on Newspapers.com

Hanson, Alice C. & Douglas, Paul H. "The Wages of Domestic Labor in Chicago, 1890-1929." Journal of the American Statistical Association Vol. 25, No. 169 (Mar., 1930), pp. 47-50 (4 pages) Published By: Taylor & Francis, Ltd.

Helmstadter, Dr. Axel. "The History of Electrotherapy of Pain." Department of Chemical and Pharmaceutical Sciences, Johann Wolfgang Goethe-University, Frankfurt/Main, Germany.

Hofer, Ronald R. "The Best Interest of the Child Doctrine in Wisconsin Custody Cases." Marquette Law Review Vol 64, Issue 2, Article 4, Winter 1980.

Holubetz, Sylvia & Burridge, George Nau, et al. l. (1981). *The Astor Historic District—Its history and Houses.* Green Bay, WI: Astor Neighborhood Association.

Kapsalis, Terri. "Hysteria, Witches, and The Wandering Uterus: A Brief History." Lithub.com. April 5, 2017.

Kasper, Madeline MPA, MPA, MPH managing legislative analyst, Jillian Slaight, PhD managing legislative analyst, Isaac J. Lee, MA research assistant intern. A Brief History of Abortion Laws in Wisconsin (rev. ed.) August 25, 2022 · Volume 6, Number 4.

Larson, Erik. (2003). *The Devil in the White City.* Vintage Book, New York.

Lerner, Paul Frederick. (2003). *Hysterical Men: War, Psychiatry, and the Politics of Trauma in Germany, 1890–1930.* Cornell University Press.

Lohman, Sarah. "Tomorrow: Living Life as a 19th Century Servant." Four Pounds Flour, Wordpress, 01/02/13.

Louis de Canonville, Christine. *The Gaslighting Syndrome.*

MacFadden, Bernarr. (1918). *Womanhood and Marriage.*

Madison Parks Foundation. "John M. Olin."Madisonparksfoundation.org.

May, Vanessa H. *Unprotected Labor: Household Workers, Politics, and Middle-Class Reform in New York, 1870-1940.* Kindle Edition.

Men Who are Making Green Bay. (1897). The Gazette Publishing Co.

Mroczkowski, Tomasz F. M.D. *HISTORY, SEX AND SYPHILIS: Famous Syphilitics and Their Private Lives.* Booklocker.com, Inc, Kindle Edition.

Noonan, John T. Jr. (1967). "Abortion and the Catholic Church: A Summary History." Natural Law Forum. Paper 126.

Oneill, T. (2016). *Unmentionable: The Victorian Lady's Guide to Sex, Marriage, and Manners.* New York: Little, Brown and Company

PBS Wisconsin Education. "Sugaring." Climate Wisconsin—Stories from a State of Change.

Peerenboom, Jean. "St. Patrick Parish celebrates 150th anniversary." The Compass. September 30, 2015.

Quétel, Claude. (1990). *History of Syphilis.* Johns Hopkins Univ. Press.

"Report and Recommendation of the Wisconsin Legislative Committee to Investigate the White Slave Traffic and Kindred Subjects." (1913). Senate Bill No. 257.

Richardson MD, B.L. *History of Medicine in Brown County, Wisconsin 1816-2000.* Quality Books.

Richardson MD, B.L. "The Minahan Trials." *Voyageur* Volume 22, Number 2— Winter/Spring 2006.

Roberts, William C., MD. "Facts and Ideas from Anywhere." Baylor Medical Center Proceedings, January 2004. ncbi.nlm.nih.gov.

Roger Minahan Papers, Box 1, Wisconsin Historical Society, Archives Section, c. 1941. Folder 1 Minahan, Folder 2-3 Dr. William E. Minahan, Folder 5 Dr. John Roger Minahan.

Ropper, Allan H., MD, and Brian David Burrell. (2019). *How the Brain Lost Its Mind: Sex, Hysteria, and the Riddle of Mental Illness.* New York. Avery (An Imprint of Penguin Random House).

Rudolph, Jack. (1983). *A Pictorial History Green Bay.* Norfolk, Virginia: The Donning Company.

Rudolph, Jack. (1976). *Birthplace of a Commonwealth.* Green Bay, WI: Brown County Historical Society.

Rudolph, Jack. (2004). *The Green Bay Area in History and Legend.* Green Bay, WI: Brown County Historical Society.

Salmon, Lucy Maynard. (2018). *Domestic Service.* Franklin Classics.

Shields, Lisa B. E. MD; Hunsaker, Donna M. MD; and Hunsaker, John C. III, MD, JD. "Trends of Suicide in the United States During the 20th Century." Forensic Pathology Reviews, Vol. 3 Edited by: M. Tsokos, Humana Press Inc., Totowa, NJ.

Sinha Dutta, Sanchari Ph.D. "History of Tuberculosis." Medical Life Science.

Stiles, C.O. (1903). *Souvenir of Green Bay.*

Spencer, Christine A. (1994). "An Analysis of the Domestic Workers' Place in the Late Nineteenth Century Household." Penn Libraries.

State Gazette—accessed on Newspapers.com

Strømskag, Kjell Erik. "Kristian Igelsrud and the first successful direct heart compression." PubMed. January 2003.

Sweet, Chris. "The Lawrenceville School House System." (2016, Jul 25).

Tarneja, P. and Duggal, BS. "Hysteroscopy: Past, Present and Future." U.S. National Library of Medicine. Published online 2011 Jul 21.

United States House of Representatives. "The Women's Rights Movement, 1848–1917." History Arts and Archives.

U.S. Department of Health and Human Services. (2007, Jan 4). Office of the Surgeon General: John B. Hamilton (1879–1891).

UWGB Archives: Brown Series 65 Brown County Circuit Court Case Files Box 803 Folder Willard J. Bent vs. Green Bay Football Corp.

UWGB Archives: Minahan Early Green Bay Family Genealogy.

UWGB Archives: Minahan vs. Cenefelt—Brown Series 65 Box 341, Folder 2 (Court box 230).

UWGB Archives: Minahan vs. Minahan divorce—Brown Series 65 Box 471 (Court box 321).

UWGB Archives: Mollie B. Minahan probate—Brown Series 144, Court Box 201, Case File 8133.

Verkuilen, Lee, Retired Postmaster from Maribel, WI—Provided Cenefelt and Cooperstown information and photos.

Wallman, Major J., Royal Army Medical Corps. (1945). "Notes on the Significance of Fever In syphilis with a Reference to Hypopyrexia."

Walter, Tony. (2020). *The Packers, My Dad, and Me.* M&B Global Solutions, Inc. Green Bay.

Warsh, Cheryl Krasnick. (1988). "The First Mrs. Rochester: Wrongful Confinement, Social Redundancy, and Commitment to the Private Asylum, 18831923." *Historical Papers.*

Wright's Directory of Green Bay & Ft. Howard. 1893, 1894. Brown County Library.

Wright, Jennifer. (2017). *Get Well Soon: History's Worst Plagues and the heroes who fought them.* New York. Henry Holt and Company.

Yeazell, Ruth Bernard. (1991). *Fictions of Modesty: Women and Courtship in the English Novel.* Chicago and London, University of Chicago Press.

Other Books by Lynda Drews

Run at Destruction: A True Fatal Love Triangle
Circle of Innocence
Desperate Parallels

Acknowledgments

The Maid and the Socialite took extensive research. To aid me in that effort I would like to thank the following individuals:

- Debra Anderson and her staff from the University of Wisconsin–Green Bay Archives and Area Research Center
- Mary Jane Herber, Brown County historian and genealogist
- Dennis Jacobs, Brown County Library
- Lee Verkuilen, retired postmaster, who aided in the discovery of Mary Cenefelt's history
- Beverly Hart Branson, married to a descendant of Mayme Comstock Warren, Mollie Bertles Minahan's friend. Bev provided photos and mementos.

I would also like to thank the following editors, readers, and publishers: Julie Tallard Johnson, Kathy Nieber-Lathrop, Melissa Wulske, Holley Bishop, Cassidy Sachs, and Kristin Mitchell.

Finally, I would like to thank my family and friends for all their support during my five-year journey to write *The Maid and the Socialite*. Without their encouragement and valued opinions, I could never have completed this book.

About the Author

Wisconsin native **LYNDA DREWS** gave the commencement speech at the University of Wisconsin–La Crosse, her college Alma mater. One lesson she shared was "to journal your life." When Lynda, a marketing executive, made the decision to retire after her thirty-year career, she returned to an earlier passion. Her true-crime memoir, *Run at Destruction*, about her Green Bay running friend's mysterious death, was the outcome. *Publishers Weekly* said, " ... the author and victim's shared moments are remarkable." Best-selling true-crime author Anne Rule said Lynda's book was "Wonderfully written ... a must for true crime readers," and Netflix and the I.D. Channel both adapted her book into true-crime segments.

Following Lynda's first book, she authored two novels before writing *The Maid and the Socialite*, a historical true crime set in Green Bay. Lynda is active in the Brown County Historical Society, the Brown County Community Women's Club, and Write On Door County where she teaches classes. She and her husband Jim have lived in Green Bay since 1974, eighteen years in the Astor Historic District where *The Maid and the Socialite* takes place.

54594015R00178